INTENSIVE CARE

INTENSIVE CARE

G.R. Park MA FFARCS
Consultant in Anaesthesia and Intensive Care
Addenbrooke's Hospital
Cambridge, UK

and

A.R. Manara FFARCS MRCP
formerly Registrar in Anaesthesia and Intensive Care
Addenbrooke's Hospital
Cambridge, UK

now Senior Registrar in Anaesthesia
Plymouth General Hospital
Plymouth, UK

Provided as a service to medicine by Bayer plc

First published in 1988 by
Castle House Publications

Reprinted 1994 by Oxford University Press

British Library Cataloguing in Publication Data

Intensive care. — (Pocket reference).
  1. Critical care medicine
  I. Park, Gilbert R.   II. Series
  616'.028   RC86.7
  ISBN 0 19 262624 8

Printed and bound in Great Britain by
Biddles Ltd, Guildford and King's Lynn

Contents

Practical Procedures:

Preface

The aim of this book is to provide guidance for junior medical staff on how to deal with the common problems that arise in patients requiring intensive care. It is not intended to replace, but to supplement, guidance, teaching and advice from more senior colleagues. Opinions may differ on some points of management; the contents of the book reflect the working practices that have been developed in the Intensive Care Unit at Addenbrooke's Hospital and expand on a series of protocols written to help our resident doctors. We have assumed a basic knowledge and skill appropriate to a senior house officer or newly appointed registrar; that the patient is in, or shortly to be admitted to, an intensive care unit. We also hope that nursing and other paramedical staff will find the information contained in this book of use.

The contents of the chapters reflect the aims of the book and assign high priorities to the investigation and management of common, everyday problems. Within the limits of this book's size, it has proved impossible to include every problem that may arise; a suggested reading-list is included for those who wish to read further. Specialist intensive care management problems (burns and cardiac surgery) have similarly been omitted. The section devoted to practical procedures should be seen as an aide memoire and is not a substitute for learning these techniques under supervision.

Drug dosages have been included for many drugs; despite careful checking, mistakes may have occurred and if a dose appears incorrect it should be checked with the package insert, British National Formulary or other suitable reference source, before the drug is administered.

We gratefully acknowledge the assistance and co-operation of the many medical, nursing, laboratory, measurement and other paramedical personnel, from whom we have received many helpful suggestions during the preparation of this book. In particular, we wish to thank Mrs S. Grant for her patient secretarial assistance.

GR Park

AR Manara

Cambridge

1988

Abbreviations

ABG	=	arterial blood gases
ACTH	=	adrenocorticotropic hormone
ADH	=	antidiuretic hormone
AF	=	atrial fibrillation
AIDS	=	acquired immune deficiency syndrome
ARDS	=	adult respiratory distress syndrome
AV	=	atrioventricular
CAVH	=	continuous arteriovenous haemofiltration
CCU	=	coronary care unit
CMV	=	continuous mandatory ventilation
CNS	=	central nervous system
CO	=	cardiac output
CPAP	=	continuous positive airway pressure
CPK	=	creatine phosphokinase
CPRC	=	cardiopulmonary cerebral resuscitation
CRC	=	concentrated red cells
CSF	=	cerebrospinal fluid
CT	=	computerised tomography
CVP	=	central venous pressure
CXR	=	chest X-ray
DC	=	direct current
DI	=	diabetes insipidus
DIC	=	disseminated intravascular coagulation
dl	=	decilitre
ECF	=	extracellular fluid
ECG	=	electrocardiogram
EEG	=	electroencephalogram
ETT	=	endotracheal tube
FDPs	=	fibrin degradation products
FEV_1	=	forced expiratory volume in one second
FFP	=	fresh frozen plasma
F_IO_2	=	fractional inspired oxygen concentration
FVC	=	forced vital capacity

f waves	=	flutter waves
GI	=	gastrointestinal
HAS	=	4.5 per cent human albumin solution
Hb	=	haemoglobin
HBeAg	=	Hepatitis B e antigen
HBsAg	=	Hepatitis B surface antigen
HIV	=	human immunodeficiency virus
HTIG	=	human tetanus immunoglobulin
ICP	=	intracranial pressure
ICU	=	intensive care unit
I:E	=	inspiratory: expiratory
IMV	=	intermittent mandatory ventilation
INR	=	international normalised ratio $\equiv$ prothrombin ratio
iu	=	international unit
IV	=	intravenous(ly)
J	=	joule(s)
JVP	=	jugular venous pressure
kg	=	kilogram
kPa	=	kilopascals
KPTT	=	kaolin partial thromboplastin time
LAP	=	left atrial pressure
LDH	=	lactate dehydrogenase
LVF	=	left ventricular failure
MAP	=	mean arterial pressure
mcg	=	micrograms
MCH	=	mean cell haemoglobin
MCV	=	mean cell volume
mg	=	milligrams
MI	=	myocardial infarction
MMV	=	mandatory minute ventilation
MW	=	molecular weight
NG	=	nasogastric
$PaCO_2$	=	partial pressure of carbon dioxide in arterial blood
PAFC	=	pulmonary artery flotation catheter
PaO_2	=	partial pressure of oxygen in arterial blood
PAP	=	pulmonary artery pressure
PCV	=	packed cell volume
PCWP	=	pulmonary capillary wedge pressure
PD	=	peritoneal dialysis
PE	=	pulmonary embolus

PEEP	=	positive end-expired pressure
PPM	=	parts per million
PR	=	per rectum
PT	=	prothrombin time
PVR	=	pulmonary vascular resistance
RAP	=	right atrial pressure
RCC	=	red cell count
RVEDP	=	right ventricular end diastolic pressure
SA node	=	sinoatrial node
SaO_2	=	percentage oxygen saturation
SC	=	subcutaneous
SIADH	=	syndrome of inappropriate antidiuretic hormone secretion
SIMV	=	synchronised intermittent mandatory ventilation
SPA	=	salt-poor albumin
SV	=	spontaneous breathing
SVE	=	supraventricular extrasystoles
SVR	=	systemic vascular resistance
SVT	=	supraventricular tachycardia
TPN	=	total parenteral nutrition
TT	=	thrombin time
TURP	=	transurethral resection of prostate
U	=	unit
U & E	=	urea and electrolytes
VE	=	ventricular extrasystoles
V/Q	=	ventilation/perfusion
VSD	=	ventricular septal defect
WCC	=	white cell count
WPW	=	Wolff–Parkinson–White syndrome

Normal Values

The values quoted may vary slightly between laboratories.

Parameter	Specimen tube	Normal range
BIOCHEMICAL		
Blood urea and electrolytes		
Sodium		132–142 mmol/l
Potassium		3.4–5.0 mmol/l
Bicarbonate		22–30 mmol/l
Glucose	5 ml lithium heparin	3.5–9.0 mmol/l
Urea		up to ≤ 7.5 mmol/l
Creatinine		35–125 μmol/l
Chloride		95–106 mmol/l
Liver function tests		
Total protein		63–83 g/l
Albumin		30–44 g/l
Bilirubin	10 ml clotted blood	2–17 μmol/l
Alkaline phosphatase[a]		30–135 U/l
Alanine aminotransferase		7–40 U/l
Total calcium	2 ml clotted blood	2.2–2.6 mmol/l
Ionised calcium	2 ml lithium heparin[b]	1.18–1.30 mmol/l
Phosphate	2 ml clotted blood	0.8–1.4 μmol/l
Zinc	5 ml clotted blood	12–23 μmol/l
Magnesium	5 ml clotted blood	0.7–1.0 mmol/l
Arterial blood gases		
Hydrogen ion		36–45 nmol/l
$PaCO_2$	2 ml arterial blood in	4.7–6.0 kPa
PaO_2	a heparinised, sealed	9.3–14.0 kPa
Base excess	syringe kept on ice	+/− 2.5 mmol/l
Standard bicarbonate		21–25 mmol/l

Parameter	Specimen tube	Normal range
Urine		
Sodium	⎫	50–200 mmol/24 hr
Potassium	24-hour collection	20–60 mmol/24 hr
Urea	of urine necessary	330–500 mmol/24 hr
Creatinine		9–16 mmol/24 hr
Protein	⎭	<0.1 g/24 hr
Creatinine clearance[c]		90–120 ml/min[a]
HAEMATOLOGY[d]		
Haemoglobin	⎫	Men 14.0–17.0 g/dl[e]
		Women 11.5–16.0 g/dl[e]
Red cell count		Men 4.5–6.5×10^{12}/l
		Women 3.9–5.6×10^{12}/l
Haematocrit (PCV)		Men 0.40–0.54%[e]
		Women 0.36–0.47%[e]
Mean cell volume (MCV)	5 ml	75–96 fl
Mean cell haemoglobin	EDTA	
(MCH)	tube	27–32 pg
Reticulocyte count		0–2
		(% of red cell count)
Platelet count		150 000–300 000 $\times 10^9$/l
White cell count (WCC)		4000–11 000 $\times 10^9$/l
Differential white cell counts	⎭	Neutrophils 40–75%
		Lymphocytes 1.5–4%
		Monocytes 2–10%
		Eosinophils 1–6%
		Basophils <1%
Prothrombin time (PT) (above control)		
	Citrate 5 ml	<2 sec
Kaolin partial thromboplastin time (KPTT)		
(above control)	Citrate 5 ml	<7 sec
Bleeding time		<7 min
Clotting time		<10 min

[a] Varies with age
[b] Arrange specimen with laboratory
[c] Requires estimation of plasma creatinine during the period of collection.
[d] Sizes of blood tubes vary. If the tube contains an anticoagulant a line usually indicates the correct amount of blood to put in the tube.
[e] Lower values may be accepted in critically ill patients.

CHAPTER 1

Cardiopulmonary Cerebral Resuscitation

Effective support of the circulation and respiration must occur within four minutes of cardiac arrest if cerebral hypoxia, and subsequent permanent cerebral damage, is to be avoided. Rapid recognition of potentially fatal arrhythmias can occur in intensive care units (ICU) because most patients have continuous electrocardiogram (ECG) displays.

Three arrhythmias result in absent cardiac output, ventricular fibrillation, asystole and electro-mechanical dissociation (Figures 1.1, 1.2, 1.3).

Other arrhythmias may result in a low cardiac output which can then precipitate one of these three previous arrhythmias.

Once the diagnosis of cardiac arrest has been made on the ECG and confirmed, by the absence of a pulse (or arterial blood pressure if this is being monitored), several actions need to be taken simultaneously; although these are listed below the patient's condition, availability of equipment and other factors may alter the order in which they are performed.

1 Get help from other staff and start resuscitation.
2 Note the time.
3 Check the equipment around the patient.
   (a) Ensure that the monitor is still properly connected to the patient and that the apparent arrhythmia has not been caused by one of the chest electrodes falling off.
   (b) Check that the ventilator has not become disconnected and is still working correctly.

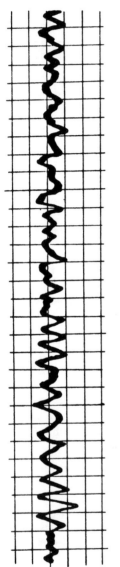

Figure 1.1   Ventricular fibrillation

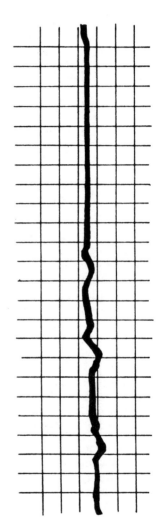

Figure 1.2   Asystole

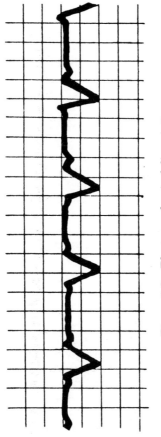

Figure 1.3 Electromechanical dissociation

(c) Ensure that the gas pipelines are still functioning normally and be suspicious that oxygen supply may have become contaminated with another gas.

(d) Check the IV fluids to ensure that a large dose of potassium chloride has not been given.

4 After each manoeuvre or drug administration continue the external cardiac massage and artificial ventilation for two minutes and then pause to see if cardiac output has returned. If it has not, continue with external cardiac massage and artificial ventilation while the next step is performed.

Circulatory support

The circulation should be maintained using external cardiac massage at a rate of 80–100 compressions per minute. The hands should be placed with the 'heel' of one hand overlying the junction of the upper two-thirds with the lower third of the sternum and the other hand placed over it; sufficient force should be exerted to compress the sternum 4–5 cm. Confirmation of the adequacy of external cardiac massage can be obtained by feeling a femoral pulse. External cardiac massage needs to be combined with artificial ventilation; cardiac massage should stop after every five compressions for one lung inflation.

Respiratory support

This will be essential, unless there is immediate return of the circulation and breathing. It is best provided via an endotracheal tube, if the patient already has one in place, or if the operator is proficient at inserting one (see Practical Procedure 1); time must not be wasted in repeated intubation attempts. If difficulty in intubation is encountered an oropharyngeal airway should be inserted (size 2 for small adults, size 3 for average-sized adults and size 4 for large adults), the head extended, and a self-inflating bag and closely fitting mask used to inflate the lungs until help can be obtained.

Metabolic acidosis

Unless the period of cardiac arrest is very short (less than two or three minutes), a metabolic acidosis develops. The administration of increments of 8.4 per cent sodium bicarbonate (1 mmol/kg at five minutes and 0.5 mmol/kg every 10 minutes thereafter) should correct this.

Frequent checking of ABG enables the accurate correction of the acidosis.

Management of Arrhythmias

Ventricular fibrillation

This is the disco-ordinated contraction of ventricular muscle fibres. Its treatment requires electrical defibrillation to stop aberrant myocardial activity and allow the SA node to re-establish control.

Defibrillation

1 Place the defibrillation paddles on the chest; one on the area of the apex of the heart and the other over the upper part of the right chest.
2 Ensure that either electrode pads or conductive jelly have been placed between the paddles and the skin to give good electrical contact.
3 Make sure that no-one is in contact with the patient's bed or equipment.
4 Give a single DC shock of 200 joules (J). Note that there is often a delay in the return of the ECG trace after a DC shock.
5 If ventricular fibrillation is still present, give a second shock at 200 J followed, if necessary, by a third shock at 400 J.
6 If these shocks are unsuccessful give lignocaine (50–100 mg IV over two minutes) followed by a period of external cardiac massage to circulate the drug and then a fourth DC shock at 400 J.
7 Give adrenaline (10 ml 1 in 10 000 IV).
8 Give a further DC shock at 400 J.
9 Resistant ventricular fibrillation may be treated with a further bolus of lignocaine. Alternatively give bretylium tosylate (500 mg by slow IV injection); this can take 10–15 minutes to work.

10 If ventricular fibrillation persists consider changing the defibrillator or repositioning the paddles to an anterior and posterior position.

Asystole

All electrical activity in the heart has ceased and the aim of treatment is to restore this either pharmacologically or by electrical means.

Once adequate oxygenation and cardiac massage have been established, and the metabolic acidosis has been corrected, if there is still no cardiac output:

1 Give atropine (0.6–1 mg IV).
2 Administer isoprenaline (25 mcg IV). If no electrical activity returns administer further isoprenaline (50–100 mcg IV).
3 If there is no response administer adrenaline (10 ml 1 in 10 000 IV). This should be repeated if necessary.
4 Check ABG and plasma potassium during the cardiac arrest.
5 Consider the need for a pacemaker.

Use of a transvenous, oesophageal or external pacemaker may be of value in patients in asystole. Experience is necessary for the insertion of a transvenous pacemaker, but an oesophageal pacemaker can be used by inexperienced personnel (see Practical Procedure 5).

Electromechanical dissociation

This can follow asystole, and although there is electrical activity seen on the ECG there is no cardiac output. The ECG is often bizarre. Adrenaline (10 ml of 1 in 10 000 IV) or isoprenaline (25–100 mcg IV) and calcium gluconate (20 ml 10 per cent IV) should be administered.

Intravenous access

The transit time of a drug from a peripheral vein to the heart can be in excess of three minutes, due to a low cardiac output and tricuspid incompetence. Suitably experienced personnel should insert a central venous line remembering the risk of pneumothorax (see Practical Procedure 3). The use of intra-

Table 1.1 Drug doses used in cardiac arrest[a]

Drug	Intravenous	Endotracheal
Adrenaline	10 ml of 1 in 10 000	20 ml of 1 in 10 000
Atropine	1 mg	2 mg
Bretylium tosylate (slow injection; may take 15 minutes to work)	500 mg	—
Calcium chloride (must not be injected with bicarbonate)	10 ml of 10%	—
Isoprenaline (infusion 2 mg in 500 ml 5% dextrose. Rate as appropriate)	25–100 mcg	—
Lignocaine	100 mg (1–3 mg/min IV as infusion)	200 mg
Sodium bicarbonate (Not as routine. ABG should be measured as soon as possible)	50 ml of 8.4%	—

[a] All doses based on 70 kg man.

cardiac injections is an unsatisfactory alternative, carrying with it a high risk of pneumothorax, direct myocardial damage and intramural injection of drugs.

If difficulties in venous access are encountered, drugs can be administered by the intratracheal route, through a suction catheter or long venous cannula into the endotracheal tube (Table 1.1).

Management of Patients after Cardiac Arrest

Following successful resuscitation patients will require intensive care. If the patient is conscious he will usually be managed in a CCU, if unconscious usually in an ICU.

1 If the patient has regained consciousness he should be turned on his side and then extubated (to lessen the risk

of aspiration). Supplemental oxygen should be administered.

2 Consciousness may not have been regained because of cerebral hypoxia during the period of cardiac arrest (vide infra).

3 Antiarrhythmic drugs should be continued; in particular following ventricular fibrillation lignocaine should be infused at 1–3 mg/hr. (See Chapter 2.)

4 The following investigations should be performed:
   (a) CXR (pneumothorax, correct placement of lines and endotracheal tube, fractured ribs, evidence of aspiration of stomach contents).
   (b) ABG (acidosis, oxygenation and ventilation).
   (c) U&E (plasma potassium).
   (d) 12-lead ECG (arrhythmia, evidence of infarction).

Impaired conscious level

1 If consciousness has not been regained, further treatment to prevent coughing and straining and other factors exacerbating cerebral oedema (see Chapter 12) may be necessary.

2 Prophylaxis against stress-induced gastric ulceration (see Chapter 9) and treatment of aspiration pneumonia (see Chapter 6) may be necessary.

3 The routine period of intensive treatment following a cardiac arrest should be 48 hours. At this time, all sedative and paralysing drugs should be discontinued to permit formal assessment of cerebral state.

Convulsions

Initially these should be treated with small bolus doses of diazepam (5–10 mg IV). Should the fits continue, refer to Chapter 13.

Blood sugar

This should be measured regularly and if necessary an IV insulin infusion used to maintain blood glucose concentrations between 4 and 9 mmol/l. Avoidance of hypo- and hyperglycaemia lessens any neurological damage present.

NOTES

CHAPTER 2

Cardiac Arrhythmias

Cardiac tissues have the electrical characteristics of automaticity, excitability, conductivity, velocity of conduction and the refractory period. Changes in any of these can result in arrhythmias. The cardiac rate and rhythm are controlled by the SA node, which has the highest automaticity, and is situated near the superior vena cava in the right atrium. The impulse travels down the atrium, across the atrioventricular (AV) node and down the bundle of His and depolarises the ventricles.

Arrhythmias may be caused by any one of three mechanisms:

1 Change in automaticity. Pacemaker sites arise elsewhere other than in the SA node and suppress it. Alternatively, the SA node itself may be diseased and have a low automaticity allowing either escape or rapid ectopic rhythms to develop.

2 Re-entry may occur when the propagating impulse continues to re-excite the heart, after the end of its refractory period. Arrhythmias most commonly arise when underlying organic heart disease is present.

3 Disorders of conducting pathways.

Arrhythmias arise both in the diseased and the normal heart, when factors regulating normal cardiac muscle are disturbed. These include changes in potassium concentration, acid–base imbalance, drugs, catecholamines, hypoxia and hypercarbia.

Principles of treatment of arrhythmias are:

1 Identify the arrhythmia.

2 Arrhythmias causing severe haemodynamic disturbance need immediate correction usually with DC cardioversion or pacing.
3 Identify and correct any precipitating or exacerbating factor (pain, hypokalaemia or hyperkalaemia, hypoxia, hypercarbia or hypocalcaemia).
4 Antiarrhythmic agents are usually negative inotropes and many can induce arrhythmias. The use of multiple agents should be avoided.

Arrhythmias may be of two sorts:

1 Disorders of impulse formation.
2 Disorders of impulse conduction.

Disorders of Impulse Formation

Arrhythmias of this type are either supraventricular or ventricular.

Supraventricular arrhythmias

Sinus arrhythmia

This is normal, especially in young people.

ECG

The R-to-R interval varies with respiration, but the shape of the P waves and the duration of the PR interval are constant. The rate increases during inspiration (see Figure 2.1). It is important to differentiate this from other arrhythmias. No treatment is needed.

Sinus tachycardia

A heart rate above 100 per minute is very common in patients requiring intensive care. It is associated with anxiety and pain, pregnancy, pyrexia, hypovolaemia, thyrotoxicosis, CO_2 retention, heart failure and anaemia. It can be induced by drugs such as atropine. Tachycardia may precipitate angina in patients with ischaemic heart disease.

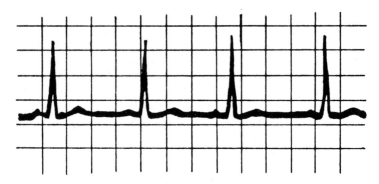

Figure 2.1   Sinus arrhythmia

Treatment is directed at the underlying cause. Beta-blockers are used to reduce the rate in thyrotoxicosis.

Sinus bradycardia

A heart rate of below 60 per minute is normal in sleep and in athletic subjects. It is pathological in myxoedema, raised intracranial pressure, sick sinus syndrome, obstructive jaundice, hypothermia, following myocardial infarction and following the administration of drugs such as beta-blockers, verapamil and digoxin.

1. Treat the underlying cause, when indicated.
2. Atropine (0.3–0.6 mg IV) may be given to increase the ventricular rate if the bradycardia is causing hypotension, oliguria or confusion.
3. Do not treat the bradycardia unnecessarily after MI if it is asymptomatic; it may exert a protective effect by reducing myocardial oxygen requirements.

Supraventricular extrasystoles

These are induced by ischaemic heart disease, stress, coffee and alcohol consumption, smoking, drugs such as digoxin and theophylline, and electrolytic and metabolic disorders. They are usually asymptomatic and only become significant if they progress to atrial tachycardia or fibrillation.

ECG

Atrial extrasystoles are diagnosed by the appearance of a premature P wave of abnormal morphology, followed by a QRS-complex and T wave of the same configuration as a sinus beat (see Figure 2.2). If the extrasystole arises in the region of the AV node, the P wave may be close in front of, or close behind, the QRS complex, or buried in the QRS complex.

Treat only if they are causing haemodynamic upset, in which case give a beta-blocking agent such as practolol (1–5 mg IV in increments to a total of 20 mg).

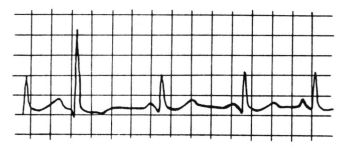

Figure 2.2   Supraventricular extrasystole

Supraventricular tachycardia (SVT)

SVT may follow myocardial infarction and is associated with thyrotoxicosis, mitral valve disease and the Wolff–Parkinson–White (WPW) syndrome. SVT with 2:1 block is characteristic of digoxin toxicity.

The patient usually complains of palpitations and dizziness; dyspnoea, syncope and chest pain are less frequent. There may be signs of cardiac failure and polyuria.

ECG

A rapid rate of between 140 and 250 beats per minute is present. The P waves, if not obscured completely, are abnormal and in fixed duration to each QRS complex (see Figure 2.3). The QRS is normal unless aberrant conduction is also present, in which case differentiation from ventricular tachycardia can be difficult. The T wave has the same shape as in the sinus beat.

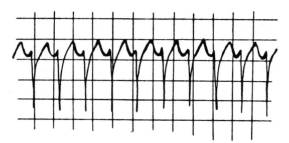

Figure 2.3   Supraventricular tachycardia

Treatment

1 Carotid sinus massage is diagnostically and occasionally therapeutically useful, as it may slow the rate, or revert the rhythm to sinus rhythm. Massage one side only at a time.

2 Verapamil (5–10 mg IV) is the most effective drug.

Have 10 ml of 10 per cent calcium gluconate available to reverse any unwanted effects of verapamil. *Do not use beta-blockers if you have given verapamil.*

3 Beta-blockers (e.g., practolol).

4 Second-line drugs:
  (a) Disopyramide (2 mg/kg IV over 5 minutes, to a maximum of 150 mg). This can be followed by 200 mg orally every eight hours, or 400 mcg/kg/hr by IV infusion.
  (b) Amiodarone: 5 mg/kg IV over 30 minutes (maximum of 1.2 g/24 hr).
  (c) Digoxin.

5 DC shock.

6 Pacing: Overdrive or underdrive pacing (using a pacing rate above or below the arrhythmia rate, respectively) may be used to suppress automaticity, or interrupt a re-entry mechanism.

Atrial flutter

This arrhythmia occurs in the abnormal heart, usually in the presence of ischaemic or rheumatic heart disease. It may precipitate the onset of cardiac failure. Unlike other supraventricular tachycardias, it is rarely a manifestation of digoxin toxicity.

ECG

The atrial rate is about 300 per minute; the P waves are replaced by flutter waves, giving a sawtooth appearance to the baseline (see Figure 2.4). The AV node does not conduct all the atrial beats and a 2:1- or 3:1-block results. Flutter waves may be confused with a T wave. The flutter waves may be made more obvious on the ECG by carotid sinus massage, which slows down AV conduction and, hence, the ventricular rate.

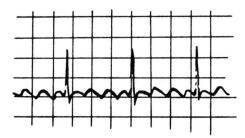

Figure 2.4   Atrial flutter

Treatment

1 DC cardioversion is the treatment of choice.
2 Otherwise use digoxin, verapamil or beta-blockers to control the ventricular rate.
3 Overdrive pacing may be used, instead of cardioversion, if the patient is already receiving digoxin.

Atrial fibrillation (AF)

Chronic AF is associated with ischaemic heart disease, mitral valve disease and cardiomyopathies. Paroxysmal AF is a feature of the WPW syndrome, pulmonary embolus, hypoxia, thyrotoxicosis and chest trauma, including thoracotomy. Digoxin toxicity may be a cause of AF if it is associated with a slow ventricular rate and frequent ventricular ectopics. AF can cause palpitations, hypotension, and may precipitate cardiac failure.

ECG

Absent P waves are replaced by a totally irregular ECG baseline (fibrillation waves) and a rapid, irregular ventricular rate (see Figure 2.5). The QRS complexes are usually of normal configuration.

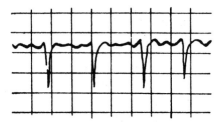

Figure 2.5   Atrial fibrillation

Treatment

1 Digoxin slows the ventricular rate and is the drug of choice for the treatment of chronic atrial fibrillation.
   How to digitalise a patient. Ensure the patient has not received digoxin recently (excretion is delayed in renal failure).
   Give 0.5 mg IV over 30 minutes.
   A further 0.25 mg should be given IV over 30 minutes after three hours.
   Give 0.125 mg after 12 and 18 hours depending on the response.
   Do not exceed 1.0 mg in 24 hours.
   Lower doses are required in the elderly and in patients with poor renal function. Further doses should be guided by serum digoxin levels, which should be performed six hours after the last dose.
2 A beta-blocker may be added to the digoxin, to control the ventricular rate.

In paroxysmal atrial fibrillation the aim of treatment is to restore sinus rhythm, using digoxin, beta-blockers or DC cardioversion.

3 Consider the use of anticoagulants, if time permits, to prevent arterial embolisation on the return of sinus rhythm.

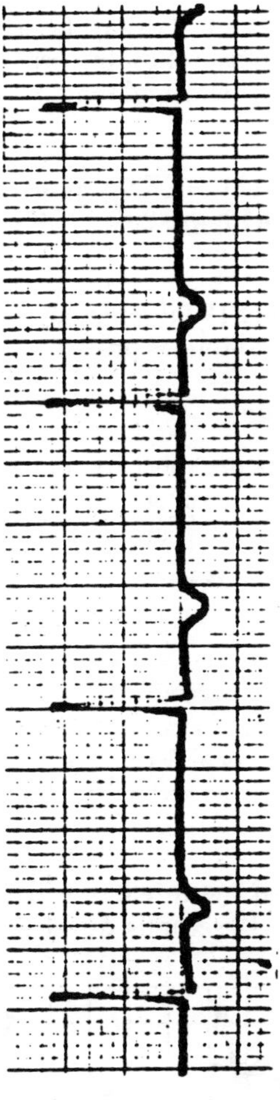

Figure 2.6 Nodal rhythm

Nodal rhythm

When the SA node discharges slowly the AV node may take over the role of pacemaker. It may be a manifestation of digoxin toxicity, or it may follow myocardial infarction or procedures causing excessive vagal tone.

ECG

The rhythm is regular and the QRS complexes normal, but not preceded by P waves (see Figure 2.6).

Treatment

Give atropine (0.3–0.6 mg IV) if haemodynamic disturbances occur, or if excessive vagal tone is present.

Ventricular arrhythmias

Ventricular arrhythmias are most frequently associated with ischaemic heart disease, the severity of the arrhythmias being a reflection of the extent of the coronary artery disease.

Ventricular extrasystoles (VE)

These result from myocardial ischaemia and infarction, digoxin toxicity, endogenous or exogenous catecholamines, valvular heart disease, myocarditis and cardiomyopathy. Frequent unifocal VEs may occur in normal individuals after exercise. However, multifocal VE are found in patients with cardiac disease and increase cardiovascular mortality.

ECG

A sinus beat is followed by an early wide and bizarre QRS complex (of more than 0.12 seconds' duration), not preceded by

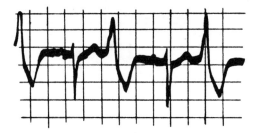

Figure 2.7   Ventricular extrasystoles

a P wave (see Figure 2.7). The VE is followed by a compensatory pause. When the extrasystole appears on the T wave of the preceding beat (R on T), it may precipitate ventricular tachycardia or fibrillation.

Treatment

Drug therapy is *not* generally required in most cases of asymptomatic VEs. There is no evidence that suppressing or reducing VEs improves prognosis. Precipitating causes should be corrected.

Ventricular tachycardia

This is defined as three or more consecutive VEs at a rate above 100 beats per minute. If the rate is below 100 beats per minute, the rhythm is idioventricular and requires no treatment. Ventricular tachycardia may be asymptomatic or it may cause syncope, marked haemodynamic impairment and cardiac arrest. It may progress to VF.

ECG

Abnormally shaped, broad (more than 0.12 seconds' duration) irregular QRS-complexes rhythm (see Figure 2.8). P waves, when present, are dissociated from the QRS complex.

Treatment

1 DC cardioversion is indicated in the presence of haemodynamic impairment, or if drug therapy is ineffective.

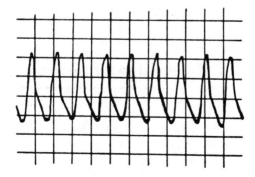

Figure 2.8   Ventricular tachycardia

2 Intravenous lignocaine is the drug of choice. Give 100 mg as a bolus over two minutes. If reversion to sinus rhythm occurs, the bolus should be followed by an infusion of 4 mg/min for 30 minutes, 2 mg/min for two hours and then 1 mg/min.

3 Disopyramide, mexiletine, tocainide and amiodarone are useful second-line drugs.

4 Correct any acid–base balance and plasma potassium abnormalities.

5 Overdrive pacing is useful, if ventricular tachycardia recurs enough to necessitate frequent cardioversion.

Torsades de pointes

Congenital or acquired (usually drug-induced) prolongation of the QT interval may lead to atypical ventricular tachycardia (Torsades de pointes).

ECG

Torsades de pointes is rapid ventricular tachycardia with a changing QRS morphology and may progress to ventricular fibrillation (see Figure 2.9).

Treatment

1 Antiarrhythmics may aggravate the arrhythmia in Torsades de pointes and are contraindicated.

2 Stop any drug that may prolong the QT interval.

3 Overdrive pacing is the treatment of choice, when indicated.

Ventricular fibrillation and asystole

See Chapter 1.

Disorders of Impulse Conduction

The impulse may:

1 Be slowly conducted – first-degree heart block or aberration of ventricular complexes.

2 Be completely blocked – second- and third-degree heart block.

3 Travel down an abnormal pathway – WPW syndrome.

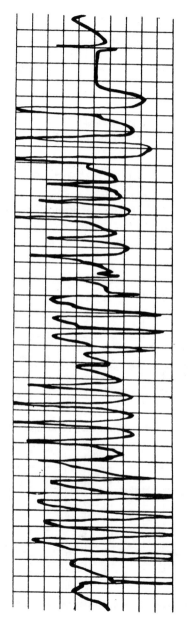

Figure 2.9   Torsades de pointes

Atrioventricular block

The causes of AV block are ischaemic heart disease, drugs such as digoxin, beta-blockers, fibrosis of the AV node, myocarditis, hypoxia, hyperkalaemia, aortic stenosis and cardiomyopathy. It is also caused by congenital abnormalities.

ECG

First-degree block. Every P wave is followed by a normal QRS complex, but the PR interval is more than 0.2 seconds (see Figure 2.10).

Second-degree block. This is of two types:

1   In Mobitz-type I block (Wenckebach), the PR interval progressively lengthens, until one P wave is not conducted, thus failing to produce a QRS complex (see Figure 2.11). This is then followed by a conducted beat

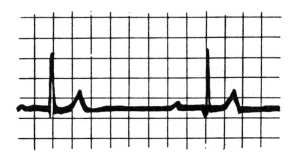

Figure 2.10   First-degree atrioventricular block

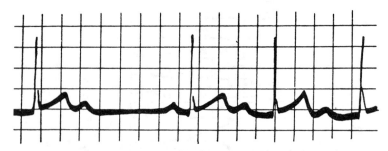

Figure 2.11   Mobitz-type I second-degree atrioventricular block

with a short PR interval, and a repetition of the sequence.

2· Mobitz-type II block occurs when, despite a constant PR interval, some P waves are not conducted, the ratio of conducted to non-conducted beats being variable (2:1 or 3:1 block) (see Figure 2.12).

Third-degree block. There is no relationship between the P waves and QRS complexes (see Figure 2.13).

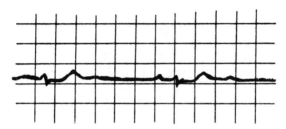

Figure 2.12   Mobitz-type II second-degree atrioventricular block

Bundle branch blocks

Right bundle branch blocks (RBBB)

RBBB may be normal or secondary to pulmonary embolus, atrial septal defect or myocarditis. It may follow right heart catheterisation.

ECG

RBBB causes an RSR pattern in V1, a wide, slurred S wave in V6 and an increase in QRS duration to more than 0.12 seconds (see Figure 2.14).

Left bundle branch block (LBBB)

LBBB almost always indicates underlying heart disease, be it ischaemic, hypertensive or valvular. The left bundle is divided into anterior and posterior fascicles, either of which may fail to conduct (hemiblock).

ECG

LBBB produces an M pattern in V6 and an increase in QRS duration to more than 0.12 seconds (see Figure 2.15).

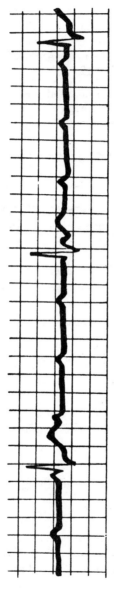

Figure 2.13   Third-degree atrioventricular block

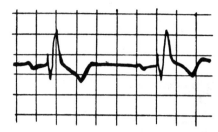

Figure 2.14   Right bundle branch block (lead V1)

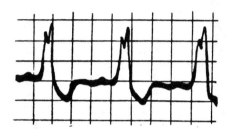

Figure 2.15   Left bundle branch block (lead V6)

Left anterior hemiblock causes left axis deviation (see Figure 2.16).

Left posterior hemiblock causes right axis deviation (see Figure 2.17). Combined RBBB and left hemiblock is bifascicular block.

Treatment of the heart blocks

1 Stop any drug that may be causing or exacerbating the conduction defect.

2 Observe first-degree heart block and Wenckebach closely. Pacing may be indicated, if they progress to more advanced conduction defects, or compromise cardiac function.

3 The decision to pace is *not* made on the presence of specific arrhythmias, but on the associated symptoms (Stokes–Adams attacks) and haemodynamic effects.

4 Pacing is normally required in bifascicular block, Mobitz-type II and third-degree heart block following an MI.

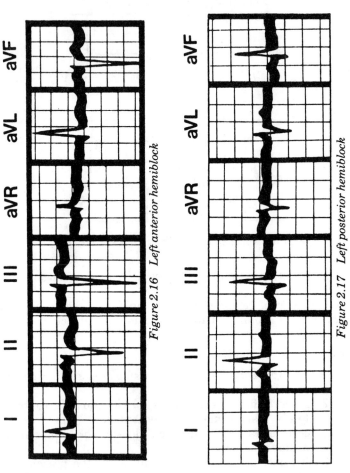

Figure 2.16   Left anterior hemiblock

Figure 2.17   Left posterior hemiblock

5 Isoprenaline infusion (1 mg in 500 ml 5 per cent dextrose) may be used to increase the heart rate temporarily, until pacing is instituted. The infusion rate is titrated to the heart rate.

Wolff–Parkinson–White syndrome (WPW syndrome)

This consists of pre-excitation, complicated by paroxysmal supraventricular tachycardia of the re-entry type. Anterograde conduction takes place via the AV node and retrograde conduction through an anomalous pathway (usually the bundle of Kent).

ECG

In sinus rhythm the WPW syndrome is diagnosed by a PR interval less than 0.12 seconds and a widened QRS complex with a slurred upstroke (delta wave) (see Figure 2.18).

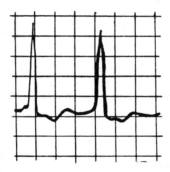

Figure 2.18   Wolff–Parkinson–White syndrome

Treatment

1 Treatment of supraventricular tachycardia (SVT) and WPW is similar to that of SVT of any other aetiology. Recognition of WPW is, however, important since special considerations are necessary when treating paroxysmal atrial fibrillation and WPW.
2 In this situation digoxin, verapamil and beta-blockers are contraindicated, since they do not increase the refractoriness of the anomalous pathway.

3 Disopyramide (2 mg/kg IV) injected over at least five minutes, is the drug of choice, but may take 15 minutes to work.

Digoxin toxicity

Various arrhythmias may result from digoxin toxicity, and this should be suspected in anyone taking the drug who develops a rhythm or conduction problem, especially in the presence of renal failure, dehydration or diuretics. Characteristic rhythm disturbances include supraventricular tachycardia with block, slow atrial fibrillation with VE, bigeminy, ventricular tachycardia and heart block. Associated symptoms include anorexia, nausea, confusion, lassitude and visual disturbances. Serum digoxin levels should be performed, although toxicity may occur in the presence of hypokalaemia or hypercalcaemia even if digoxin levels are normal. Plasma digoxin levels above 4 nmol/l indicate toxicity is likely.

Treatment

1 Stop digoxin.
2 Correct hypokalaemia. Do not give potassium if hyperkalaemia or AV block is present.
3 Usually these measures are all that is necessary.

Other measures include:

4 Perform gastric lavage if toxicity is due to deliberate oral overdosage.
5 Phenytoin (3.5–5 mg/kg IV at a maximum rate of 50 mg/min) or lignocaine are useful for serious ventricular arrhythmias, but combination of these drugs should be avoided.
6 Beta-blockers are useful, but may worsen AV conduction.
7 Temporary pacing is indicated for high degrees of AV block.
8 Cardioversion is used only if life-threatening arrhythmias are present, as it may induce dangerous ventricular rhythms. Use low energy levels and give prophylactic lignocaine (100 mg IV).
9 Digoxin Fab antibodies are potentially life-saving in severe toxicity.

Appendix

ECG paper

Vertical axis represents voltage
1 mm square = 0.1 mV
Horizontal axis represents time
5 mm square = 0.2 second (i.e. 25 mm/sec).

ECG variables

PR interval	0.12–0.20 second
QRS complex	0.04–0.10 second
P wave	Less than 0.11 second
QRS axis	−30' to +110'
	More positive than 90' = right axis deviation
	More negative than −30' = left axis deviation

$$\text{Corrected QT interval} = \frac{\text{Measured QT interval}}{\text{Square root of cycle length}}$$

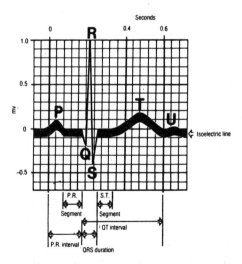

Figure 2.19   Normal ECG recorded at 25 mm/sec with 10 mm = 1 millivolt

NOTES

CHAPTER 3

Shock

Shock is the failure of the cardiovascular system to provide the tissues with essential nutrients and to remove the waste products. In many clinical circumstances the rule of 100 is a helpful guide to the presence of shock in adults: when the patient has a heart rate in excess of 100 beats per minute and a systolic blood pressure of less than 100 mmHg shock is present. Although this rule is useful, it does not always apply, as patients may have high blood pressures or low heart rates and still be shocked.

Blood pressure depends on the cardiac output and systemic vascular resistance (afterload).

Cardiac output

This is the product of heart rate and stroke volume. Stroke volume is determined by preload, afterload and myocardial contractility. Raising preload increases the tension in the myocardial muscle and produces a reflex rise in the strength of myocardial muscle contraction with an increase in stroke volume. Excessive preload, however, will overdistend the muscle fibres, with a resultant fall in stroke volume. In addition, fluid will leak into the lungs and may result in pulmonary oedema. In clinical practice, preload of the right side of the heart is measured by introducing a catheter into a large central vein and measuring the pressure within it (central venous pressure). If myocardial function is normal, it can also be used as a guide to left heart filling pressures; in more critically ill patients, who may have abnormal myocardial function, pulmonary capillary wedge pressure is a better measure of left heart filling pressures (see Practical Procedure 4).

Systemic vascular resistance

Afterload is the resistance of the vascular system that the heart pumps against. The vascular resistances in the pulmonary and systemic circulations are different. The pulmonary circulation has a low resistance (155–255 dyne sec cm^{-5}), whereas the systemic circulation has a high resistance (950–1300 dyne sec cm^{-5}). The right ventricle therefore has less muscle than the left ventricle, despite pumping the same amount of blood per minute. Changes in systemic vascular resistance (SVR) can only be measured when the cardiac output is known, and this usually entails the use of a thermodilution flow-directed pulmonary artery flotation catheter (PAFC), although non-invasive methods may become available.

An increase in SVR may be recognised clinically as vasoconstriction. It is seen in hypovolaemic states and in states where a low cardiac output occurs, such as cardiogenic shock.

A low systemic vascular resistance is recognised clinically as vasodilatation. It occurs in septic and anaphylactic shock.

Adrenergic System

There are three major adrenergic receptor systems recognised in the cardiovascular system.

Alpha-receptors

Two types of alpha-receptors (alpha$_1$- and alpha$_2$-receptors) have been identified – both are predominantly concerned with the maintenance of systemic vascular resistance.

Alpha$_1$-receptors produce vasoconstriction when stimulated and are found on vascular smooth muscles.

Alpha$_2$-receptors are found on the presynaptic nerve terminal and cause a decrease in noradrenaline release when they are stimulated.

Beta-receptors

These are subdivided into beta$_1$- and beta$_2$-receptors.

Beta$_1$-receptors are found in the heart and when stimulated increase contractility, heart rate, conduction velocity and decrease the refractory period.

Beta$_2$-receptor stimulation causes relaxation of uterine muscle and of the bronchial muscle, resulting in bronchodilatation. They are also located in blood vessels supplying muscles, where stimulation leads to vasodilatation.

Dopamine receptors

These receptors are located in the splanchnic and renal circulation. Stimulation of these receptors results in vasodilatation leading to an increase in splanchnic and renal blood flow, which may cause hypotension.

Normal values and formulae for calculating derived variables are included in the appendix to this chapter.

Aetiology and Treatment

Shock is a common emergency encountered in the ICU and is usually due to one of the following causes.

1 Hypovolaemia
2 Sepsis
3 Pump failure (cardiogenic shock)
4 Anaphylaxis
5 Pulmonary embolism (see Chapter 6)

Although these are discussed separately below, it is important to remember that several causes for shock may coexist at the same time in the same patient. In all patients who are in shock, for whatever reason, certain common steps in treatment and resuscitation should be undertaken. The order in which these steps are taken will vary according to the patient's condition. They include the following:

1 Establish venous access with a large (14 G) cannula and, if hypovolaemia is suspected, infuse a volume expander. Further intravenous cannulae may be necessary.
2 Monitoring
   (a) In the profoundly shocked patient, the insertion of a

radial artery catheter will allow the prompt recognition of any change in the patient's condition and facilitate the collection of arterial blood.

(b) A continuous ECG to display heart rate and rhythm.

(c) Central venous pressure (CVP) measurement. The insertion of a central venous catheter (see Practical Procedure 3) allows measurement of CVP, an invaluable guide to the adequacy of intravascular volume replacement. If the pressure is low (less than 2 mmHg), fluid replacement can be given rapidly, without fear of overloading the circulation and causing pulmonary oedema. If it is high and the patient's blood pressure is still low, a bolus of fluid (200–300 ml) should be given; if the CVP rises, and then falls again, further boluses can be given. If it rises and stays up, further fluid administration may not be indicated. The usual upper limit of CVP is 10–12 mmHg during artificial ventilation and 8 mmHg during spontaneous ventilation. Patients with impaired myocardial function may benefit from a PAFC to help in their resuscitation and management.

(d) A urinary catheter is inserted, and hourly urine output measured.

(e) Core and peripheral temperature measurement. The normal core (rectal or oesophageal) to peripheral (great toe) difference is 2–5°C. The difference increases with shock, and the changing difference can be used as an indicator of the effectiveness of treatment.

3 Adequate ventilation and oxygenation must be ensured, and it is safer to ventilate the patient artificially at an early stage if respiratory insufficiency is clinically evident. All shocked patients should receive supplemental oxygen.

4 Early correction of severe acid–base deficit (base excess > 10 mMol/l) should be effected with small increments of 8.4 per cent sodium bicarbonate into a central venous catheter, or 1.4 per cent sodium bicarbonate into a peripheral vein. Acidaemia is a myocardial depressant and will exacerbate the shock.

5 Adequate analgesia must be administered to a shocked patient in pain (see Chapter 17). Opiates must not be administered IM, as they will not be absorbed because of vasoconstriction, until resuscitation is complete; when they may then be absorbed in large amounts, causing toxicity. Small doses of morphine (1–2 mg) should be given IV and repeated every three minutes until the pain is relieved.

6 To prevent renal vasoconstriction and subsequent renal impairment, a dopaminergic stimulator (dopamine 2 mcg/kg/min) should be infused as soon as shock is diagnosed.

Hypovolaemic Shock

Hypovolaemic shock is caused by excessive loss of fluid from the body.

1 Blood loss – following trauma or surgery.
2 Plasma loss – following burns or gastrointestinal loss.
3 Salt and water loss – dehydration following diarrhoea, excessive or prolonged exposure to heat, diabetes mellitus or Addison's disease.

Treatment

Hypovolaemia should be treated by intravascular volume expansion with an appropriate fluid.

If the patient has lost blood, then whole blood should be used to replace the loss. When the losses are a mixture of blood and exudate (such as following abdominal surgery), the haematocrit should be measured after every 2 l of blood and maintained at approximately 0.35, using a mixture of blood, human albumin solution (HAS), fresh frozen plasma (FFP), etc. If large volumes of blood are infused measure the ionised calcium and give bolus doses of 10 ml of 10 per cent calcium gluconate IV to maintain the ionised calcium between 1 and 1.5 mmol/l.

Hypovolaemia from other causes, resulting in hypotension and shock, should be treated initially with plasma volume expansion, using a colloid solution. This can be 4.5 per cent

HAS or a synthetic plasma volume expander, such as gelatin solution or hydroxyethyl starch. (Some centres prefer to use crystalloid solutions, e.g., Hartmann's solution, for resuscitation.)

Adequacy of volume replacement can be gauged by a falling heart rate, increasing blood pressure, increasing urine output and warming of the peripheries (i.e. falling core to peripheral temperature difference). Further guidance, if necessary, can be obtained from CVP measurement.

Once intravascular volume has been restored other fluids can be administered, as necessary, to replace extravascular fluid losses, such as those seen in dehydration.

Cardiogenic Shock

This follows damage to the myocardium by ischaemia, infarction or myocardial toxins. The patient is peripherally cold and clammy with his skin blue and mottled, and he may have an obtunded conscious level. As the myocardium is damaged, CVP may not accurately reflect filling pressures on the left side of the heart, and the insertion of a thermodilution PAFC is invaluable in assessing whether hyper- or hypovolaemia is present. In addition the measurement of cardiac output enables the rational choice of inotropes or vasodilators and determination of their correct dose.

Treatment

1 Correct any arrhythmias.
2 Inotropes to improve contractility in a failing heart. Dobutamine at a starting dose to 5 mcg/kg/min by infusion is the inotrope of first choice; the dose is increased by increments of 5 mcg/kg/min up to 40 mcg/kg/min. If doses of more than 40 mcg/kg/min fail to produce an adequate cardiac output, other inotropes may need to be added. The choice of inotrope should be made on the basis of the underlying haemodynamic disturbance (Table 3.1).

Table 3.1 *Receptor selectivity of common used inotropes. Suggested dose ranges are intended as a guide only.*

Drug	Dose[a]	Alpha	Beta$_1$	Beta$_2$	Dopamine	Note[b]
Adrenaline	B 0.2–0.5 mg	++	++	++	—	T
	I 0.05–0.3[d]	—	++	++	—	T
	I > 0.3	++	++	++	—	T
Dobutamine	I 2–40	—	++	+	—	
Dopamine[c]	I 0.5–2[d]	—	—	—	++	E
	I 2–5	—	++	—	++	E
	I 5–10	+	++	++	—	E
	I > 10	+++	++	++	—	E
Dopexamine	I 2–8[d]	—	+	++	++	T
Isoprenaline	B 10–20 mcg	—	++	++	—	T
	I 0.05–0.3	—	++	++	—	T
Noradrenaline	I 0.026–0.3	++	+	—	—	E
Phenylephrine	B 0.1–0.5 mg	++	+	—	—	
	I 1–5	++	+	—	—	

[a] B = bolus dose; I = infusion dose in mcg/kg/min. All can be diluted in 5 per cent dextrose.
[b] T = care in the presence of tachydysrhythmias; E = tissue necrosis if extravasation occurs.
[c] Dopamine hydrochloride is best reserved for use as a dopaminergic agonist to preserve renal blood flow during periods of shock.
[d] May produce a fall in blood pressure at low doses.

3 Afterload reduction to reduce peripheral vasoconstriction by infusing a short-acting vasodilator such as:

   (a) Nitroglycerin (10 mcg/min increasing by 10 mcg/min every 10 minutes).
   (b) Sodium nitroprusside (10–15 mcg/min increasing by 10–15 mcg/min to a maximum of 1.5 mcg/kg/min with a maximum total dose of 3.5 mg/kg).
   (c) Isosorbide dinitrate (2–10 mg/hr).

All decrease the amount of work performed by a damaged heart. If the patient has a low cardiac output, the addition of an inotrope will be necessary to prevent hypotension, and this combination will be better than either alone. In these circumstances, a thermodilution PAFC is essential.

4 Correction of hypovolaemia, which may have been induced by aggressive diuretic therapy.

5 Balloon assistance of the circulation may be useful to support the patient while awaiting surgery, or in the immediate postcardiac surgery period, when myocardial function is expected to improve.

Septic Shock

This can be caused by any organism, but is most commonly caused by Gram-negative bacteria. In all patients requiring intensive care whose general condition deteriorates in a non-specific way (such as failure to absorb nasogastric feeds), sepsis must be excluded. It may arise not only from their original illness or injury, but also from organisms colonising, or gaining access by, the monitoring lines. In addition to antibiotics, other general supportive treatment may be necessary, including the institution of assisted ventilation. Three components may contribute to cardiovascular dysfunction in septic shock.

1 In the early stages, peripheral vasodilation may occur, with a low systemic vascular resistance (SVR). Later on, vasoconstriction occurs, leading to a markedly increased SVR.

2 Hypovolaemia: the capillaries become leaky and allow protein-rich fluid to leak into the tissues; in particular, into the lungs. In addition, vasodilation may lead to an increased capacitance of the intravascular compartment.

3 Myocardial depression: the combined effects of bacterial toxins and a metabolic acidosis lead to a deterioration in myocardial function.

On the basis of the peripheral circulation and the cardiac output, two subclassifications of septic shock are commonly used.

Warm septic shock

This occurs early on and is characterised by warm peripheries, a high cardiac output, a low systemic vascular resistance and, often, decreased right and left atrial filling pressures, indicative of hypovolaemia (if untreated).

Cold septic shock

This follows if delayed or ineffective treatment is given to a patient with warm septic shock and is characterised by marked peripheral vasoconstriction, with blue and mottled peripheries (resulting from an increase in SVR), a fall in cardiac output and, possibly, a rise in left and right atrial filling pressures, indicating myocardial depression.

Treatment

1 Antibiotics (see Chapter 19), but only after blood cultures and other specimens (sputum, urine, etc.) have been sent for microbiological examination.
2 Restoration of circulating blood volume with a colloid solution (i.e. HAS), with guidance from CVP measurement, in patients with warm septic shock, or from PAFC readings, in patients with cold septic shock, or in those who develop pulmonary or renal dysfunction.
3 Inotropic support of a depressed myocardium initially using dobutamine as described under cardiogenic shock.
4 Manipulation of the SVR.
   (a) Low: a peripheral vasoconstrictor should be infused (phenylephrine 2–5 mcg/kg/min). This may decrease renal blood flow, with a consequent fall in urine production and may be overcome by infusing dopamine in a dopaminergic dose.
   (b) High: a peripheral vasodilator should be given to decrease myocardial work, in the manner described under cardiogenic shock.

Methylprednisolone in pharmacological doses (30 mg/kg) is currently thought to be contraindicated in septic shock and may increase mortality.

In any patient who requires large doses of vasoactive drugs, but fails to respond to them, consider the possibility of acute adrenal hypofunction. Perform a short ACTH (tetracosactrin

Synacthen) test and, without waiting for the result, give IV
hydrocortisone (see Chapter 14).

Anaphylactic Shock

This follows the administration of a substance to which a
patient is allergic. The term is used loosely and is applied to
patients who have undergone true anaphylaxis involving IgE,
as well as to those who have had an anaphylactoid reaction,
when the complement system has been activated via the
alternate pathway. Although different mechanisms are
involved, both result in a clinically indistinguishable picture
of shock. The major pathophysiological disturbance is the
release of pharmacologically active peptides, which may cause
vasodilation, vasoconstriction, increase capillary leakiness,
bronchoconstriction and which act as myocardial toxins.

Clinical features

Symptoms include shock, bronchospasm, cough, flushing and a
rash in addition to intense central and peripheral cyanosis.

Investigation

Venous blood (5 ml) should be put into EDTA tubes (pink) and
5 ml into a plain tube as soon as possible after the onset of the
reaction and thereafter at 10 minutes, 20 minutes, 30 minutes,
one hour, three hours, six hours and 24 hours, after the onset of
the reaction. Send the EDTA samples to the haematology
laboratory for WBC + differential. The serum in the plain
tubes should be separated off (in a centrifuge), clearly labelled
(date and time) and deep-frozen. Subsequent analysis by an
immunological laboratory can be arranged later.

Treatment

Early treatment is necessary to halt the progress of rapid
profound shock, with poor tissue perfusion, acidosis and
myocardial depression resulting in further hypotension.

1 Intravascular volume expansion using large quantities of a colloid solution (i.e. HAS). There is little place for blood transfusion as haematocrits are often high, because of the loss of plasma from the circulation.
2 Acidosis should be corrected with 25 mmol increments of sodium bicarbonate IV.
3 Ventilatory support may be needed.
4 Adrenaline (2–5 ml of 1 in 10 000 IV), injected very slowly, is an alpha- and beta-agonist, reversing bronchospasm and acting as an inotrope. In addition, its alpha-stimulating effect may stabilise mast cell membranes, preventing further release of active peptides into the circulation. Great care is necessary with this drug in a patient who may be hypotensive, acidotic and possibly hypoxic to prevent further arrhythmias. It may need to be repeated several times.
5 Hydrocortisone (100–200 mg IV) may also stabilise mast cell membranes and reduce bronchospasm.
6 An antihistamine, such as chlorpheniramine (10 mg IV), is administered to block any further peripheral effects of histamine.
7 Bronchospasm should resolve following the administration of adrenaline (see above), but if it does not and further adrenaline is thought inadvisable due to hypertension or arrhythmias, then aminophylline (250 mg slowly IV) should be given.

It is important to document all events and possible precipitating drugs a patient may have received, in his notes so that further investigation of the collapse can be undertaken at a later date. Only true allergies should be documented on the front of a patient's notes and warrant the issuing of a warning letter or bracelet to the patient.

Appendix

Normal cardiovascular parameters and their calculation

Measured variables (mmHg)

Right atrium
  Mean -1 to $+7$

Right ventricle
  Systolic   15 to 25
  End diastolic   0 to 8

Pulmonary artery
  Systolic   15 to 25
  Diastolic   8 to 15
  Mean   10 to 20

Pulmonary capillary wedge pressure
  Mean   6 to 12

Derived variables

Mean arterial pressure (MAP) =

$$\text{diastolic} + \frac{(\text{systolic} - \text{diastolic})}{3} \text{ mmHg}$$

Systemic vascular resistance (SVR) $= \dfrac{(\text{MAP} - \text{CVP}) \times 80}{\text{CO}}$ (range: 950–1300 dyne sec cm^{-5})

Pulmonary vascular resistance (PVR) $= \dfrac{(\text{PAP} - \text{PCW}) \times 80}{\text{CO}}$ (range: 155–255 dyne sec cm^{-5})

Cardiac index $= \dfrac{\text{CO}}{\text{body surface area}}$ (range: 2.5–3.5 l/min/m^2)

NOTES

CHAPTER 4

Myocardial Infarction and Cardiac Failure

Myocardial Infarction (MI)

Myocardial ischaemia is the result of an imbalance between myocardial oxygen supply and myocardial oxygen demand. It most commonly arises in the presence of coronary athero-sclerosis, but may also be caused by anaemia, hypotension, arrhythmias or increased myocardial oxygen demands.

If ischaemia is severe or prolonged, MI (death of myocardial cells) results. Patients may be admitted to the ICU or CCU for the management of complications of myocardial infarction, or may suffer a myocardial infarction during the course of another illness.

Presentation

1 In the ICU, a change in the ECG may be the only sign.
2 Severe central crushing chest pain radiating to the arms or jaw.
3 Unexplained hypotension.
4 A third or fourth heart sound, or a pericardial rub, may be heard on auscultation.
5 A mild pyrexia.

Investigations

It is often more difficult to prove that infarction has *not* occurred.

Cardiac enzymes

Plasma levels of creatine phosphokinase (CPK) and serum glutamate-oxaloacetate transaminase (SGOT) rise and fall within two days. The lactate dehydrogenase (LDH) level reaches a peak at about three or four days and returns to normal within two weeks. As these enzymes are also found in liver, skeletal muscle, gut and kidney, a variety of other non-cardiac conditions can also cause elevation in serum enzyme levels. The use of the more specific isoenzymes (CK/MB and LDH1) is helpful in aiding the diagnosis of myocardial infarction. Cardiac enzymes should be measured each day for three days.

ECG

A twelve-lead ECG should be performed daily for three days in anyone suspected of MI. The changes associated with MI are T wave inversion, ST segment elevation and, later, development of pathological Q waves and loss of voltage in the QRS complexes in the leads facing the infarcted areas. Reciprocal changes (i.e. depressed ST segments and upright T waves) may occur in the leads opposite the region of acute infarction.

1 The changes of inferior infarction are seen in leads AVF, II and III.
2 Those of anterior infarction are confined to leads V3 and V4.
3 Anterolateral infarction causes changes in leads AVL and V4 to V6.
4 In anteroseptal infarction, the changes are seen in V1 to V4.

Full blood count

A polymorphonuclear leucocytosis is common. Any anaemia should be corrected by careful blood transfusion to increase the oxygen-carrying capacity of the blood.

Plasma urea and electrolytes

Correct any abnormalities of plasma potassium as these may precipitate or aggravate arrhythmias.

Chest X-ray (CXR)

A CXR should be obtained in every case of suspected or proven MI:

1 Cardiomegaly may indicate a dilated, poorly-functioning left ventricle, or pre-existing heart disease; rupture of a valve, the ventricular septum or ventricular wall (resulting in tamponade) may also cause this.

2 Look for signs of left ventricular failure: upper lobe venous diversion, Kerley B lines and pulmonary oedema. Radiographic signs of left ventricular failure tend to lag behind clinical improvement or deterioration.

3 Widening of the mediastinum should arouse suspicion of a dissecting aortic aneurysm.

Complications and their management

1 Arrhythmias should be managed along the lines described in Chapter 2.

2 Cardiogenic shock is described in Chapter 3. It should be regarded as a severe form of left ventricular failure. Cardiogenic shock after MI has a very high mortality rate (85–95 per cent). Following MI, inotropic agents should be used in the smallest effective dose and for the shortest possible time, as these drugs tend to increase myocardial oxygen demands thereby exacerbating myocardial ischaemia.

3 Cardiac failure: this is discussed below.

4 Pericarditis is common after MI; a pericardial rub is frequently heard during the course of the illness. The patient complains of chest pain which is related to posture and is pleuritic in nature. It is treated with aspirin or indomethacin.

5 Myocardial rupture is uncommon. It presents acutely with the signs of cardiac tamponade (hypotension, pallor, pulsus paradoxus, distended neck veins and distant heart sounds). Survival is dependent upon surgical repair.

6 Patients developing a ventricular septal defect (VSD) present with severe pulmonary oedema. A thrill is palpable and a pansystolic murmur is heard at the left sternal edge.

7 Mitral regurgitation is the result of papillary muscle dysfunction or rupture. A pansystolic, or late systolic, blowing murmur is heard at the apex in papillary

muscle dysfunction. When the muscle is ruptured, a pansystolic murmur is associated with severe pulmonary oedema. The differential diagnosis between a VSD and a mitral regurgitation can be made if a pulmonary artery catheter is in place, large V waves are seen on the wedged trace, in mitral regurgitation. If a VSD is suspected, blood samples are taken from the proximal and distal lumina of the catheter; a higher oxygen saturation seen in the blood taken from the distal lumen confirms a VSD. Echocardiography may also be helpful in differentiating the two conditions. The treatment of both conditions is to control the heart failure and to seek advice from a cardiothoracic surgeon.

8 Ventricular aneurysms are clinically recognisable as a palpable dyskinetic segment which bulges outward during systole. The CXR may show a prominent left ventricular bulge, while ST segment elevation persists on the ECG. There is a danger of systemic emboli in these patients. Surgical resection of the aneurysm is occasionally indicated in refractory heart failure, or when there is persistent systemic embolisation despite adequate anticoagulation.

9 Deep venous thrombosis and pulmonary and systemic emboli may all complicate MI, but are less frequent following the adoption of early mobilisation and subcutaneous heparin.

10 Patients with persistent angina after MI, in the absence of pericarditis and left ventricular failure, should be treated with beta-blockers, calcium antagonists or nitrates. If angina still persists, an intravenous infusion of isosorbide dinitrate (2–10 mg/hr) or nitroglycerin (10–200 mcg/min) should be commenced and titrated to the patient's response. The patient should be referred to a cardiothoracic centre for possible cardiac catheterisation and coronary artery bypass grafting.

Management of uncomplicated myocardial infarction

1 Adequate analgesia is essential to relieve pain and reduce the concomitant sympathetic stimulation which results in increased myocardial oxygen demands and

arrhythmias. Small incremental IV doses of opiate, such as diamorphine (2 mg), are given until the pain is relieved. Avoid IM administration as this will cause elevation of the serum CPK.

2 The anxious patient should be prescribed small doses of a sedative, such as diazepam 5 mg eight hourly orally.

3 A laxative may be necessary to prevent straining at stool.

4 The patient should rest in bed in a peaceful atmosphere for three days. There should be a specific area set aside for this purpose; most general ICUs are too noisy. Mobilisation should be commenced early, in the absence of complications.

5 If urinary retention occurs, catheterisation may be necessary.

6 Give oxygen by mask or nasal cannulae to all patients.

7 Give subcutaneous heparin 5000 IU twice daily to all patients with suspected or confirmed MI, unless contra-indicated (e.g., peptic ulceration).

8 Prescribe a beta-blocker, such as atenolol (100 mg orally daily) for all patients without contraindications (e.g., heart failure, heart block, asthma).

9 Do not give diuretics routinely, as a high filling pressure may be required to maintain cardiac output; they should only be prescribed in the presence of clinical or radiological evidence of pulmonary congestion.

Cardiac Failure

Cardiac failure is the inability of the heart to maintain a cardiac output sufficient to meet the body's demands, in spite of an adequate venous return.

Cardiac failure may be due to:

1 Pressure overload: pulmonary or systemic hyper-tension, aortic or pulmonary stenosis, coarctation of the aorta.

2 Volume overload: valvular regurgitation, excess fluids, thyrotoxicosis, AV fistulas, anaemia, beriberi.

3 Pump failure:
  (a) Primary myocardial disease: ischaemia, sepsis, myocarditis, cardiomyopathy.
  (b) Reduced ventricular compliance reducing diastolic filling of the ventricles: chronic pericarditis, restrictive cardiomyopathy, cardiac tamponade.
  (c) Arrhythmias: tachyarrhythmias reduce both diastolic filling of the ventricles and diastolic coronary blood flow. Severe bradyarrhythmias may cause marked falls in cardiac output.
4 A combination of the above factors.

It is important to identify any acute precipitating cause that may have exacerbated a chronic lesion, such as infection, myocardial infarction, pulmonary embolism, arrhythmias, thyrotoxicosis, anaemia, hypertension and infective endocarditis.

Clinical features

Left ventricular failure may occur in isolation, whereas right heart failure without left ventricular failure is uncommon.

Left ventricular failure (LVF)

The patient complains of dyspnoea, orthopnoea and paroxysmal nocturnal dyspnoea. On examination a tachycardia, pulsus alternans, cardiomegaly, triple or gallop rhythm and basal inspiratory crepitations, with or without an expiratory wheeze, may be present. Pleural effusions, when present, are more common on the right side. Cheyne–Stokes respiration is seen in advanced LVF.

Right ventricular failure

The jugular venous pressure (JVP) is elevated, pitting sacral or ankle oedema, hepatomegaly and possibly jaundice are present. A loud second heart sound is heard if pulmonary hypertension is present.

CXR findings include enlargement of cardiac chambers (e.g., left atrial enlargement in mitral stenosis) and signs of congestion in the lung fields. Pleural effusions may be present. Other investigations are directed at identifying the underlying or precipitating cause.

Management

Underlying and precipitating causes of cardiac failure *must be* identified and treated or controlled.

1 Reduce cardiac work:
   (a) Prescribe a sedative, if necessary, to reduce anxiety.
   (b) The patient should rest in bed.
   (c) Control persistent hypertension (diastolic >100 mmHg).
   (d) Reduce salt intake.
2 Reduce preload if congestion is present:
   (a) Give frusemide 40 mg IV (administer over several minutes to avoid toxicity) and repeat if necessary.
   (b) An intravenous infusion of a nitrate, such as isosorbide dinitrate (2–10 mg/hr IV) or oral prazosin may reduce preload that fails to respond to frusemide.
   (c) Remember that patients with cardiac dysfunction may require a higher than normal venous pressure to maintain cardiac output.
3 Improve myocardial contractility:
   (a) Correct hypoxia, acidosis or electrolyte disturbances.
   (b) Consider digitalising the patient (see Chapter 2).
   (c) If the cardiac output remains low in spite of a high pulmonary capillary wedge pressure, start an IV infusion of dobutamine (see Chapter 3).
4 Reduce the afterload. If the above measures do not result in improvement, and the systemic vascular resistance is high afterload reduction can be achieved using:
   (a) Infusion of 0.01 per cent sodium nitroprusside IV in 5 per cent dextrose at a rate of 10–15 mcg/min initially increasing every five to 10 minutes to a maximum of 6 mcg/kg/min. The dose is titrated to the response. Direct intra-arterial blood pressure monitoring is essential.
   (b) Hydralazine 25 mg twice daily orally.
   (c) Oral prazosin. The first dose may cause a precipitate fall in blood pressure. Give 0.5 mg and observe the

blood pressure. The maintenance dose is 1 mg eight hourly.

(d) Captopril is combined with diuretics in the treatment of heart failure. The first dose can markedly drop blood pressure. Give 6.25 mg orally and observe the blood pressure. The maintenance dose is usually 25 mg eight hourly orally.

5 To avoid hypotension ensure an adequate filling pressure before starting vasodilator therapy.

Acute cardiogenic pulmonary oedema

Cardiac failure is managed as described above, but the following additional measures should also be instituted:

1 If possible sit the patient up with his legs hanging over the edge of the bed.
2 Give oxygen by mask or nasal cannula.
3 Give 5–10 mg of morphine IV to reduce anxiety and promote venodilation.
4 Aminophylline (250 mg slowly IV) reduces bronchospasm and enhances contractility.

If there is no improvement, the following should be considered:

1 Removing 0.5 l of blood by venesection.
2 Artificial ventilation (with PEEP), which increases intra-alveolar pressure, and will improve oxygenation.

NOTES

NOTES

CHAPTER 5

Respiratory Failure

Pulmonary function has two major components:

Gas exchange (diffusion), abnormalities of which affect oxygenation.

Flow in and out of the lungs of large quantities of air (ventilation), which controls the removal of carbon dioxide.

Acute respiratory failure is said to occur when the $PaCO_2$ is more than 6 kPa (failure of ventilation) and the PaO_2 is less than 8 kPa with the patient breathing room air (failure of diffusion). Although much information can be gained from the regular estimation of ABG, the need for repeated clinical examination and observation should not be forgotten.

Causes of Respiratory Failure

Pulmonary conditions

Many acute conditions can cause abnormalities in function of the lungs including the adult respiratory distress syndrome, pulmonary oedema and pneumonia. They will usually result in poor oxygen transfer.

Failure of central respiratory drive

This may follow depression of the respiratory centre by drugs (sedatives, opioids, etc.), poisoning or trauma and both hypoxia and hypercarbia. Ventilation will be inadequate leading to a rise in $PaCO_2$.

Mechanical failure of respiration

To create a negative pressure during inspiration, an intact rib cage and diaphragm are necessary. When either of these is damaged a failure of ventilation will result.

Peripheral neuromuscular failure

Many pathophysiological processes affect neuromuscular transmission including the residual effects of muscle relaxant drugs and a variety of neuromuscular diseases. These result in a failure of ventilation.

Monitoring of Respiration

Clinical signs

Much can be gained from clinical examination. A patient who is deteriorating will look tired and anxious, and will use his accessory muscles of respiration. A tracheal tug may be present; in addition there may be central cyanosis. With central respiratory depression the respiratory rate will be slow; with other causes, tachypnoea will be present which increases as respiratory failure progresses. Auscultation of the chest may reveal a wheeze, fine crackles (pulmonary oedema), coarse crackles (infection), bronchial breathing (consolidation), or decreased air entry (pneumothorax, collapse or consolidation).

Spirometry

The tidal and minute volumes may be measured, using a Wright's respirometer on a face mask or attached to a tracheal tube. Intermittent measurements of forced expiratory volume in one second (FEV1) and forced vital capacity (FVC) may help assess the benefits of bronchodilator therapy.

Arterial blood gases (ABG)

Regular estimation of ABG (PaO_2, $PaCO_2$) can be used as a guide to the inspired oxygen concentration (F_IO_2) necessary and the amount of artificial ventilation the patient may require.

Chest X-ray (CXR)

A routine CXR should be taken in critically ill patients each morning. This gives valuable information on the state of the lung fields and the heart. In addition, it can be used to diagnose pneumothoraces and to confirm the correct positioning of the tracheal tube and other monitoring lines. Whenever possible, the film should be taken with the patient erect, which will demonstrate the presence of pneumothoraces and help to differentiate between basal effusions and consolidation better than a supine film. Even when an erect CXR is available, differentiation between an effusion and consolidation can be difficult; the use of ultrasound is invaluable for this.

Oxygen Face Masks

Most patients will need an increased F_IO_2 during their intensive care period. This is usually delivered by one of the several different types of face masks available. Before administering high concentrations of oxygen ensure that the patient does not have chronic hypercarbia (see Chapter 6).

Methods of oxygen delivery

Oxygen tents/head boxes

Increasing the ambient F_IO_2 around the head or body of the patient is a successful technique in children. It is not widely used when treating adults, except when burns to the face make oxygen masks unsuitable.

Low-flow systems

These include nasal cannulae and simple, low-volume, oxygen face masks. They work by displacing air from the naso- and oropharynx with oxygen. The resulting F_IO_2 is variable and will depend not only on the flow of oxygen, but also on the minute ventilation of the patient. As the patient becomes more dyspnoeic, the F_IO_2 will fall.

High-flow systems

Some masks use the high pressure of the delivered oxygen to entrain air through a venturi. This leads to a great increase in the amount of fresh gas going into a face mask. The degree of air entrainment and the subsequent F_IO_2 can be accurately predicted. The high flow generated is able to meet the peak inspiratory flow rate of all but the most dyspnoeic patient, resulting in a known F_IO_2, independent of patient ventilation. The masks usually have cutouts or holes to avoid any back pressure on the system. They are more expensive, noisy and uncomfortable than the low-flow delivery systems.

Management of the Patient with Respiratory Failure

1 If the patient is *in extremis* due to respiratory failure intubate the trachea (or use a self-inflating bag, mask and oropharyngeal airway) and artificially ventilate the patient.
2 Identify the cause of respiratory failure (infection, drugs, neurological disease, adult respiratory distress syndrome, fluid overload, MI, etc.).

Opioid overdose

1 If respiratory failure is thought to be due to opioid overdose (whether iatrogenic, accidental or self-induced), administer naloxone at a rate of 0.1 mg IV every 15 seconds. When the respiratory depression has been reversed and consciousness has returned, observe the patient carefully for several hours. The effect of naloxone may wear off 20 minutes after administration.
2 Care is necessary with naloxone in patients following surgery, as excessive doses of naloxone may produce reversal of analgesia, resulting in pain. Similarly, an acute abstinence syndrome may be induced in addicts. (See Chapter 17.)
3 Ventricular fibrillation and other arrhythmias have been reported following the administration of naloxone.

Other causes

1 Estimate the ABG.
2 If the patient is hypoxaemic (PaO_2 less than 8 kPa) increase the F_IO_2.
3 Obtain a CXR (pneumothorax, pneumonia, etc.).
4 If the patient has pulmonary oedema give a diuretic (frusemide 40 mg IV slowly). Check the plasma potassium to detect hypokalaemia.
5 If the patient has a wheeze give a bronchodilator (such as salbutamol 2.5 mg nebulised).
6 Chart the patient's heart rate, blood pressure, respiratory rate and urine output.

The following trends may indicate the need for artificial ventilation:
Increasing heart rate.
Increasing respiratory rate.
Decreasing conscious level.
Use of the accessory muscles.
Fall in PaO_2 despite increasing F_IO_2.
Rising $PaCO_2$ despite therapy.

Artificial Ventilation

Respiratory support may be necessary while the causes of respiratory failure are receiving treatment. It may also be applied to facilitate other forms of treatment, such as the treatment of tetanus, or status epilepticus or head injuries.

Equipment

Although artificial ventilation may be performed during resuscitation either by the expired air method or with the use of a face mask and self-inflating bag, any long-term artificial ventilation requires the use of a mechanical ventilator, a tracheal tube and some means of humidifying and warming the inspired gases.

Mechanical ventilator

Three broad types of ventilators (all of which are referred to as mechanical ventilators) can be identified.

1 Simple electrically driven ventilators, usually allowing variation only of the respiratory frequency and tidal volume. Alteration in the F_IO_2 is usually made by changing the amount of oxygen delivered to the air-entrainment device.

2 Gas-driven ventilators working on the fluid or pneumatic logic principle, which allow more control over the pattern of ventilation, with alteration in the inspiration:expiration (I:E) ratio being possible. The control system may be used to drive a set of bellows, with air/oxygen entrainment used to alter the F_IO_2.

3 Electronically controlled ventilators. These are sophisticated ventilators usually requiring connections to compressed air and oxygen pipelines and electricity. They have many inbuilt sensors, measuring such variables as inspiratory and expiratory flow, airway pressure and F_IO_2. Comprehensive alarm systems for excessive pressure, high and low minute volume and disconnection are built in. The user can control almost every variable in the respiratory cycle, and the sensors will accurately perform and monitor what has been set. With the increasing complexity of patient conditions requiring intensive care, these ventilators can also be used to assist ventilation intermittently (intermittent mandatory ventilation – IMV) rather than continuously artificially ventilating patients (continuous mandatory ventilation – CMV). The IMV mode in these sophisticated ventilators can be made to synchronise with the patient's own respiratory effort (synchronised intermittent mandatory ventilation – SIMV). In addition, IMV or SIMV can be used as a means of weaning patients from ventilation.

Ancillary equipment

Unless the machine already incorporates it, the following additional equipment will also be required:

Oxygen analyser

This accurately measures F_IO_2 and is usually placed in circuit before the humidifier, so that excess moisture does not interfere with the measuring cell.

Respirometer

This enables the accurate measurement of tidal and minute volumes. It is always placed in the expiratory limb of the ventilator, to ensure that the measurement incorporates what has come out of the patient's lungs, rather than on the inspiratory side, where any leaks in the circuit may lead to discrepancies between what the patient is receiving and what the ventilator is generating.

Alarms

The minimum alarm permissible on a ventilator is a discon-nection alarm, which usually works by detecting the absence of the pressure wave generated by the resistance of the patient's lungs to the tidal volume coming from the ventilator.

While many other ancillary devices are available, which allow the measurement of end tidal CO_2, lung compliance and metabolic rate, they are beyond the scope of this book.

Tracheal tube

Whenever prolonged artificial ventilation is necessary, an artificial airway is required to allow connection of the venti-lator to the trachea. Artificial airways are introduced through the mouth or nose, or surgically directly into the trachea. All the tracheal tubes designed to remain in place for more than a few hours are made of non-irritant plastic and have high-volume, low-pressure cuffs, except those used in children. These ensure a gas-tight seal during the inspiratory phase of ventilation, when intracuff pressure rises, but due to the fall in intracuff pressure during expiration (to allow capillary blood flow to the mucosa) they do not prevent aspiration of fluids from the pharynx into the trachea. After the insertion of an endotracheal tube (ETT), a CXR should be obtained to confirm correct placement (above the carina and well below the larynx).

Oral endotracheal intubation

This technique is described in Practical Procedure 1. Oral intubation is suitable for periods of artificial ventilation of up to seven days. The ETT is difficult to secure when inserted by this route, which can lead to excoriation of the angle of the mouth and its mobility can erode the vocal cords.

Nasotracheal intubation

This is sometimes more comfortable for the patient, with the tube being away from the mouth; it allows more efficient mouth care and firmer fixation due to its support by the nose. This route can be tolerated for periods of up to three weeks, after which time tracheostomy should be considered. Difficulties include those caused by having to use a smaller ETT than can be passed by the oral route and the risk of damage to the cuff by the turbinates during insertion. Tracheal suction can be difficult due to the smaller size, longer length and tortuous course of the ETT.

Tracheostomy

Tracheostomy is usually performed if long-term ventilation is required, or if excessive sputum production is expected. It requires a surgical operation, with its attendant hazards to introduce the tube into the trachea. Until a tract is formed (after 48 hours), removal of the tracheostomy tube is hazardous because the trachea may be difficult to find again. If the tube needs changing during this period the patient should be returned to the operating theatre and the tube changed with a surgeon available. The disadvantages of this technique include the need for a surgical operation, a residual scar and the possibility of postoperative bleeding for 24–48 hours if the patient has a coagulopathy. During weaning, the cuffed tube can be changed for a fenestrated tube to allow speech. Some designs enable an inner tube to be inserted, to allow both ventilation and speech through the same tube.

Humidification

Medical gases contain no water, which does not pose a problem if the patient is breathing spontaneously through his nose. When the nose is bypassed by an ETT, lack of humidification leads to drying of secretions, a deterioration in ciliary function and damage to the endothelial cells of the trachea and bronchi; this may give rise to both blockage of ETT with sputum and deterioration of gas exchange. While patients are receiving artificial ventilation, humidification is necessary and two methods are in common use.

Heated water bath humidifiers

These contain water that is heated to 40–42°C and are placed on the inspiratory limb of the ventilator. The inspired gases, which are bubbled through or over the water, emerge fully saturated and will reach the patient still fully saturated at approximately body temperature. Condensation occurs as the humidified gas cools during its passage through the ventilator tubing, and water traps are provided in the ventilator circuit to collect this water.

Heat and moisture exchangers (condenser humidifiers)

These rely on the warm and humid air that the patient exhales condensing on a special element that is placed close to the tracheal tube. During inspiration the cold, dry fresh gases pick up the water and the heat from this element before entering the patient. Recent improvement in the design of these devices has led to them becoming efficient enough to replace heated water baths. They should not be used in patients who have excessive pulmonary oedema or sputum production, both of which may block the humidifier, leading to respiratory obstruction. In addition, they must not be used with a water bath humidifier, as this can also block the heat and moisture exchanger. Newer types are available which also act as a bacterial filter, protecting the ventilator and environment from the patient's bacteria and vice versa.

Positive end-expired pressure/constant positive airway pressure (PEEP/CPAP)

When a tracheal tube is in place at the end of expiration airway and atmospheric pressure are equal. Collapse of alveoli may therefore occur, which may not re-expand with the next inspiration. This can lead to a progressive increase in ventilation/perfusion (V/Q) mismatch and worsening hypoxaemia. If, during spontaneous ventilation, a valve and a high-flow gas supply are attached to the breathing circuit, a constant positive airways pressure (CPAP) can be maintained in the lungs during all phases of ventilation. This enables alveoli that are collapsed to be reinflated, decreasing the V/Q mismatch within the lungs and leading to a higher PaO_2 for the same F_IO_2. During artificial ventilation a similar system can be used and is referred to as PEEP. Excessive levels of PEEP or CPAP may be detrimental, and it is now uncommon to exceed 15 cm H_2O pressure. PEEP and CPAP are used in patients with pulmonary oedema, ARDS and similar pathologies. They must not be used in patients with obstructive airways disease. Shocked patients may suffer a fall in cardiac output, when PEEP or CPAP is used which may require treatment with volume expansion or inotropes.

Establishing the Patient on Artificial Ventilation

1 Once it has been decided that a patient requires artificial ventilation, establish an intravenous line and such monitoring as is appropriate. Insert an ETT (obtain help with this if you are not proficient with endotracheal intubation). The patient may require anaesthesia and neuromuscular paralysis to allow this.

2 Set the ventilator to deliver approximately 10 ml/kg tidal volume, at a respiratory frequency of approximately 12 breaths per minute.

3 Apply 5 cm H_2O PEEP if indicated.

4 Set the F_IO_2 0.2 higher than the F_IO_2 the patient was breathing by mask before needing artificial ventilation (assuming the PaO_2 was adequate at that time).

5 Look at the chest to ensure that it is moving (i.e. the ventilator is working and connected).

6 Auscultate to ensure bilateral air entry.

7 Aim for a PaO_2 of between 8 and 10 kPa and a $PaCO_2$ in the normal range, unless hyperventilation is required. Measure the ABG. If the PaO_2 is too high, decrease the F_IO_2, if too low, increase the F_IO_2; if the $PaCO_2$ is too high, increase the minute volume and if it is too low, decrease the minute volume.

8 Obtain a CXR, to confirm correct placement of the ETT.

9 Recheck the ABG until satisfactory PaO_2 and $PaCO_2$ are obtained. Try to keep the F_IO_2 below 0.6, to avoid the risk of oxygen toxicity. If necessary, increase the PEEP.

Pneumothorax

Any patient receiving artificial ventilation is at risk, at any time, of developing a pneumothorax. The risk is further increased if the patient has had a CVP line inserted, has received intercostal blocks, has fractured ribs or is receiving PEEP. The initial signs include an increase in airway pressures, asymmetry of breath sounds on the two sides (but note that they may still be present during artificial ventilation even with a large pneumothorax). The patient may be seen to be distressed. ABG estimation demonstrates hypoxaemia.

The pneumothorax may be under pressure (tension pneumothorax); the increased intrathoracic pressure prevents return of blood to the heart, leading to severe cardiorespiratory embarrassment. This can develop rapidly and result in cardiac arrest.

An erect CXR should be obtained, but if the patient's condition is deteriorating, do not wait for this; insert a chest drain (see Practical Procedure 7).

A supine CXR may be misleading, with lung markings going out to the periphery; depression of the hemidiaphragm and increased lucency of the lung field may be the only indicators of a pneumothorax. If the patient's condition precludes an erect CXR, obtain a cross-bed lateral or lateral decubitus film if doubt exists.

Weaning from Artificial Ventilation

As the patient recovers from his illness, less respiratory support will be required. For patients who have required artificial ventilation following elective surgery (a period of 12 hours or less), all that is required is to ensure that an adequate tidal volume and rate can be maintained when breathing spontaneously; the trachea can then be extubated. For patients who have been more severely ill and have required artificial ventilation for some time, a period of weaning may be necessary. Weaning is usually attempted in such patients when they have an adequate PaO_2 on a low F_IO_2 (usually less than 0.45), without high levels of PEEP. In addition, they should be haemodynamically stable, apyrexial, with no major fluid or electrolyte problems and in no pain.

Two methods of weaning are commonly employed:

Machine-assisted weaning

Sophisticated ICU ventilators have weaning modes, such as intermittent mandatory ventilation (IMV), incorporated in them. As the patient's condition improves, so the number of mandatory breaths per minute can be gradually reduced and more spontaneous breathing allowed, until no further machine assistance is necessary. Other weaning modes exist on some machines, including mandatory minute ventilation (MMV); if the patient has a spontaneous minute volume equal to, or greater than, the preset one, no mandatory breaths are given; if the patient's minute volume is less than the preset one, the machine makes up the difference automatically.

Intermittent disconnection from the ventilator

In this method, the patient is disconnected from the ventilator for increasing periods and allowed to breathe spontaneously humidified oxygen-enriched air, through a suitable breathing-circuit (usually a T piece). It may be necessary to start with a patient breathing spontaneously for 15 minutes in each hour and for the remaining 45 minutes being reconnected to the ventilator. As the patient improves, the period of spontaneous breathing in each hour is increased.

Alternatively the patient may be disconnected for several hours until he is tired and then reconnected to the ventilator, rested and later on given another period of spontaneous breathing.

During weaning, clinical signs are more valuable than ABG estimation; a rising heart and respiratory rate, with a change in blood pressure, indicates the need for reconnection to the ventilator.

High-frequency Jet Ventilation

High-frequency ventilation differs from ordinary ventilation in having a much faster respiratory frequency (100–200 breaths per minute) and a tidal volume that is less than the physiological dead space. The exact mechanism of how this achieves gas exchange is not known at present. It is a very effective method of decreasing mean intrathoracic pressure and of CO_2 elimination. There remain design problems with the machines and with the provision of adequate humidification.

This method of ventilation has not achieved widespread use; before embarking on this technique, expert assistance should be sought.

Indications

1 To reduce barotrauma.
2 In the management of bronchopleural fistula, where the leak may be diminished.
3 During shock, where the lower intrathoracic pressure impairs venous return less than conventional ventilation.
4 To assist in weaning of patients. High-frequency ventilation is tolerated with less sedation.

NOTES

NOTES

CHAPTER 6

Common Respiratory Problems

Adult Respiratory Distress Syndrome (ARDS)

ARDS is a common accompaniment of many severe illnesses or may follow trauma. Some of the causes of this syndrome are listed in Table 6.1

The pathophysiology is of non-cardiogenic pulmonary oedema due to increased permeability of the alveolar capillary endothelium. The alveoli are full of a proteinaceous oedema fluid. It must be differentiated from cardiac causes of pulmonary oedema, and this is easily done following the insertion of a PAFC. In ARDS, the PCWP is less than 12 mmHg, whereas in cardiogenic pulmonary oedema the PCWP is greater than 15 mmHg. Lung compliance falls, and increasing difficulty is found in oxygenating the patient. (Oxygen by face mask is ineffective in raising PaO_2.) Type 2

Table 6.1

Shock of any aetiology	Inhaled toxins
Infection	Haematological disorders
Trauma	Metabolic disorders
Head injury	Aspiration of gastric contents
Drug overdose	

pneumocytes proliferate, and a hyaline membrane is formed in the alveoli. A full recovery is possible from this condition.

Management

1 Treat the cause (e.g., antibiotics for infection).
2 Increase the F_IO_2.
3 Consider early artificial ventilation if the patient is developing signs of respiratory failure. Apply PEEP from the outset.
4 Do not give unnecessary sodium chloride and restrict water administration to 1.5–2 litres/day.
5 If hypovolaemia occurs, it should be treated with a suitable volume expander salt-poor albumin (SPA), hydroxyethyl starch or blood (if the patient is anaemic).
6 The use of steroids remains controversial in this condition. Methylprednisolone (30 mg/kg IV) may be administered as soon as the condition is recognised, and repeated six hours later. No further doses of methyl-prednisolone should be given to treat ARDS. Steroids may work by preventing lysozymal release of active polypeptides and by stabilisation of the complement activation system. After six hours all of these sub-stances will have been released or activated, and further administration of steroids is pointless.
7 Prophylactic antibiotics are not indicated, unless there is a proven site of infection.
8 If hypoxaemia persists despite a high F_IO_2, application of PEEP and diuretic therapy, the following additional measures should be considered:
   (a) Turning the patient prone will increase the PaO_2.
   (b) CAVH (see Practical Procedure 8) may be useful in removing excess salt and water.
   (c) Extracorporeal membrane oxygenation has been used in some centres with good results.

Pulmonary Aspiration

Pulmonary aspiration can occur when a patient has decreased airway protective reflexes, such as during anaesthesia, coma from any cause, or neurological disease affecting the upper airway reflexes. It is an underdiagnosed condition.

Presentation

Aspiration can present in one of four ways.

Mendelson's syndrome

This occurs when a few millilitres of gastric contents with a low pH (less than 2.5) is aspirated. Within minutes, the patient is dyspnoeic and hypoxaemic, with widespread wheeze and fine crackles on auscultation. Profuse frothy pulmonary oedema is produced in such large amounts that hypovolaemia may occur, with the attendant signs of shock.

Bacterial pneumonia

This is the commonest presentation of an aspiration pneumonia in the ICU. Fluid from the pharynx leaks past a high-volume, low-pressure ETT cuff and usually results in right lower lobe consolidation. It may progress to a lung abscess.

Foreign body

Following trauma, parts of teeth, bone or other foreign bodies may be found in the bronchial tree. They may be demonstrated radiographically and require removal by a rigid bronchoscopy. Children may aspirate peanuts, and these must be removed to prevent an additional lipoid pneumonia.

Lipoid pneumonia

The ingestion of lubricating or other oils and their subsequent aspiration can give rise to a severe chemical pneumonitis.

Prevention

Assume all critically ill patients with respiratory failure who require endotracheal intubation have full stomachs. Use a rapid induction sequence, with cricoid pressure being applied by a suitably trained person.

Ranitidine, cimetidine or antacids may be used in selected patients, to raise gastric pH before intubation.

When high-volume, low-pressure cuffs are being used do not

use fine-bore nasogastric tubes which cannot be aspirated. Routine aspiration of the stomach will prevent large collections of stomach contents that may result in regurgitation.

Prior to extubation of the trachea, fast the patient and aspirate the nasogastric tube immediately before extubation.

Treatment of Mendelson's syndrome

1 Intubate the trachea and, if aspiration has been witnessed, aspirate the trachea before artificial ventilation is started, if possible, to prevent dissemination of material.
2 Give artificial ventilation with PEEP.
3 Do not aspirate pulmonary oedema fluid from the ETT.
4 Give methylprednisolone (30 mg/kg IV) or, if this is unavailable, hydrocortisone (500 mg/IV).
5 If wheeze is present, nebulise 2.5 mg salbutamol into the circuit.
6 Treat hypovolaemia; guidance from a PAFC may be helpful.
7 If the aspiration is life-threatening, or has occurred in the presence of gastrointestinal obstruction, or the patient has been receiving H_2-antagonists, administer antibiotics. Penicillin (1 MU four hourly IV) [substitute erythromycin (1 gm six hourly IV) if the patient is penicillin-sensitive] gentamicin (see Chapter 19) and metronidazole (500 mg eight hourly IV).
8 Do not bronchoscope the patient, unless upper airway obstruction is present due to large foreign bodies in the trachea or bronchi.

Blunt Chest Trauma

Blunt injury to the chest may follow a road traffic accident, when the chest strikes a steering wheel (crushed chest injury), or blows to the chest during cardiopulmonary cerebral resuscitation. The exact injury sustained will depend on the age and general physical condition of the patient. Children and young adults have flexible ribs which are able to absorb shocks without fracturing, whereas more elderly patients have brittle ribs which fracture easily.

Investigations

1 Other injuries are common in association with chest trauma and must be looked for carefully and investigated.
2 An erect CXR – pneumothorax, haemothorax, fractured ribs, mediastinal injuries, cardiac tamponade, ruptured diaphragm.
3 ECG – myocardial contusion, arrhythmias.
4 Cardiac enzymes – myocardial contusion.
5 Other more specialised investigations, including angiography – aortic rupture.

Management

Rib fractures

The problems associated with rib fractures include pain, which can be severe. This must be promptly treated either with intercostal nerve blocks (see Practical Procedure 11) or a thoracic epidural (see Practical Procedure 10), unless the patient is to receive artificial ventilation, in which case IV opiates may be used. Failure to provide adequate analgesia in spontaneously breathing patients will result in ineffective ventilation, with small rapid breaths and failure to expand the lungs adequately. Coughing is impaired and, gradually, respiratory function deteriorates, as secretions build up within the lungs.

A flail chest may result if three or more ribs are fractured. The initial CXR may not show all of the fractured ribs which may only become apparent a few days later. Diagnosis of a flail segment is, therefore, made on clinical grounds when a segment of the chest wall moves paradoxically during spontaneous ventilation. All patients with flail chests must be admitted to the ICU, for observation. As the compliance of the lungs decreases, so the flail will increase and artificial ventilation may become necessary. In severe injuries, artificial ventilation may be required soon after arrival in hospital, but in the majority of patients a period of observation is possible first.

Other injuries

The patient may need continuing resuscitation and treatment to deal with these.

Treatment

1 Minimal sodium input. Restrict water administration to 1–1.5 litres per day. (This does not include fluid needed for resuscitation.)
2 Provide good analgesia.
3 Give salbutamol 2.5 mg nebulised if wheeze is present.
4 Use diuretics liberally.

If these measures fail to produce improvement and the patient's condition is deteriorating, then the patient will require artificial ventilation. This is usually required for a period of 10–14 days, during which period pneumatic stabilisation of the fractured ribs has occurred. Intermittent mandatory ventilation (IMV) has been used with some success for this purpose, lessening the risk of barotrauma.

Pneumothorax

Pneumothorax can occur in any patient after chest trauma and needs drainage. If the patient is to be artificially ventilated or receive a general anaesthetic, the pneumothorax must be drained before these are started.

Haemothorax

If a haemothorax is seen and contains more than 500 ml of blood, a chest drain must be inserted. Continuing blood loss from a chest drain may indicate damage to an intrathoracic structure and a surgical opinion should be sought.

Pulmonary contusion

This is demonstrated radiographically as areas of diffuse opacification. The appearances may not be noted for 24–48 hours and usually occur in the area of chest trauma. Hypoxaemia may result and the treatment is as indicated above.

Myocardial contusion

The features of this are similar to a myocardial infarction. The ECG and cardiac enzyme changes are similar, as are the complications which include cardiac failure, arrhythmias and the development of a VSD.

Diaphragmatic injuries

The majority of these will occur on the left side and may be unrecognised for some time. The presence of bowel sounds in the chest or seeing loops of bowel or stomach in the chest on CXR will demonstrate this. Severe respiratory embarrassment can be caused if the stomach distends with gas; this should be relieved with a nasogastric tube. Surgical repair of this condition is necessary.

Shear forces

The intrathoracic contents do not all decelerate at the same rate. Shearing forces will be set up where structures are held or attached to other structures that decelerate at a different rate and may result in:

Aortic rupture

Aortic damage may occur and may not be immediately fatal, the haematoma forming under the outer layers of the aorta delaying rupture. However, rupture will occur in most patients within 10 days, unless surgical repair is undertaken. The CXR will show a widened mediastinum, and there may be a difference in the blood pressure between the left and the right arms. The definitive investigation is arch aortography. Surgical repair is indicated.

Bronchial rupture

This presents with a large pneumothorax and, following the insertion of a chest drain, the lung fails to expand and a continual air leak is present. Haemoptysis may also occur. It is diagnosed by bronchoscopy. Surgical repair is indicated.

Lung cysts

These may occur throughout the lungs, and tend to occur after several days in the ICU. They do not require treatment unless they become so large as to interfere with ventilation, in which case a surgical opinion should be sought.

Near-drowning

Other problems may be associated with near-drowning and it should be remembered that alcohol, drugs, attempted suicide, non-accidental injury to children or epilepsy may be a contributory factor.

Investigations

CXR, Hb, U&E, ABG and measurement of temperature (with a low-reading thermometer, if necessary) should be performed.

Treatment

Four groups of patients can be identified:

Group 1

These patients have received expired air resuscitation, but are conscious on arrival and not hypoxic. They should be admitted to a ward for 48 hours. Hypothermia should be corrected if it is less than 35°C, and metabolic acidosis should be corrected if the pH is less than 7.2. The risk to these patients is of late-onset cerebral or pulmonary oedema.

Group 2

These patients have aspirated water, now have adequate spontaneous ventilation, but remain hypoxaemic. They must be admitted to the ICU. Correct hypoxaemia by supplemental oxygen, correct hypothermia and metabolic acidosis. Give methylprednisolone (30 mg/kg IV); antibiotics may be indicated if they have aspirated contaminated water or sewage.

Group 3

These patients have aspirated water and have inadequate spontaneous ventilation. They require artificial ventilation with PEEP. They may become hypovolaemic (circulatory overload is uncommon), which requires correction, guided by central venous pressure measurement or a PAFC. If they require rewarming, peritoneal dialysis can be used (see Practical Procedure 9).

Group 4

Cardiac arrest is present on admission. CPRC should be started and must not be discontinued in any patient who is hypothermic, unless the period of immersion has been in excess of several hours. Full recovery from submersion periods of up to 60 minutes has been reported. Do not abandon resuscitation attempts until the core temperature is greater than 31°C. This may again necessitate the insertion of a peritoneal dialysis catheter (packing the patient with hot-water bottles, or immersing them in a bath, does not work). Cerebral oedema may need treatment (see Chapter 12).

In all unconscious patients, insert a nasogastric tube, as there may be several litres of water in the stomach.

Chronic Obstructive Bronchitis and/or Emphysema

This disease is common in the western world and occurs in 10 per cent of all cigarette smokers. It is a combination of airway obstruction and emphysema. Airways obstruction greatly increases the work of ventilation, and emphysema results in wasted ventilation. Initially the respiratory drive is normal and responds to changes in carbon dioxide production. As the work of breathing increases, some patients control ventilation from their hypoxic drive rather than responding to changes in $PaCO_2$. If these patients are given excessive oxygen, their respiratory drive will be removed, and they will become hypercarbic; apnoea and unconsciousness rapidly supervene. Acute decompensation can occur in both types of patients, following a viral or bacterial infection, an episode of aspiration, a pneumothorax, surgery, electrolyte abnormalities, or if they are given a large carbohydrate load during total parenteral nutrition (which increases CO_2 production).

Treatment

During an episode of acute decompensation patients may require:

Bronchodilators

Some degree of airway spasm reversibility may be present, and it is worth administering nebulised salbutamol (2.5 mg four hourly) or ipratropium bromide (an anticholinergic bronchodilator) (0.1–0.5 mg six hourly).

Steroids

A short course of steroids may be beneficial (see below).

Antibiotics

If a patient is seriously ill, use a broad-spectrum antibiotic, such as amoxycillin (500 mg eight hourly oral) or ampicillin (1 gm eight hourly) during acute exacerbation. If influenza is prevalent add an antistaphylococcal antibiotic (flucloxacillin 500–1000 mg six hourly IV).

Diuretics

Increased ADH secretion will occur, leading to water retention. Diuretics may be useful.

Supplemental oxygen

If the patient has a normal $PaCO_2$, then hypoxaemia can be corrected. If, however, the $PaCO_2$ is already elevated, then low concentrations of oxygen should be administered and the ABG estimated frequently to ensure that the $PaCO_2$ is not rising.

Artificial ventilation

This will be required if there is an increasing hydrogen ion concentration with progressive CO_2 retention and disco-ordinated breathing (lack of co-ordination between the thoracic and diaphragmatic components). Fatigue, hypoxaemia and a decrease in conscious level are further indicators for the need for artificial ventilation. This should not be undertaken lightly because, although patients are initially easy to oxygenate and artificially ventilate, there can be great difficulty restoring spontaneous ventilation when the acute period is over. Tracheostomy can ease these difficulties in some patients.

Severe Acute Asthma

The airways become obstructed because of a muscle spasm, decreased mucociliary clearance and increased formation of secretions. There is a fall in the flow rate of air, especially during expiration, and consequent air trapping within the lung. Hypoxaemia results from the V/Q abnormalities, the work of breathing is increased, and transpulmonary pressure can become very high. In the majority of patients this can be rapidly reversed by the administration of bronchodilators, but some patients will require admission to the ICU for careful observation and frequent estimation of ABG. A few patients will require assisted ventilation.

Investigations

1 FEV_1/FVC should be regularly measured and the response to bronchodilators noted.
2 ABG estimation.
3 CXR – pneumothorax.

Treatment

Nebulised salbutamol (2.5 mg every four hours). This may be increased to two hourly administration, with a further increase in dose to 5 mg, if necessary, until a tachycardia is seen. Do not administer it using intermittent positive pressure breathing, which increases the risk of pneumothorax.

Theophyllines

It is important to know if the patient has been taking oral theophyllines before admission to hospital. If he has, measure the serum level before administering further bolus doses; failure to do this will expose the patient to the risk of toxicity (convulsions and cardiac arrest). If they have not received theophyllines before give 5 mg/kg over 15 minutes. Infuse 0.4–0.6 mg/kg/hr aminophylline. 12 hours after the start and then 12 hours later, estimate the serum level. This should lie between 55 and 110 μmol/l. The dose must be reduced in liver or heart failure, or with concurrent adminis-tration of cimetidine or erythromycin.

Steroids

These speed the resolution of an attack; an initial dose of hydrocortisone (2 mg/kg IV) should be administered. This should be followed with an IV infusion of hydrocortisone at 0.5 mg/kg/hr, for 24 hours. If the patient has been on steroids before, they should be continued after this period.

Other agents

Ether, halothane and ketamine have all been used to treat resistant bronchospasm.

Sedation

This must not be given to spontaneously breathing asthmatics as it increases both the need for artificial ventilation and the mortality rate.

Hydration

Patients are frequently dehydrated due to the increased work they have been performing in breathing and the difficulties in eating and drinking they may have experienced during this period.

Artificial ventilation

This is indicated if there is resistant hypoxaemia, a rising $PaCO_2$ and an increasing hydrogen ion concentration. The patient will look tired, and the respiratory rate will often increase. The importance of continual assessment of the patient over several hours is essential in this condition. When artificial ventilation is embarked upon, the following points should be noted:

1 Use a large endotracheal tube to lessen airways resistance.
2 Use a volume preset ventilator to overcome the problems that are associated with changing airways resistance.
3 Use a low tidal volume to lessen intrathoracic pressure.
4 Adjust the expiratory time on the ventilator to the longest possible; listen to the chest and ensure expiration has occurred before the start of the next inspiration.
5 Measure the thoracic circumference; if this starts to

increase air entrapment is occurring, so reduce the minute volume.

6 Do not attempt to bring the $PaCO_2$ back to normal quickly. This will take several hours to achieve.

7 Ensure the patient is adequately sedated. Struggling, coughing and straining increase the risk of pneumothorax.

8 Pneumothorax may occur and is difficult to diagnose clinically in these patients. If in doubt obtain a CXR.

Pneumonia

Pneumonia may develop in a patient already receiving intensive care, or it may be the reason for admission. If it develops during the course of another illness, the sputum should be cultured and examined by Gram film. Microbiological advice is usually available about such patients, but if sputum is unavailable, start broad-spectrum antibiotics such as ceftizoxime (1 gm six hourly IV). Pneumonias acquired in the community can be bacterial (pneumococcal), atypical (mycoplasma, *Legionella*) or viral. A suitable antibiotic regimen to treat bacterial and atypical pneumonias is erythromycin (1 gm six hourly IV) and ceftizoxime (1 gm six hourly IV). Full supportive measures, including high-flow oxygen and artificial ventilation, may be required in these patients. Septic shock is a frequent accompaniment of a severe pneumonia.

Pulmonary Embolus (PE)

The commonest cause of pulmonary embolism is thrombus becoming detached from veins, usually in the lower limbs. Thrombus forms in veins because of stasis (due to immobility in bed), hypercoagulability (which follows injury or illness) or trauma to the veins (pelvic and orthopaedic surgery or injury). These factors are common in most patients requiring intensive care, and autopsy studies have revealed a very high incidence of thromboembolic disease which is underdiagnosed clinically.

Presentation

There is a wide spectrum of presentation ranging from a mild fever, pleuritic chest pain, sinus tachycardia and unexplained hypoxaemia when small particles of thrombus embolise to sudden, unexpected cardiovascular collapse if a large thrombus embolises. On examination the patient may have a pleural rub, loud and split second heart sound, a parasternal heave and a raised CVP.

Investigations

Chest X-ray

This may show oligaemic areas, consolidation, pleural effusions and large pulmonary arteries.

Arterial blood gases

Hypoxaemia and a compensatory respiratory alkalosis will be seen unless it is a massive PE when a metabolic and respiratory acidosis will be present.

ECG

Sinus tachycardia and signs of right ventricular strain (S wave in lead I; Q wave and T wave inversion in lead III) may be demonstrated.

Ventilation/perfusion isotope scan

Areas of underperfusion may be demonstrated. For the less ill patient this investigation is usually sufficient evidence on which to base therapy.

Pulmonary angiography

This investigation definitively demonstrates the presence (or absence) of pulmonary emboli, their site and the amount of thrombus present.

Treatment

Prevention of thromboembolic disease with intermittent calf compression or subcutaneous heparin (5000 U 12 hourly SC) may be used in patients who are going to be immobile for several days or longer. Anticoagulants or thrombolytic agents are used to treat this condition. In certain groups of patients, including those immediately following surgery, cerebro-vascular accidents, cranial and cavity trauma and peptic ulceration, the benefits of treatment must outweigh the risk to the patient of bleeding.

No or minimal haemodynamic disturbance

1 Supplemental oxygen should be given to correct hypoxaemia.
2 Give adequate analgesia.
3 Anticoagulate the patient.
   (a) Give 10 000 U heparin IV as a bolus.
   (b) Infuse heparin 500–1500 U/hr IV. Check the kaolin partial thromboplastin time (KPTT) and maintain it in ratio 1.5–2.5 (patient/control) by changing the rate of infusion.
   (c) On day 1 or 2 start oral anticoagulation with warfarin. Give 10 mg each day for three days. Maintenance dose 2–5 mg/day. Monitor to keep INR between 2.5 and 3.5. Adjust dose accordingly.

Major haemodynamic disturbance (massive embolism)

1 Resuscitate the patient.
   (a) CPRC may be necessary. External cardiac massage may break up the embolus.
   (b) Use colloids to expand the intravascular volume – a high CVP is necessary.
   (c) Inotropes may be necessary. Isoprenaline may dilate the pulmonary circulation and decrease the work of the right ventricle; its use may be limited by tachycardia.
   (d) Respiratory failure may need treatment.
   (e) Treat any metabolic acidosis that may arise from poor peripheral perfusion (see Chapter 7).
2 Confirm the diagnosis by pulmonary angiography. Injection of radiocontrast media may produce vasodila-tion and a fall in blood pressure; vasoconstrictors may be necessary. The radiologist may be able to break up the clot with the catheter or use it to infuse thrombo-lytic agents.
3 Consider lysis or removal of the embolus.
   (a) *Pulmonary embolectomy.* If cardiopulmonary

bypass facilities are rapidly available the thrombus may be removed surgically, especially if angiography has demonstrated a single large thrombus.

(b) *Percutaneous embolectomy.* This technique allows a steerable suction catheter to be introduced by the venous route to the area of the embolus. A special cup at the end of the catheter is held against the thrombus by suction and the catheter and thrombus removed together.

(c) *Lysis.* Streptokinase may be infused to lyse the thrombus. After an initial bolus dose of 250 000–600 000 U IV over 30 minutes, a maintenance dose of 100 000 U/hr IV is required. Expert haematological advice over the exact dose is necessary. Anaphylaxis (see Chapter 3) may occur if the patient has streptococcal antibodies and necessitating the use of urokinase. Further episodes may need to be prevented with an inferior vena caval filter.

NOTES

NOTES

CHAPTER 7

Fluid and Electrolyte Balance

Fluid and Solute Balance

Correct management of fluid, electrolyte and nutritional balance in critically ill patients is essential. Particular problems in the critically ill patient include:

1 Reduction in sodium excretion, due to an increased secretion of aldosterone.

2 Retention of water, because of an increased release of ADH.

3 Excessive sodium and water administration will result in peripheral and pulmonary oedema.

4 In some patients large losses from bowel, wound drains, etc. may lead to water or electrolyte depletion.

5 All seriously ill patients become catabolic, requiring intravenous or nasogastric feeding, and effective management demands a knowledge of nitrogen losses.

For all these reasons, it is important to monitor not only the plasma levels of electrolytes, but also the amounts given, together with the excretion or loss of electrolytes and nitrogenous waste and to estimate the balance between input and output.

The daily requirements in adults of water and electrolytes are: sodium, 1–2 mmol/kg; potassium, 1 mmol/kg; calcium, 5–10 mmol; magnesium, 5–10 mmol; phosphate, 0.5 mmol/kg.

The methods described below are all based on routine

laboratory investigations. All critically ill patients should have 24-hour urine collections which are analysed for sodium, potassium, creatinine and urea levels. Plasma electrolytes, urea and creatinine are usually measured in the mornings, but may be repeated at more frequent intervals. The use of morning values to represent 24-hour periods has limitations.

Methods

Water balance

1 Record and calculate the totals of all intravenous and other fluids given. Include all drugs and fluids used to flush monitoring lines.

2 Record the hourly urine output and other outputs (drain losses, etc.) at appropriate times. Calculate the total output.

3 The following losses cannot be measured, but should be estimated and included in the final calculation:

   (a) *Insensible loss (mouth/nose breathing)*. These include sweat, respiratory and faecal losses. For an average adult, an additional input of 500 ml/day is necessary.

   (b) *Insensible loss (artificial humidification)*. Additional water will be given to the patient if inspired gases are humidified efficiently. Halve the insensible allowance.

   (c) *Insensible loss (fever)*. As the patient's temperature rises so will the amount of water lost in sweat increase. For each 1°C of temperature rise, allow an additional 13 per cent for insensible losses. If the ambient temperature is high, even though the patient's temperature is normal, increase the insensible allowance to take account of sweating.

   (d) *Faecal losses*. These may be excessive in diarrhoeal illnesses.

   (e) *Other losses*. These may also require an allowance, such as fluid loss into the tissues following surgery, or the accumulation of ascites.

4 Total fluid volume balance is the difference between input (1) and output (2 + 3).

Electrolyte balance

1   Calculate amounts of sodium, potassium and nitrogen in the intake. A list of fluids and their solute contents is shown in the Appendix.

2   The amounts of sodium, potassium, urea and creatinine are measured in 24-hour urine samples. The results may require converting to outputs per 24 hours (based on the volume of urine actually passed in that period) if less than the whole 24-hour output is sent to the laboratory.

3   Measure the sodium, potassium and nitrogen contents of wound drain, nasogastric, bowel and other losses, if the volume exceeds 250 ml/24 hr. If measurement is not possible, assume the values listed in Table 7.1.

Table 7.1

	Sodium (mmol/l)	Potassium (mmol/l)
Wound	66	2.5
Bowel	77	12

4   Calculate electrolyte balance from the difference of fluid input (1) and output (2 + 3).

Nitrogen balance

1   Calculate the nitrogen input in all IV fluids (see Appendix).

2   Calculate nitrogen loss from the urinary urea output, using the following formula:

N output (gm) = (urine urea $\times$ 0.035) +

(Δ plasma urea $\times$ body wt (kg) $\times$ 0.046)

(urine urea is in mmol/24 hr and plasma urea in mmol/l). Δ plasma urea is the difference between one day's result and the previous day's. If the level has risen, add the difference, but if the difference is not known, or the level has fallen, make no correction. Measure urinary protein loss if the patient has excessive proteinuria.

3 Measure nitrogen (and protein) in any fluids being lost in excess of 250 ml/day.

4 Nitrogen balance is the difference between input (1) and output (2 + 3).

Creatinine clearance

$$\text{Creatinine clearance} = \frac{U \times V}{P}$$

where U = urine creatinine excretion/min
      V = urine volume/min
      P = plasma creatinine

The laboratory results for plasma creatinine must be converted from μmol/l to mmol/l and the urine volume from ml/24 hr to ml/min. In practice this formula can be expressed as:

$$\frac{\text{Creatinine}}{\text{clearance}} \text{ (ml/min)} = \frac{\text{urine creatinine (mmol/24 hr)} \times 694}{\text{plasma creatinine (}\mu\text{mol/l)}}$$

For a 'spot' creatinine clearance, take samples of blood and urine at the same time. Note the urine output during the preceding hour and divide by 60 to give the volume per minute. The normal range is 90–120 ml/min.

Plasma osmolality

The most accurate way of obtaining this is to measure it directly. This takes account of osmotically active substances such as mannitol, glucose and alcohol. If direct measurement is unavailable, or if it is certain that interfering substances are not present, it can be calculated as follows:

$$\text{Osmolality (mosmol/kg)} = 2 \times (\text{Na} + \text{K}) + \text{urea} + \text{glucose}$$

(Plasma, sodium, potassium urea, and glucose are all expressed in mmol/l.)

Urine osmolality may also be measured. It is an accurate indication of the concentrating power of the kidneys. It may be compared with the osmolality of the plasma as the urine/plasma osmolality ratio (see Chapter 8). The normal range of plasma osmolality is 280–300 mosm/kg.

Common Electrolyte Problems

Hypokalaemia

Hypokalaemia can be caused by diarrhoea, vomiting, large nasogastric aspirates, excessive urinary losses (often attributable to the use of potent loop diuretics) and inadequate supplementation. High-concentration dextrose solutions used during TPN, necessitating the administration of insulin, will also lead to a marked fall in potassium.

Clinically the patient will be weak and may develop arrhythmias (supraventricular or ventricular extrasystoles and tachycardias). The ECG shows a depressed ST segment with a low T wave and a prominent U wave. Death supervenes once the plasma concentration is less than 1.5 mmol/l.

Correction can take place gradually, if no arrhythmias are present; in an adult, up to 120 mmol/day is usually sufficient. If arrhythmias are present, rapid correction is indicated and up to 20 mmol/hr may be administered carefully, either through an electronically controlled pump, or by diluting 20 mmol in 100 ml of 5 per cent dextrose and administering this over one hour through a microdrop-giving set whilst carefully monitoring the ECG.

Hypocalcaemia

Common reasons for this include: inadequate supplementation; excessive renal loss (when tubular damage has been sustained); citrate (an anticoagulant in stored blood may bind calcium and render it inactive); during acute pancreatitis saponification may bind calcium.

The patient will exhibit features of an excitable nervous system, including tingling and numbness of the peripheries and, in severe cases, may have fits.

When the facilities exist, it is preferable to measure ionised calcium rather than total calcium. Ionised calcium is the unbound fraction of all the calcium present in plasma; it is ionised calcium that exerts physiological effects. Calcium is bound to albumin and, in hypoalbuminaemic states, measurement of the total calcium may be misleading; even with very low plasma albumin concentrations, ionised calcium may be normal. Treatment is by administering 2 mmol of calcium gluconate (10 ml of 10 per cent solution) by slow IV injection, repeated until the symptoms disappear, or the plasma calcium returns to normal.

Hypophosphataemia

Hypophosphataemia is usually due to failure of supplementation, especially during TPN. High-concentration dextrose solutions and insulin lead to large falls in plasma phosphate. In addition phosphate excretion is increased by the use of loop diuretics and the infusion of low dose dopamine.

Hypophosphataemia results in weakness of skeletal and cardiac muscle, decreased leucocyte function through depletion of ATP and inefficient oxygen carriage by the red blood cells due to depletion of 2,3-diphosphoglycerate (2,3-DPG). It should be treated by the infusion of 5–10 mmol of sodium or potassium phosphate over six hours, repeated until the level is normal.

Hypomagnesaemia

This may result from failure to supply an adequate intake, from excessive nasogastric drainage, or from saponification in acute pancreatitis. It is usually accompanied by a loss of intracellular potassium. The patient may become confused and irritable, with neuromuscular twitching. It is treated by the administration of 4–5 mmol of magnesium sulphate IV over six hours and repeated until the plasma concentration is normal, or the effects of hypomagnesaemia disappear.

Hyponatraemia

This can be caused by:

1 Low sodium intake, usually due to avoidance of sodium intake.
2 Large sodium loss.
  (a) Gastrointestinal tract losses (vomiting, nasogastric aspiration).
  (b) Renal losses (diuretic therapy, diabetic ketoacidosis, adrenal insufficiency).
  (c) Excessive sweating.

  3 Increased water intake.
   (a) Polydipsia (psychological or in beer-drinkers).
   (b) TURP syndrome (water absorption from the irrigation solution used during the procedure)
  4 Increased retention of water by the kidneys. The syndrome of inappropriate diuretic hormone secretion (SIADH). This may follow trauma, head injury, sepsis or small cell carcinoma of the lung and results in a failure to excrete water.

Clinical features

  1 The features of excessive sodium loss will be those of a depleted extracellular fluid compartment (hypotension, tachycardia, thirst, oliguria, etc.).
  2 Excessive water administration or retention will result in peripheral oedema.
  3 The features of hyponatraemia itself are cerebral signs. When the plasma sodium is in the range 110–120 mmol/l, the patient exhibits confusion and nausea; as the plasma sodium falls to a level below 110 mmol/l severe neurological features are seen, including unconsciousness and fits.

The syndromes resulting in inadequate body sodium and excessive body water can usually be differentiated by careful examination of the patient and close scrutiny of the sodium and water balance. Further information can be gained from measuring the urinary sodium concentration if renal function is normal. If the urinary sodium is less than 10 mmol/l on an unrestricted sodium intake, sodium retention is occurring; this reflects a low body sodium, depleted ECF, or the administration of minerals or glucocorticoids. If the urinary sodium is equal to, or higher than, the sodium intake, further excessive water has been administered, or SIADH or adrenal insufficiency is present.

The management of patients with a low body sodium involves replacing the sodium deficit, using 0.9 per cent saline or Hartmann's solution. If the patient has excessive body water, water restriction may be indicated, if the symptoms are severe.

Do not overtreat hyponatraemia, which rarely causes problems unless the plasma concentration drops below 120 mmol/l. Treatment with concentrated saline solutions is potentially dangerous and may produce rapid disequilibrium across membranes, resulting in further neurological deterioration and is only rarely indicated.

Pseudohyponatraemia occurs when excessive amounts of lipids or protein are present in the plasma and may cause confusion. When a plasma specimen is centrifuged, layers of lipids or proteins can be identified, and the plasma sodium can be accurately estimated in the aqueous phase. An alternative is to use ion-selective electrodes, which are not interfered with by the presence of lipids or proteins in the plasma.

Acid–Base Balance

The acidity or alkalinity of the blood is measured using either a logarithmic expression of the hydrogen ion concentration (i.e. the pH scale; normal range: 7.35–7.45), or the hydrogen ion concentration (normal range: 35–45 nmol/l). The body is able to excrete the large amounts of acid made by the normal body metabolic processes, either through the lungs, as carbon dioxide, or through the kidneys, as an acid. The excretory mechanisms and buffering ability of blood combine to maintain the hydrogen ion concentration within narrow limits. When there is a failure of excretion, or there is excessive administration of either acid or alkali, the patient will become acidotic or alkalotic, respectively.

Arterial blood gases (ABG)

In addition to the measurement of PaO_2 and $PaCO_2$, ABG estimation gives information on the acid–base status of a patient. The following information is also reported:

1 Standard bicarbonate (HCO_3^-). This is the plasma concentration of bicarbonate, equilibrated at a $PaCO_2$ of 5.3 kPa. The measurement of standard bicarbonate avoids the problems caused at high $PaCO_2$, when excess carbon dioxide artificially elevates the plasma bicarbonate. The normal range is 21–25 mmol/l.

2 Base excess. This represents the buffering capacity of the blood and is determined with an acid or alkali. If the base excess is negative, the blood is acid; if it is positive the blood is alkaline. The measurement is again performed after the specimen is equilibrated at a $PaCO_2$ of 5.3 kPa. The result therefore only reflects the metabolic component of excess acidity or alkalinity. The normal range is -1 to $+2$ mmol/l.

Respiratory acidosis

The accumulation of carbon dioxide may result from acute or chronic respiratory failure, equipment failure or incorrect adjustment, poisoning, inadequate reversal of neuromuscular relaxants, or respiratory centre depression due to narcotic analgesics. The ABG estimation shows an increased $PaCO_2$, increased hydrogen ion concentration, a slightly low PaO_2 and a raised HCO_3^- concentration.

Respiratory alkalosis

This may follow excessive artificial ventilation, pulmonary oedema or a central nervous system disorder. The $PaCO_2$ is decreased, as is the hydrogen ion concentration, the PaO_2 is normal, the HCO_3^- may be slightly decreased and the base excess is normal.

Metabolic acidosis

This may occur:

1 When there is an accumulation of acid such as in renal failure, lactic acidosis, or diabetic ketoacidosis.
2 Following a cardiac arrest.
3 Excessive ingestion of acid (such as a salicylate overdose).
4 Loss of bicarbonate from pancreatic, small intestine or biliary tree fistulas.

The body compensates for the excess acid by increasing respiration to lose more carbon dioxide.

The following ABG abnormalities will result: hydrogen ion increased (unless respiratory compensation is complete when it may be normal); $PaCO_2$ decreased; PaO_2 normal; HCO_3^-

decreased; base excess decreased. Metabolic acidosis decreases the cardiac output, leads to a deterioration in renal function and may precipitate hyperkalaemia.

Treatment

This can be corrected with sodium bicarbonate ($NaHCO_3$), which is available in the concentrations 1.4, 4.2 and 8.4 per cent. The 8.4 per cent solution contains 1 mmol/ml. Excessive use of $NaHCO_3$ can result in:

1 A large sodium load (producing left ventricular failure in patients with ischaemic heart disease).
2 Hyperosmolality, if the 8.4 per cent solution is used.
3 An increased CO_2 production, which may result in respiratory failure in patients with poor respiratory reserve.
4 Tissue necrosis will follow extravasation of the 8.4 per cent solution; infuse through a central venous line only.
5 In diabetic ketoacidosis, the oxygen carriage of the blood is decreased; rapid reversal of the metabolic acidosis will worsen this.
6 Production of a metabolic alkalosis.

If ABG estimation is readily available, give 25–50 mmol $NaHCO_3$ over five minutes and recheck the acid–base status. Repeat as necessary. If ABG estimation is not readily available, the amount of $NaHCO_3$ necessary can be calculated from:

$$\frac{\text{base deficit (mmol/l)} \times \text{body weight (kg)}}{3}$$

It is best to give half the calculated amount and then recheck the ABG.

Lactic acidosis

Type A. This form of lactic acidosis is common and follows disease states where tissue hypoxia occurs (e.g., shock). Some initial correction may be necessary, but treatment of the cause will also result in its correction, as long as renal, respiratory and hepatic function are adequate or supported.

Type B. This occurs without the presence of tissue hypoxia and is usually related to the administration of a precipitating drug (such as the biguanide oral hypoglycaemic, phenformin), the use of fructose in TPN, renal or liver failure, or septicaemia. It is more serious than type A, with a mortality rate of approximately 50 per cent. Treatment must be aggressive with large amounts of $NaHCO_3$, in addition to treating the cause and supporting other body systems.

Metabolic alkalosis

This is uncommon and may result from excessive ingestion of alkali (as in the milk alkali syndrome), large blood transfusions (when the sodium citrate anticoagulant is metabolised to bicarbonate) or excessive loss of gastric acid from vomiting (as in pyloric stenosis) or nasogastric drainage. Typically, the hydrogen ion concentration is reduced, the $PaCO_2$ is elevated and the HCO_3^- and base excess are raised.

The body attempts to conserve hydrogen ions by exchanging and excreting potassium in the kidneys. This leads to a large body deficit of potassium.

The detrimental effects of an alkalosis include a fall in cardiac output, hypokalaemia and a shift of the 2,3-DPG levels in red cells to the left (leading to a fall in oxygen delivery to the tissues).

Treatment with large amounts of IV potassium chloride is usually sufficient. The use of a H_2-antagonist may prevent hydrogen ion loss from nasogastric drainage. Only very rarely is the infusion of a dilute acid solution necessary.

NOTES

Appendix

Contents of the commonly used solutions in patients requiring intensive care.
Many other solutions are available and space has been left for readers to add others.

Solution	Na (mmol/l)	K (mmol/l)	Ca (mmol/l)	HCO3 (mmol/l)	PO4 (mmol/l)	Acetate (mmol/l)	Carbohydrate (g/l)	Fat (g/l)	N2 (g/l)	Energy (Cal/l)	pH	Osmolality (mosm/kg)
Crystalloid solutions												
0.18% NaCl	30	0	0	0	0	0	0	0	0	0	5.9	61
0.45% NaCl	77	0	0	0	0	0	0	0	0	0	5.2	154
0.9% NaCl	150	0	0	0	0	0	0	0	0	0	5.5	308
1.8% NaCl	308	0	0	0	0	0	0	0	0	0	5.9	616
5% NaCl	855	0	0	0	0	0	0	0	0	0	5.9	1710
0.18% NaCl +4% dextrose	30	0	0	0	0	0	40	0	0	160	4.5	300
0.45% NaCl +2.5% dextrose	77	0	0	0	0	0	25	0	0	100	4.5	300
5% dextrose	0	0	0	0	0	0	50	0	0	200	5.6	278
20% dextrose	0	0	0	0	0	0	200	0	0	800	5.6	1250
50% dextrose	0	0	0	0	0	0	500	0	0	2000	5.6	3800
Hartmann's Solution	131	5	2	29[a]	0	0	0	0	0	0	6.5	280
1.4% NaHCO3	167	0	0	167	0	0	0	0	0	0	9.0	484
8.4% NaHCO3	1000	0	0	1000	0	0	0	0	0	0	9.0	2008
Colloid solutions												
Haemaccel[b]	145	5	6	2	0	0	0	0	5.5	160	7.3	290
Hetastarch	154	0	0	0	0	0	0	0	0	0	5.5	310
4.5% HAS[c]	150	2	0	2	0	0	0	0	7.1	180	6.9	280
Blood[d]												

continued

Appendix — contd

Contents of the commonly used solutions in patients requiring intensive care.
Many other solutions are available and space has been left for readers to add others.

Solution	Na (mmol/l)	K (mmol/l)	Ca (mmol/l)	HCO$_3$ (mmol/l)	PO$_4$ (mmol/l)	Acetate (mmol/l)	Carbohydrate (g/l)	Fat (g/l)	N$_2$ (g/l)	Energy (Cal/l)	pH	Osmolality (mosm/kg)
Diuretics												
10% mannitol	0	0	0	0	0	0	0	0	0	0	5.0	550
20% mannitol	0	0	0	0	0	0	0	0	0	0	5.0	1100
Parenteral nutrition solutions												
Synthamin 14 with electrolytes	73	60	0	0	30	130	0	0	14	363	6	1140
Synthamin 14 without electrolytes	5	0	0	0	0	68	0	0	14	363	6	875
Aminoplex 12[e]	35	30	0	0	0	5	0	0	12.4	316	7.4	830
Aminoplex 24[e]	35	30	0	0	0	5	0	0	24.9	620	7.4	1564
Perifusin[f]	40	30	0	0	0	10	0	0	5	130	7.0	396
10% Intralipid	0	0	0	0	0	0	23	112	0	1100	7.0	300
20% Intralipid	0	0	0	0	0	0	23	212	0	2000	7.0	350
Enteral nutrition solutions[g]												
Clinifeed Favour	30	28	12	0	35	0	140	33	4.1	1000	6.8	335
Clinifeed Iso	15	38	15	0	50	0	131	41	3.1	1000	6.7	270
Nutrauxil	33	32	12.5	0	63	0	138	34	6	1000	6.5	350

[a] As lactate.
[b] Gelofusin is a similar solution but contains less calcium (0.4 mmol/l).
[c] Blood Products Laboratory (Elstree) product.
[d] Values for whole blood and concentrated red cells will vary with the length of storage and anticoagulant used.
[e] Magnesium 2.5 mmol/l.
[f] Magnesium 5.0 mmol/l.
[g] All contain trace elements and vitamins.

NOTES

CHAPTER 8

Oliguria and Anuria

The mortality of uncomplicated renal failure is low, but in those patients who develop it while receiving artificial ventilation the mortality is high. Prevention, recognition, diagnosis and treatment are of great importance. Oliguria is defined as a urine output of less than 0.5 ml/kg/hr; anuria is defined as almost no urine output. Both are of concern, because low urinary outputs indicate either an existing or an impending problem with renal function.

Pathophysiology

Three well-defined causes of renal failure are recognised:

1 Prerenal. A fall in intravascular volume, due to shock or dehydration, leads to a fall in renal blood flow, with a consequent fall in glomerulofiltrate production. Increased reabsorption of salt and water occurs in the tubules, and a diminished output of concentrated urine is seen. Providing treatment is started promptly, this form of oliguria can be corrected with appropriate treatment.

2 Renal. The kidney itself can be damaged by many causes and result in renal failure. Some of the causes are listed in Table 8.1.

3 Acute obstructive uropathy. Obstruction to the renal tract outflow may result in renal failure. It may follow an abdominal operation or be due to a hypertrophic

Table 8.1 Causes of renal damage

Ischaemia	Shock
Nephrotoxic drugs	Aminoglycosides (especially in combination with loop diuretics) Sulphonamides Mercurials Radiographic contrast media
Circulating pigments	Myoglobinuria Haemoglobinuria
Glomerulonephritis	
Metabolic	Hypercalcaemia Oxaluria Amyloid Myelomatosis Gout
Collagen vascular disease	Systemic lupus erythematosus Polyarteritis nodosa Haemolytic–uraemic syndrome
Renal arterial disease	Aortic aneurysm

prostate, or to the prolonged administration of certain drugs (e.g., practolol) which may cause retroperitoneal fibrosis. Obstructive uropathy may be the cause of the development of acute renal failure in 10 per cent of patients and should be considered in all patients, especially those with intermittent or variable urine outputs.

A further mechanism as a cause of oliguria can be identified in some patients, following abdominal surgery. Postoperative intra-abdominal bleeding will result in oliguria if the abdomen is allowed to tamponade. The cause is in part hypovolaemia, but in addition the rise in intra-abdominal pressure obstructs both the urinary tract outflow system and either the venous drainage from, or the arterial inflow to, the kidney. If surgical drainage of the abdomen is performed promptly, good recovery of renal function ensues.

Investigation

1 Review the patient's fluid and electrolyte balance (see Chapter 7).

2 Review the drug chart and ensure that no nephrotoxic drugs are being administered; if any aminoglycosides are being administered, ensure the plasma concentrations are not in the toxic range.

3 Measure the plasma urea, electrolytes, creatinine and osmolality.

4 Measure the urinary urea and electrolytes and urine osmolality.

5 The results of (3) and (4) can be interpreted from Table 8.2.

6 Urinary specific gravity can also be used as a bedside test if urine osmolality is unavailable. It gives false results if the urine contains mannitol, glucose or alcohol.

7 If haemodialysis is to be performed, check the hepatitis B status of the patient.

8 When an acute obstructive uropathy is suspected obtain an ultrasound of the kidneys.

9 Other more specialised investigations include abdominal CT, renal biopsy and isotope scans.

Management

The early involvement of renal physicians is essential in all patients who do not promptly respond to simple measures. Anuria is uncommon; if absolutely no urine output is produced ensure that the urinary catheter is not mechanically obstructed, by performing a bladder washout before proceeding any further. If this does not effect any improvement, change the urethral catheter.

Prerenal failure

The patient will demonstrate the clinical signs of hypovolaemia or dehydration, including tachycardia and hypotension. The infusion of a volume expander, or fluid appropriate to replace the losses (see Chapter 3), should result in an improved urine output. To improve renal blood flow, an

Table 8.2

	Normal	Prerenal	Renal	Obstructive
Plasma				
Urea	≤7.5 mmol/l	Slight ↑	↑↑	↑↑
Potassium	3.4–5 mmol/l	Normal	↑↑	↑ or ↑↑
Creatinine	35–125 µmol/l	Normal	↑↑	↑↑
Osmolality	285–300 mosm/kg	Slight ↑	↑↑	↑ or ↑↑
Urine				
Osmolality (mosmol/kg)	400–1400	>400	285–295	260–330
Urine/plasma osmolality	>1.5:1	>2:1	1.1:1	1.1:1
Urinary specific gravity	1000–1040	>1020	1010	1010
Urine/plasma urea	>20:1	>10:1	<4:1	<4:1
Creatinine clearance (ml/min)[a]	90–120	Normal or slight ↓	Low	Low

[a] Twenty-four-hour urine collection for creatinine clearance.

infusion of dopamine hydrochloride (2 mcg/kg/min) may be advantageous.

Renal failure

Ensure that hypovolaemia and other prerenal and obstructive postrenal causes have been excluded.

1 Start a dopamine infusion at 2 mcg/kg/min.
2 Give frusemide (20 mg IV) or bumetanide (0.5 mg IV) and, one hour later, if there is no response, give a further dose (frusemide 80 mg IV or bumetanide 2 mg IV).
3 If there is no response to the frusemide or bumetanide, give mannitol (1 gm/kg IV) over one hour. Mannitol produces an increase in intravascular volume, and care is necessary if the patient is at risk of developing pulmonary oedema.
4 If there is no response give frusemide (250 mg IV) or bumetanide (6 mg IV) over one hour (faster rates of infusion risk the development of toxicity).
5 When a diuresis commences, either because of treatment or during recovery from acute renal failure, tubular function is impaired and sodium conservation is limited. Failure to replace the sodium loss will result in hypotension. Measure the urinary sodium and use an appropriate replacement fluid (usually 2.5 per cent dextrose and 0.45 per cent NaCl).
6 If a diuresis is produced with frusemide or mannitol, but the effect is transient (two to three hours), it may be maintained with an infusion of mannitol at a rate of 1.5–2 g/kg/24 hr, or frusemide at a rate of 5–10 mg/hr.
7 If there is no response to these measures, restrict the fluid input (including monitoring line flushes and drugs) to the urine output plus an allowance for insensible loss (see Chapter 7). Restrict the intake of nitrogen (in nutrition) to 7 g/day, which may allow an increase in the number of calories it is possible to give. Obtain advice on renal support.

Renal support

When renal function is inadequate, support may be necessary for the following reasons:

1 Rising plasma urea or potassium.
2 Severe metabolic acidosis.
3 Fluid overload, pulmonary oedema.
4 Symptoms or signs of uraemia (e.g., pericarditis).
5 Making room for nutrition, transfusion.
6 Drug toxicity.

Three methods of support available are haemodialysis, peritoneal dialysis and haemofiltration. The choice of method will depend on the patient's needs and the availability of equipment and staff. Transfer to a specialised unit may be appropriate if local facilities are inadequate. The situations that may influence the choice of method are listed in Table 8.3.

Table 8.3 Choice of renal support

Haemodialysis	Peritoneal dialysis	Haemofiltration
Rapid correction required	CVS instability	CVS instability
Hypercatabolic patient	Haemodialysis unavailable	Haemodialysis unavailable
	Small children	
Following abdominal surgery	Removal of high MW substances	Salt and water overload
Respiratory disease	Coagulopathy	
Removal of low MW substances	Diabetes mellitus	
Hyperkalaemia		

Peritoneal dialysis and haemofiltration are procedures that may be performed outside specialist centres and are described elsewhere (see Practical Procedures 8 and 9, respectively). Both haemodialysis and haemofiltration require access to the circulation, which is described in Practical Procedure 8, whereas peritoneal dialysis requires the insertion of a peritoneal catheter. Haemodialysis is a procedure that requires specialist equipment and personnel, and is outside the scope of this book.

Obstructive uropathy

Obstructive uropathy is treated by ureteric or urethral catheterisation, or percutaneous drainage of the renal pelvis if necessary.

Intra-abdominal tamponade

Prompt surgical drainage of blood and clot usually results in a prompt diuresis. In addition to lowering the intra-abdominal pressure removal of blood and clot prevents a rise in plasma potassium when breakdown of the blood clot occurs.

A spontaneous diuresis usually occurs, but if it has not started by the end of the operation, the regimen for renal failure should be followed.

Hyperkalaemia

A continued rise of plasma potassium to more than 6.0 mmol/l can result in cardiac arrhythmias and, in particular, asystole. The ECG should be monitored continuously; it may show tall-peaked T waves, a widened QRS complex and conduction defects.

Management

Hyperkalaemia may develop acutely, over a few hours, or more slowly, over two or three days.

Acute hyperkalaemia

1 If it is an unexpected finding and the patient does not have any cardiac arrhythmia, recheck the result.

2 If an arrhythmia is present administer 5 mmol calcium chloride or calcium gluconate IV and repeat as necessary.

3 Give 50 ml 50 per cent dextrose and 10 U soluble insulin. Check the blood glucose 10 minutes later to exclude hypoglycaemia.

4 If the patient has a metabolic acidosis, correct it with sodium bicarbonate; this will produce a further fall in potassium.

5 Sodium polystyrene sulphonate (Resonium A), an ion exchange resin, can be given orally (15 g six hourly), or rectally (30 g in 100 ml 2 per cent methylcellulose as a retention enema once daily), when the enema must be retained for at least nine hours.

6 Haemodialysis can be used to lower the plasma potassium rapidly.

Drug Dosage in Renal Impairment

Drugs may be excreted unchanged or require metabolism before being excreted in the urine. Some water-soluble metabolites excreted by the kidney may be active and exert pharmacological effects. Care is necessary with all drugs in renal failure and in particular with the following:

1 Antibiotics
    Aminoglycosides
    Vancomycin
    Penicillin (in massive dosage)
    Some cephalosporins
2 Sedatives and analgesics
    Barbiturates
    Morphine
    Pethidine
    Salicylates
3 Cardiovascular drugs
    Digoxin
4 Renal drugs
    Diuretics
    Mannitol
5 Others
    Cimetidine
    Some muscle relaxants (gallamine)

The following drugs have unchanged effects in the presence of renal disease:

1 Antibiotics
    Penicillins (normal dosage)
    Most cephalosporins
2 Sedatives and analgesics
    Fentanyl
3 Cardiovascular drugs
    Lignocaine

    4 Others
            Theophyllines
            Corticosteroids

Drugs not mentioned are variable in their response, and the appropriate literature should be consulted.

Opiates and renal failure

Morphine and other opiates stimulate ADH secretion, which causes a fall in urine output. Opiates may also have other effects on the renal vasculature. If a patient who has received opiates develops oliguria, a small dose of naloxone (0.1 mg IV) should be administered; this may be followed by a diuresis. This should be repeated, up to a total dose of 0.4 mg. Ensure that adequate analgesia is maintained, by the use of regional analgesia, or other techniques (see Chapter 17) during this period.

Therapeutic drug monitoring

Assays are available for many drugs in most clinical chemistry/microbiological laboratories to aid correct dosing in renal failure: digoxin; aminoglycosides; theophylline; anti-convulsants.

NOTES

NOTES

CHAPTER 9

Liver and Gastrointestinal Problems

Acute Liver Failure

Acute liver failure may follow:

1 Viral infections (hepatitis A or B, non A–non B hepatitis).
2 Bacterial infections (leptospirosis).
3 Drug reactions (rifampicin, paracetamol, halothane).
4 Exposure to toxic chemicals (carbon tetrachloride).
5 Alcohol abuse.
6 Fatty liver (pregnancy).
7 Septic and hypotensive episodes.
8 Acute or chronic liver failure (precipitated by illness, injury, drugs, haemorrhage, etc.).

The aim of intensive care in this situation is to support the patient and prevent further liver damage, while regeneration occurs. The major problems include hepatic encephalopathy, hypoglycaemia, renal and respiratory failure, and electrolyte and acid–base disturbances. Death in this condition follows cerebral oedema and tentorial herniation in two-thirds of patients, massive gastrointestinal haemorrhage (with 50 per cent of all patients developing it at some stage), sepsis and haemodynamic complications in the remainder.

Investigations

The following investigations should be performed to aid in the diagnosis and management of these patients:

1 Liver function tests.
2 Clotting screen.
3 Plasma glucose – hypoglycaemia.
4 Plasma urea and electrolytes (to assess renal function).
5 Haemoglobin and white cell count (to assess blood loss from gastrointestinal bleeding and the presence of infection).
6 ABG estimation (to assess the need for oxygen supplementation and determine acid–base disturbances).
7 Toxicology screen (looking for ingested drugs).
8 Hepatitis B markers and viral titres.
9 Liver biopsy.
10 Specialised imaging techniques (including ultrasound and CT scanning).

Clinical features

The patient becomes rapidly jaundiced (unless death occurs before jaundice develops). Foetor hepaticus, a coarse, flapping tremor of the hands and hepatomegaly (followed by the liver shrinking) may all develop in addition to the features listed below.

Hepatic encephalopathy

Deterioration in conscious level follows severe liver damage. The exact mechanism that produces this is unclear; toxic metabolites from gut (metabolism of ingested foodstuffs or altered blood), false neurotransmitters and an increase in gamma-aminobutyric acid (GABA) or similar substance have all been implicated.

To follow the course of hepatic encephalopathy, it is usual to grade the condition as follows:

Grade 1. Slowness in cerebration, intermittent mild confusion and euphoria.

Grade 2. Confused most of the time, increasing drowsiness.

Grade 3. Severe confusion, rousable, responds to simple commands.

Grade 4. Unconscious, responds to painful stimuli.

Coagulation defects

Absorption of vitamin K and other fat-soluble vitamins from the gastrointestinal tract may be impaired, due to the lack of bile salts. In addition, the failing liver does not synthesise clotting factors. A coagulopathy may result, with depletion of Factors II, V, VII, IX and X. Thrombocytopenia may also occur and require treatment with platelet concentrate (see Chapter 15). Prothrombin time is an indicator of both clotting abnormalities and the synthetic function of the liver.

Renal failure

Patients with liver failure are prone to renal failure, either acute tubular necrosis or a salt-losing nephropathy. Treatment of both types is as described in Chapter 8.

Electrolyte- and acid-based disturbances

Hyponatraemia is common and may be due to water intoxication or the aggressive use of diuretics. The use of concentrated sodium chloride solutions is rarely indicated in this group of patients. Metabolic alkalosis occurs in the early stages of liver failure and does not require treatment.

Management

Emptying the gastrointestinal tract

1 Do not give any protein or amino acid by mouth.
2 Empty the bowel of any protein (food or blood from gastrointestinal bleeding), by giving lactulose (a non-absorbed disaccharide which has a low pH and acts as a purgative) 50 ml every four hours orally.

Hypoglycaemia

1 The damaged liver is unable to store glycogen, and failure of gluconeogenesis, combined with increased sensitivity to insulin, leads to episodes of hypoglycaemia. This will aggravate any neurological deterioration due to hepatic encephalopathy.

2 Measure the blood sugar using a reflectance meter at least four hourly. Large amounts (up to 3 l) of 10 per cent glucose may need to be administered by peripheral vein. If more concentrated solutions are required, these must be given by a centrally placed venous catheter.

3 Hypoglycaemia must be excluded before attributing changes in conscious level to a deterioration in hepatic encephalopathy.

4 Hypophosphataemia and hypomagnesaemia may also occur (see Chapter 7) and require treatment.

Neurological complications

Cerebral oedema may develop and prove life-threatening. It should be managed as described elsewhere (see Chapter 12), without steroids (which worsen the prognosis in these patients). Papilloedema is not always present.

Confused patients with liver disease are exposed to an increased risk of head injury and consequent subdural haematoma (aggravated by deranged clotting). If focal neurological signs develop cranial CT is indicated.

Branched-chain amino acids may improve hepatic encephalopathy, but at present they are not an accepted method of treatment.

Infection

Spontaneous bacterial peritonitis may occur, but is especially common in patients with alcoholic liver disease.

Vitamin supplementation

1 Vitamin K (10–20 mg once a day IV) should be administered.

2 Thiamine hydrochloride (100 mg twice daily orally), folic acid (15 mg orally) and ascorbic acid (500 mg/day orally) should be given.

3 Patients suffering from alcoholic liver disease may require additional vitamin B supplementation, which should be given daily.

Respiratory failure

Hypoxaemia is common due to venoarterial shunts developing within the lungs, and supplemental oxygen is usually required. If the conscious level deteriorates, endotracheal intubation may be necessary to protect the airway. Early artificial ventilation should be considered.

Liver transplantation

Orthotropic liver transplantation may be life-saving in suitable patients, if the facility is available. Early discussion with the transplantation unit should take place.

Liver Dysfunction in Patients Requiring Intensive Care

Deterioration in liver function may occur in any critically ill patient. Liver dysfunction can follow septic shock, pneumonia, haemorrhage, cardiopulmonary bypass and myocardial infarction.

The patient is usually jaundiced, and hepatomegaly may be present. Biochemically the jaundice is usually mild, with a cholestatic picture. On rare occasions, a marked increase of the transaminases may lead to an erroneous diagnosis of hepatitis. These changes are usually of little importance and will revert spontaneously to normal when the patient's condition improves.

Some patients requiring intensive care may have long-standing and well-compensated liver disease, which has been unrecognised. A severe illness or accident may then precipitate a sufficient deterioration in liver function to cause decompensation, leading to acute hepatic failure. Treatment as suggested above is required to allow recovery.

Adjustment of Drug Dosage in Liver Disease

The effects of drugs may be altered in liver disease in the following ways:

1 Decreased metabolism leading to prolongation of action.

2 Alteration in the amount of proteins in the blood. Less drug may be bound to its carrier protein, so increasing the amount of free drug available and exaggerating its effect. Rarely, the effect of a drug (usually muscle relaxants) may be decreased, if its carrier protein concentration is increased.

3 Alteration of cerebral function (hepatic encephalopathy) makes patients extremely sensitive to sedatives and narcotics.

4 In severe liver failure, renal impairment and failure may also supervene, decreasing elimination and further prolonging the duration and action to drugs and increasing the patient's sensitivity to them.

Some drugs will require a reduced dose in liver disease:

1 Antibiotics
   Chloramphenicol
   Erythromycin
2 Analgesics
   Paracetamol
   All opioids
3 Antiarrhythmics
   Lignocaine
   Beta-blockers
   Verapamil
4 Bronchodilators
   Theophylline
5 Sedatives
   Diazepam
   Chlordiazepoxides

The changes in dosage recommended are listed in Table 9.1.

It is easier to give a small dose and repeat it if necessary, than to give a large dose and deal with toxicity.

In liver disease (uncomplicated by renal failure) the following drugs are used in normal dosage:

1 Antibiotics
   Penicillins
   Aminoglycosides

         Cephalosporins
         Trimethoprim
    2 Anti-inflammatory agents
         Prednisolone
    3 Antiarrhythmics
         Digoxin
    4 Diuretics
    5 Others
         H_2-antagonists

Table 9.1

No decrease or small decrease in dose	Mild liver disease, or elimination of the drug by the kidneys, with no alteration in drug sensitivity Large therapeutic index
Decrease dose by 25 per cent	Moderate liver disease (if alternative routes of elimination exist and there is no renal dysfunction)
Decrease dose by 50–75 per cent	Severe liver disease Hepatic encephalopathy present (any degree) Renal dysfunction present Small therapeutic index

Prevention of Stress-induced Gastric Ulceration

Critically ill patients are highly stressed, and this leads to an increased incidence of GI ulceration, usually in the fundus of the stomach. Ulceration of the gastric mucosa can lead to GI haemorrhage, which may be life-threatening. It may present as:

    1 Fresh or altered blood appearing in nasogastric aspirate.
    2 Bloody or melaena stools.
    3 A gradual fall in the haemoglobin concentration.

Acid secretion by the stomach, leading to a low gastric intraluminal pH, is thought to be important; the need to keep the intraluminal pH above 3.5–4 must be emphasised. The pH of nasogastric aspirate should be regularly tested to ensure it is above this level. Other factors also contribute, particularly hypotension, but apart from aggressive treatment of shock, the manipulation of intraluminal pH remains the only therapeutic manoeuvre commonly practised today. The risk of stress ulceration is increased in the presence of:

1 Sepsis
2 Head injury
3 Multiple trauma
4 Severe burn injuries
5 Respiratory failure
6 Fulminant hepatic failure or severe hepatic dysfunction
7 Renal failure
8 Major surgical procedures

Prevention

The routine administration of antacids or H_2-blockers to all patients in an ICU is an unnecessary risk to the less ill. Both antacids and H_2-antagonists have undesirable side-effects:

Antacids. Hypermagnesaemia, hyperaluminiumaemia, alkalosis, diarrhoea and a large sodium load.

H_2-antagonists. Drowsiness, confusion, bradycardia, hypotension, drug interactions and endocrine effects.

Routine prophylaxis should be undertaken in patients who have two or more of the risk factors described above and should be discontinued when patients are established on oral or nasogastric feeding. Although antacids may be slightly more efficacious than H_2-antagonists, they are more difficult to administer to maintain a satisfactory pH; H_2-antagonists are more commonly used. Ranitidine has several advantages over its predecessor cimetidine, causing less confusion, cardiovascular side-effects, interference with hepatic metabolism and bone marrow depression. Ranitidine should be administered in a dose of 50 mg eight hourly IV, the dose being halved in the presence of renal failure. Nasogastric pH should be checked to ensure an adequate dosage.

Other substances currently under investigation to prevent stress ulceration include sucralfate and methyl substituted prostoglandins which work as cyto protective agents.

Management of Patients Following Liver and Other Major Abdominal Surgical Procedures

Following major abdominal surgery the problems commonly encountered are:

Artificial ventilation

This may be required immediately postoperatively while haemodynamic stability, rewarming and satisfactory urine output are achieved. Initially continuous mandatory ventilation (CMV) is used until the effects of muscle relaxants wear off; subsequently IMV may be used. Successful weaning from artificial ventilation can be facilitated by the provision of adequate analgesia, using regional analgesia or parenterally administered opiates (see Chapter 17). Only when haemodynamic stability has been achieved, pain control is adequate and gas exchange is satisfactory should the patient be weaned from artificial ventilation. This may be within two or three hours of the end of operation or, more usually, the following morning.

Abdominal bleeding and other fluid losses

After any major surgical procedure, there will be a continuing ooze of blood and a protein-rich exudate into the tissues and abdominal cavity. It is therefore important to transfuse the patient with an appropriate fluid to replace these losses. Since a mixture of blood and exudate is being lost, replacement should be with whole blood and 4.5 per cent HAS. The exact volumes that need to be replaced should be dictated by the CVP and the composition of fluids guided by haematocrit measurement. After every 5 U of blood or HAS (or a mixture), measure the haematocrit, aiming to maintain it in the region of 0.3–0.35. If it is too high, use more HAS; if it is too low, use more blood.

Rewarming

Heat is lost during a major abdominal procedure, resulting in peripheral vasoconstriction. As the patient rewarms vaso-dilation occurs, and an increased intravascular volume results. Volume expansion will be required during this period and is usually provided with HAS or a gelatin solution. If excessive volume replacement is required, the guidelines about the measurement of haematocrit described above should be followed.

Renal function

With adequate volume replacement and the use of pro-phylactic dopaminergic stimulation, poor renal function should not be a problem (see Chapter 8).

Analgesia

Adequate analgesia and sedation is important during the period of artificial ventilation and during weaning (see Chapter 17).

Fluid balance

Pulmonary oedema may follow surgical procedures due to excessive sodium and water administration. Sodium is con-tained in large amounts in HAS, gelatin solutions and in whole blood. It will usually resolve with a small dose (10 mg IV) frusemide. Further information is found in Chapter 6.

Gastrointestinal Bleeding

Life-threatening GI haemorrhage can result from:

    1 Gastric ulcers.
    2 Duodenal ulcers.
    3 Stress ulcers.
    4 Bleeding from the small bowel (AV malformation, etc.).
    5 Oesophageal varices.

Investigations

The site of bleeding is usually diagnosed by endoscopy, barium studies or arteriography.

Management

1 The patient should be resuscitated using the guidelines on hypovolaemic shock in Chapter 3.
2 Small doses of benzodiazepines (1–2 mg diazepam IV) may be necessary to control anxiety. Larger amounts, causing sedation, are dangerous and may lead to loss of protective reflexes and the subsequent risk of pulmonary aspiration of gastric contents.
3 H_2-antagonists, such as ranitidine (50 mg six to eight hourly IV) may prevent the recurrence of bleeding, especially in the younger patient.
4 If bleeding continues, or repeated episodes of bleeding occur, then surgery may be necessary to control it.

Oesophageal varices

These are usually secondary to portal hypertension, resulting from liver disease. Additional measures may be necessary to control this type of GI bleeding.

Reduction of portal venous pressure

1 Vasopressin constricts the splanchnic arterioles and reduces portal pressure. It can be given as an IV infusion of 10–20 units over 15 minutes. It must not be given to patients with ischaemic heart disease, in whom it may cause angina or arrhythmias. In addition, it may cause abdominal colic and evacuation of the bowels.
2 Glypressin is a possibly safer alternative to vasopressin. It is given at a dose of 2 mg IV every six hours until the bleeding stops and then 1 mg every six hours IV for a further 24 hours.

Local measures

1 Injection of a sclerosing solution into the bleeding varices may be used to control bleeding.
2 Direct pressure on the bleeding vessels can be applied using a Sengstaken or a Linton tube, both of which

possess inflatable balloons that can apply pressure to the lower oesophagus and gastric fundus.

Surgery

Emergency transection of the oesophagus may be undertaken in patients who fail to respond to other measures, but it carries a high mortality. Orthotopic liver transplantation offers a further alternative in some critically ill patients, as a means of lowering the portal venous pressure.

Acute Pancreatitis

The pancreas is digested by its own enzymes and, in addition to the deterioration of pancreatic function, severe shock can develop. Most cases are associated with biliary disease or alcoholism; the rest are rarer, such as drugs (corticosteroids and contraceptives) and viral illness. Soaps are formed which bind both calcium and magnesium causing hypocalcaemia and hypomagnesaemia.

Clinical features

The patient complains of epigastric pain radiating to the back, associated with vomiting. On examination, the patient may be severely shocked and possibly jaundiced. Tenderness and rigidity develop in the epigastrium and become generalised.

Investigations

1 An elevated serum amylase is seen in the acute stage of the disease.
2 A plain abdominal X-ray may show evidence of gallstones, duodenojejunal ileus or pancreatic calcification.
3 An ultrasound may detect gallstones.
4 Measure the plasma glucose, calcium and magnesium and ABG.

Management

1 The patient should be resuscitated.
2 Pain relief with intravenous opiates as required. Pethidine in small IV increments (10 mg) is preferred,

producing less spasm of the sphincter of Oddi than other opiates.

3 Insert a NG tube to drain stomach contents collecting as a result of an ileus.

4 Measure the blood sugar four hourly and treat hyperglycaemia with insulin on a sliding scale (see Chapter 14).

5 Treat hypocalcaemia and hypomagnesaemia.

6 Hypoxaemia is common and respiratory failure may occur. Measure the ABG frequently. Artificial ventilation with PEEP may be necessary.

NOTES

NOTES

CHAPTER 10

Nutrition

The maintenance of adequate nutrition following severe injury, or during a critical illness, is often neglected and may prolong the patient's illness and hospital stay, or contribute to his demise. During a period of starvation, the body is able to slow down its metabolic rate and death may be slow coming. In the critically ill patient, metabolic rate and catabolism are increased and, if adequate nutrition is not supplied, death will rapidly ensue.

In health, humans are in zero nitrogen balance (input = output). When unwell, or following trauma, catabolism occurs and results in a negative nitrogen balance (input < output). During this phase, muscles are broken down (including the respiratory muscles) to provide peptides and amino acids for acute-phase proteins and energy. Failure to provide adequate nutrition will result in severe muscle wasting and consequent weakness. During recovery (the anabolic phase), wasted muscle and other proteins are resynthethised and a positive nitrogen balance occurs (input > output). The loss of muscle during the catabolic phase can be prevented by the provision of amino acids. In addition, however, adequate energy sources must be provided. The body stores of carbohydrate are limited and consist mainly of the glycogen in the liver, which will be exhausted within 24 hours. Although fat stores are plentiful in some patients, their mobilisation may be inhibited during a catabolic phase of illness. Exogenous sources of energy are therefore necessary.

1 The aim of nutrition should be to establish the patient on adequate oral nutrition at the earliest opportunity.
2 The need for nutrition must be considered daily in all patients and should be commenced, in all patients, by the second or third day of intensive care.

3 All feeding, enteral or parenteral, should be introduced gradually and be increased gradually.

Enteral Feeding

Nasogastric feeding

Equipment

When patients have a tracheal tube in place, or have impaired airway reflexes, a NG tube should be used, of sufficient size (10–12 French gauge) to allow aspiration of stomach contents. This is essential to confirm adequate gastric emptying. Silicon-coated tubes may be useful when long-term feeding is necessary. Fine-bore NG tubes must not be used in this situation; they are reserved for convalescent patients with good airway reflexes. The position of fine-bore nasogastric tubes must be confirmed by X-ray prior to the instillation of feed and checked in each subsequent X-ray.

Alternative routes of access to the GI tract may be made surgically and include gastrostomy and jejunostomy. They are particularly useful when long-term feeding is necessary, or when the oesophagus is damaged and is unable to allow the passage of a NG tube.

The use of pumps to administer enteral feeds is desirable. They allow constant infusion of the feed, as well as preventing the accidental administration of large quantities of feed from the reservoir.

Enteral nutrition feeding sets must not have connections which allow connection to IV cannulae.

Administration of the feed

1 Consider starting feeding when NG aspirates and drainage are low. Bowel sounds are an unreliable indicator of bowel function in patients receiving artificial ventilation.

2 Feeding should be in four six-hour blocks each day. The prescribed amount of fluid should be put down the NG tube over five hours. No feed should be administered during the sixth hour; at the end of that period the NG tube should be aspirated. If a significant amount of NG

aspirate is obtained (in excess of two hours' NG feed), feeding by this route should cease, as gastric emptying is not occurring. Continuing to feed in the presence of delayed or absent gastric emptying risks regurgitation or vomiting and subsequent pulmonary aspiration. Feeding should start off slowly and gradually build up in amount and concentration.

3 Assess gastric emptying using water (25 ml/hr).

4 If the water is absorbed, start feeding with half-strength proprietary feed.

5 After 12 hours, the feed should be increased in volume to 50 ml/hr, with the concentration remaining at half-strength.

6 A further 12 hours later, if there is no diarrhoea, the feed can be increased to full-strength.

7 Increases in the volume of full-strength feed should usually be at the rate of 25 ml/hr each day.

8 The maximum volume of enteral nutrition is usually 2.5 l/day.

Sip feeding

Many patients will tolerate sip feeding from a cup; in this case, an equal volume of flavoured feed can be substituted for the NG feed. Exchange of NG feed entirely for tea, coffee or squash, in large amounts, should not be permitted, as the nutritional value of these drinks is not sufficiently high.

Management of diarrhoea

Diarrhoea is common in patients being fed enterally. It is upsetting and painful for the patient, it causes excoriation of the anal skin and difficulties with fluid balance. It should be dealt with promptly.

1 Ensure that there is no mechanical cause, such as faecal impaction (opiates are a common cause of this).

2 Loperamide is effective in stopping diarrhoea. An initial dose (2 mg) is prescribed, followed by 2 mg after every loose stool. In addition, loperamide can be mixed with the NG feed (2 mg added to each 500 ml NG feed).

3 If the diarrhoea persists for more than 12 hours, the

feed should be discontinued. The antibiotic regimen should be reviewed, and specimens of stool sent to the microbiology laboratory for culture and in particular to look for *Clostridium difficile* toxin. Intolerance to one of the feed constituents may have occurred, and a different feed may be better.

Parenteral Nutrition

The use of the intravenous route for nutrition should be reserved for situations where:

1 Enteral nutrition is not possible because of a non-functioning GI tract (usually following abdominal surgery).
2 It is impossible to give sufficient nutrition enterally (the very catabolic patient).
3 When access to the gastrointestinal tract is not possible.

Parenteral nutrition is expensive and, despite the many advances that have made it safer, it is still not as safe or efficient as enteral nutrition.

Equipment

Many of these solutions are hypertonic and are irritant to peripheral veins; a centrally placed venous catheter is therefore essential (see Practical Procedure 3). Its position must be verified by X-ray and it must be possible to aspirate blood from the catheter before parenteral nutrition is commenced.

Volumetric infusion pumps should be used to administer fluids accurately.

Energy requirements

This can be estimated, using indirect calorimetry, if an assumed RQ is used (see Suggested Reading). Alternatively, tables can be consulted, to provide an estimate of energy requirements (see Appendix). It is usual to administer one-and-a-half times the basal metabolic rate, as a mixture of carbohydrate and fat, to the majority of adult patients receiving intensive care (approximately 1500–2500 Calories).

Carbohydrates

1 One gram of carbohydrate supplies 4 Calories.
2 Carbohydrate is supplied as dextrose, in solutions with a concentration of 10, 20, 40 or 50 per cent.
3 Nutrition is usually started with 200 g dextrose (1 l of 20 per cent dextrose).
4 Plasma glucose is measured two hourly at the bedside, by a reflectance meter.
5 If blood glucose rises above 12 mmol/l, an insulin infusion should be started (see below).
6 The following day, if little or no insulin is being required, the amount of dextrose per 24 hours should be increased to 400 g dextrose (1 l of 40 per cent dextrose). Again insulin should be prescribed if hyperglycaemia occurs.
7 If large amounts of insulin are not required through that 24 hours, on the following day the patient should receive 500 g dextrose (1 l of 50 per cent dextrose). This will provide 2000 Calories and is usually the maximum amount of dextrose prescribed.
8 In the event of large amounts of insulin being needed, to maintain normoglycaemia (>200 IU/day) do not increase the concentration of dextrose, but use an alternative energy source, such as lipid.
9 Dextrose infusions must be administered continuously throughout the 24 hours. Sudden stopping and starting of high concentrations of dextrose solutions are dangerous, leading to rebound hypo- or hyperglycaemia.

Insulin sliding scale

Insulin requirements vary throughout the day, as the patient's stress level alters and as the daily load of dextrose changes. In order to meet changing insulin requirements, an infusion of soluble insulin, controlled by the nurse according to a sliding scale, should be prescribed. This is based on blood glucose, measured at the bedside by the reflectance method. An example of this, along with a typical adult starting dose, is shown in Table 10.1.

Table 10.1 Adult insulin sliding scale

Blood glucose (mmol/l)	Infusion rate of insulin[a] (U/hr)	
>20	4	
15–20	2	
10–15	1	
7.5–10	0	
0–7.5	0	

[a] 50 U of insulin in 50 ml 0.9 per cent saline.

A common problem is the prescribing of *too much* insulin; this results in frequent and sudden swings of blood glucose. It is remedied by decreasing the amount of insulin prescribed for the intermediate blood glucose concentrations.

Diabetics may require the continuous administration of a low dose of insulin (approximately 1 U/hr in the plasma glucose range 7.5–10 mmol/l).

Lipid solutions

1 One gram of fat supplies 9 Calories.
2 Intralipid is the only fat source available. It is an isotonic emulsion of fat globules derived from soya, and each globule is approximately the size of a chylomicron. It is supplied in concentrations of 10 or 20 per cent.
3 The only additive that can be used in Intralipid is the fat-soluble vitamin preparation Vitlipid. Addition of other drugs cracks the emulsion, leading to larger globules of fat (which can block blood vessels). Cracking of the emulsion *is not* visible to the naked eye.
4 Caution is necessary when Intralipid is used in patients who are:

   (a) Deeply jaundiced (bilirubin >300 mcmol/l). Intralipid may produce, or exacerbate, jaundice and confuse the clinical picture.
   (b) Severely hypoxaemic (patients receiving a high F_1O_2 and artificial ventilation but still with a low PaO_2); this may be exacerbated by Intralipid.

(c) Thrombocytopenic or with a coagulopathy, where diminution of platelet efficiency by Intralipid may be important.

5 In some patients, fat may not be cleared from the plasma. Lipaemia will result and, although not harmful to the patient, it does interfere with laboratory estimations and indicates inefficient utilisation of this energy substrate. It is detected by centrifugation of an anticoagulated specimen of blood and the finding of an opalescent plasma. If it is discovered, the rate of administration should be slowed, or the daily dose decreased.

6 The average daily dose of 20 per cent Intralipid is 500 ml over at least six hours; it is usual to start with one or two days of 10 per cent Intralipid to ensure clearing of the fat from the plasma, before starting the higher concentration. When used in a patient receiving CAVH, Intralipid should be administered over a longer time period (20 hours) to prevent clogging of the haemofilter by fat droplets.

Nitrogen requirements

1 One gram of nitrogen = 6.25 grams of protein = 25 grams of wet muscle.

2 Nitrogen requirements vary from patient to patient, depending on the severity of their illness. The correct amount of nitrogen to administer can be derived from tables, or from the measurement of urinary urea (see Chapter 7).

3 Usually patients require 14–17 g of nitrogen per day, but very catabolic patients may require more.

4 The number following the name of commercial amino acid preparation indicates the amount of nitrogen (in grams) contained per litre.

5 All of the commonly available amino acid solutions contain sufficient essential amino acids for the normal adult patient.

6 Electrolyte-free amino acid solutions may be useful in patients who need sodium or potassium restriction.

7 Special amino acid preparations may be used in certain circumstances, such as branched-chain amino acids in hepatic encephalopathy.

Patients with renal failure

Assistance with nutrition should be sought at an early stage from the renal physicians. General guidelines are discussed below.

(a) *Patients not requiring haemodialysis or receiving CAVH*. Careful administration of fluid volume and electrolytes is necessary, to prevent salt and water overload. In addition, nitrogen intake is restricted to avoid raising the plasma urea.

(b) *Patients requiring haemodialysis or CAVH*. It is usually possible to give more parenteral nutrition and in particular nitrogen once renal support is established, as the increased fluid and urea load are more easily removed.

Vitamins requirements

Water-soluble vitamins

Most commercially available vitamin preparations contain enough vitamins, except folic acid and vitamin B_{12}. They can be added to dextrose solutions which may require additional supplementation.

1 Folic acid (15 mg/day IV) should be prescribed separately.
2 Vitamin B_{12} (500 mcg IM) given at the commencement of nutrition and thereafter monthly.

Fat-soluble vitamins

1 There are large body stores of these, and replacement is not needed as frequently as it is of water-soluble vitamins. They should be given as a mixture of vitamins (Vitlipid), dissolved in Intralipid, every day.
2 Phytomethadione 10 mg/day (Vitamin K) may be given when the prothrombin time is prolonged (assess response after three days).
3 In renal failure, toxicity may result from inappropriate dosing with fat-soluble vitamins.

Trace elements

Daily administration of proprietary preparations is recommended. Many hospital pharmacies make their own preparations, which can be administered less often.

Phosphate

The start of dextrose and insulin feeding results in a large drop in phosphate; this can be further exacerbated by a dopamine or frusemide infusion. Hypophosphataemia can be prevented by the administration of potassium, or sodium hydrogen phosphate, 20–30 mmol/day.

Laboratory monitoring

1 Daily Hb, WCC, plasma urea and electrolytes; blood sugar may need frequent monitoring initially.
2 Three times a week liver function tests, plasma protein and albumin, calcium and phosphate.
3 Once weekly plasma magnesium and zinc (which are easily measured) may be used as indicators of how well trace element replacement is succeeding.

Peripheral vein feeding

This may be used during the intermediary period between total parenteral nutrition and the establishment of enteral nutrition, when difficulties with venous access may be experienced, or in the less catabolic patient.

An isotonic amino acid solution (Perifusin) is used as a nitrogen source (5 g/l), with 10 or 20 per cent Intralipid, in addition to 10 per cent dextrose, as the energy source.

'Big bag' nutrition

Many centres mix the total 24-hour prescription of parenteral nutrition in a 3-l bag, under sterile conditions. This has much to commend it, including ease of administration, greater accuracy and smaller risk of infection. It may, however, lack the flexibility necessary in the management of the more seriously ill patient.

Appendix

Estimation of energy

(Reproduced with permission from *A Guide to the Operation of a TPN Service*, Allwood, M. C., McHutchinson, D. and Elia, M.)

---

1 *Determine basal MR*
  for a normal person of that weight.

---

2 *Determine energy requirements*
  (a) *Adjust* basal MR for stress (Table 10.2)
  (b) *Adjust* MR (stress) for 24-hour energy expenditure (Figure 10.1)
    +20% 'immobile'
    +30% bed bound but mobile
    +40% mobile in ward
  (c) *Add* up to 1000 kcal/day extra if increase in energy stores is required. *Reduce* energy intake if loss of excess fat is required.

Table 10.2 Basal metabolic rate estimation

| Weight | | Basal metabolic rate (MR) | |
kg	(lb)	kcal/day	(MJ/day)
30	(66)	850	(3.5)
35	(77)	950	(3.9)
40	(88)	1050	(4.3)
45	(99)	1150	(4.7)
50	(110)	1200	(5.1)
55	(121)	1300	(5.5)
60	(132)	1400	(5.8)
65	(143)	1450	(6.2)
70	(154)	1550	(6.5)
75	(165)	1650	(6.9)
80	(176)	1700	(7.2)
85	(187)	1800	(7.5)
90	(198)	1850	(7.8)
95	(209)	1950	(8.1)
100	(220)	2000	(8.4)
105	(231)	2100	(8.8)
110	(242)	2150	(9.1)

Change in metabolic rate: % of normal

Burn size

+100

+95

+90

        70%

+85

+80   60%

+75

        50%

+70

+65

        40%

+60

+55   Multiple injuries/severe infection with patient on respirator

        30%

+50

+45

+40   Multiple injuries, severe infection

+35

+30

+25   10%

+20   Long bone fracture, moderate infection

+15

+10   Postoperative, chronic sepsis, mild infection inflammatory bowel disease

+5

0   **Basal metabolic rate**

−5

−10   Partial starvation

−15

−20

NOTES

CHAPTER 11

Poisoning

Acute poisoning is common and may be accidental or deliberately self-inflicted in association with emotional disturbance. Accidental poisonings are usually industrial or farming accidents, involving a known chemical, whereas self-poisoning may involve any chemical substance to which the patient has access. The management of poisoned patients is usually supportive, and this varies from simple first aid to the maintenance of vital functions. The diagnosis of poisoning must be considered in any comatose patient admitted to the ICU. An accurate history is invaluable; it is important to interview relatives, police and ambulancemen. Clinical examination may give further clues to the diagnosis: venepuncture marks, pinpoint pupils, corrosive burns around the mouth and skin blisters. Toxicological investigation is required if the diagnosis is in doubt, or when it may influence treatment or prognosis (paracetamol, salicylates, iron, barbiturates).

Poisoning may result in:

1 Respiratory depression.
2 Cardiovascular depression.
3 Hypothermia or hyperthermia.
4 Neurological abnormalities.
5 Dehydration.
6 Metabolic derangement.

General Measures

The priorities in management, irrespective of the nature of the poison, are to ensure adequate ventilation and cardiovascular function, followed by measures to reduce absorption and increase elimination of the poison.

Respiratory

1 Ensure a clear, unobstructed airway.
2 If the gag and cough reflexes are absent, intubate the patient with a cuffed endotracheal tube, applying cricoid pressure (see Practical Procedure 1).
3 A NG tube should be inserted in patients requiring intubation.
4 Assessment of immediate need for artificial ventilation is made clinically in patients who are breathing very slowly and irregularly, or who are having periods of apnoea.
5 Measure the ABG. A $PaCO_2$ of more than 6.5 kPa suggests that artificial ventilation will be required.
6 Maintain normocapnia and avoid hypoxia; both hypoxia and hypercarbia will increase the likelihood of cardiac arrhythmias, especially in patients predisposed to them (e.g., tricyclics overdose).
7 Give 0.8 mg of naloxone IV to all unconscious patients with respiratory depression, irrespective of pupil size. Improvement in conscious level or ventilation is a positive response and further bolus doses, or an IV infusion, may be necessary to maintain the improvement. Add 2 mg naloxone to 500 ml 5 per cent dextrose and adjust the infusion rate according to the response.
8 Respiratory stimulants (doxapram, nikethamide) are dangerous and are contraindicated.
9 Exclude pulmonary inhalation of gastric contents.

Cardiovascular

1 Hypotension is the most common cardiovascular manifestation of poisoning. It may result from myocardial depression by the poison, dehydration due to diminished fluid intake or vomiting, arterial dilation decreasing systemic vascular resistance or venous dilatation resulting in hypovolaemia and hypothermia either singly or in combination.
   (a) Obtain a 12-lead ECG to detect arrhythmias.

    (b) Treat the hypotension as described in Chapter 3.

2 Arrhythmias may be a direct result of the action of the poison on the heart, or secondary to hypoxia, hypercarbia or electrolyte and acid–base disturbances.

    (a) Correct hypoxia, hypercarbia, metabolic acidosis and potassium abnormalities.

    (b) Treat arrhythmias only if they are causing haemodynamic disturbance, as outlined in Chapter 2, but note that in the case of tricyclic antidepressant toxicity, lignocaine and disopyramide may increase the cardiotoxicity. Phenytoin or physostigmine are sometimes useful in managing these patients.

3 Cardiac arrest may be due to direct cardiotoxicity, or secondary to hypoxia or metabolic derangement. Management is described in Chapter 1, but note:

    (a) Resuscitation should be prolonged since it may be successful after several hours of cardiac massage and artificial ventilation.

    (b) Pupillary signs are unreliable, especially if tricyclic antidepressants have been ingested.

Neurological abnormalities

1 CNS depression is the most common neurological manifestation of poisoning. It is usually a direct effect of the poison, but may be secondary to hypoglycaemia or trauma.

2 Always exclude hypoglycaemia as a cause of, or contributing to, coma. If in doubt, give 50 ml of 50 per cent dextrose IV, having first taken blood for plasma glucose estimation.

3 Grade the conscious level regularly to monitor progress, using a simple scale (see Table 11.1).

Table 11.1

Level	Degree of consciousness
I	Drowsy but responds to verbal commands
II	Unconscious, but responds to minimal painful stimuli
III	Unconscious, but responds to maximal painful stimuli
IV	Unconscious and unresponsive

4 Record neurological signs regularly.

5 Remember nutrition (see Chapter 10) in patients who are unconscious for long periods (more than two days).

6 Brain stem death tests cannot be performed on poisoned patients until it is certain that all possible cerebral depressants have been eliminated. Repeated analysis of blood and urine may be necessary to show that any drug depressing brain function has been eliminated.

7 Convulsions may be caused by the toxic agent, or be secondary to hypoxia or metabolic derangement. They should be rapidly terminated, as they can exacerbate hypoxaemia and cerebral damage, and may, rarely, cause rhabdomyolysis. Treatment is as described in Chapter 13. Note that anticonvulsants may cause further respiratory depression and artificial ventilation may be required.

8 Cerebral oedema is usually secondary to hypoxia. Once diagnosed, measures to reduce and prevent further rises in intracranial pressure should be instituted (see Chapter 12).

Hypothermia

1 Several factors contribute to the development of hypothermia including reduced heat production and increased heat loss. It predisposes to ventricular fibrillation.

2 Use a low reading rectal thermometer to obtain accurate temperature. If the temperature is below 30°C, insert a rectal probe and monitor temperature continuously.

3 Monitor the ECG continuously. A 12-lead ECG may show sinus bradycardia and J waves.

4 Cover the patient with a foil reflecting blanket, to prevent further heat loss.

5 If possible, maintain an environmental temperature of 28°C.

6 Warm all intravenous fluids.

7 A warming blanket may be used.

8 In the case of ventricular fibrillation, a long period of cardiopulmonary resuscitation may prove successful.

Reducing absorption

The methods employed to reduce absorption of the poison depend on the site from which it is being absorbed; this is most commonly from the gastrointestinal (GI) tract. The techniques involved are gastric lavage, emesis and the use of oral adsorbents. Both gastric lavage and emesis are procedures that are usually performed as soon as the patient arrives in hospital usually in the accident and emergency department. Activated charcoal may be given orally or left in the stomach at the end of gastric lavage.

Increasing elimination

The methods available to increase elimination of the poison are seldom indicated and are potentially dangerous. They are forced alkaline or acid diuresis, peritoneal dialysis, haemodialysis and haemoperfusion. They should only be used in the severely poisoned patient and when appropriate (i.e. the drug is minimally protein-bound, has a small volume of distribution, undergoes little metabolism and is mainly excreted unchanged in its toxic form). Expert assistance should be sought before they are instituted.

Psychiatric assessment

When the patient is fully conscious and able to talk, psychiatric help should be available.

Specific measures

In addition to the general principles described above, certain poisons require specific further management. Specific antidotes are few.

Paracetamol

Overdosage of paracetamol may result in severe hepatocellular and renal tubular necrosis. This is preventable, if acetylcysteine can be administered promptly. Symptoms in the first 24 hours are limited to anorexia, nausea and vomiting. Hepatic damage follows, usually two to three days after ingestion, and may lead to death.

Management

1 Measure plasma paracetamol levels, on admission to hospital and four and 12 hours after *ingestion*

2 Acetylcysteine is given if the plasma paracetamol level exceeds 1.3 mmol/l four hours after ingestion. The risk at other times can be assessed from Figure 11.1.

Give 150 mg/kg acetylcysteine in 200 ml 5 per cent dextrose by IV infusion over 15 minutes followed by 50 mg/kg in 500 ml over four hours, then 100 mg/kg in 1000 ml over 16 hours. Start the infusion as soon as possible if there is any doubt; it can be stopped later, if the paracetamol levels are not in the toxic range.

3 Measure baseline liver function tests, urea and electrolytes, glucose and prothrombin time.

4 Give Vitamin K (10 mg IV) if the prothrombin time is prolonged

5 If hepatic necrosis develops, liver failure will result and should be treated as described in Chapter 9.

6 Remember that paracetamol may be combined with dextropropoxyphene and the latter may be causing coma and respiratory depression. Treat with naloxone.

Salicylates

Features of salicylate toxicity include tinnitus, nausea and vomiting, tachypnoea, a mixed respiratory alkalosis and metabolic acidosis, hypokalaemia, hyper- or hypoglycaemia, and hypoprothrombinaemia. In children, a metabolic acidosis develops quickly and respiratory alkalosis is rare.

Management

1 Measure plasma salicylate levels. Concentrations between 3.6 and 5.5 mmol/l are associated with moderate toxicity, and those above 5.5 mmol/l are potentially fatal.

2 Monitor plasma electrolytes and glucose, and the prothrombin time.

3 Always perform gastric lavage and NG aspiration since salicylates stay in the stomach for prolonged periods. Use ipecacuanha syrup for children.

4 Correct dehydration and hypokalaemia, with IV fluids and potassium supplements. Large doses of potassium may be required if forced alkaline diuresis is employed.

5 Sodium bicarbonate may be required in the presence of a severe metabolic acidosis. Again the plasma potassium may fall and supplements be required.

6 Tetany may occur secondary to the respiratory alkalosis and excessive administration of sodium bicarbonate. It is treated with 10 ml of 10 per cent calcium gluconate IV.

7 Forced alkaline diuresis is used if symptoms are severe or if the plasma salicylate levels are above 3.6 mmol/l. The procedure is hazardous in the elderly and in patients with renal or cardiac disease.

   (a) Catheterise the patient.

   (b) Infuse 500 ml of 5 per cent dextrose, 500 ml of 1.4 per cent sodium bicarbonate and 500 ml of 5 per cent dextrose, in that order, over 90 minutes. Add 5–10 mmol of potassium chloride to every 500 ml of fluid. The same sequence is adjusted and repeated to produce a urine output of 200–500 ml/hr. Potassium supplements are adjusted according to plasma potassium.

   (c) Use bolus doses of IV frusemide to initiate and maintain a diuresis. Dopamine (2–5 mcg/kg/min) may also be used for this purpose.

   (d) Stop the procedure if <200 ml of urine are passed in the first hour. Reassess the patient to exclude renal failure or dehydration.

   (e) Measure urine pH every 30 minutes. Aim for a pH of 7.5–8.5. This may be difficult if the plasma potassium is not kept in the normal range.

   (f) Measurement of CVP is a useful guide to the presence of fluid overload.

   (g) Complications include pulmonary and cerebral oedema due to fluid overload and electrolyte and acid–base imbalance.

8 Give Vitamin K (10 mg IV) if the prothrombin time is prolonged.

Organophosphates

These chemicals are widely used as insecticides and are rapidly absorbed through the skin and mucous membranes and via the respiratory and GI tracts. The toxic effects are secondary to inactivation of acetylcholinesterase and a resultant accumulation of acetylcholine at cholinergic synapses.

Clinical features include bradycardia, increased salivation and bronchosecretion, abdominal cramps, sweating, miosis, muscle fasciculation, drowsiness and possibly coma and convulsions.

Management

1 Muscle weakness and increased secretions contribute to inadequate ventilation. Measure ABG and start artificial ventilation if necessary.
2 Give atropine 1.2 mg IV every 10 minutes until atropinisation is complete (i.e. the pulse rate is above 70 beats per minute and the mouth dry). Repeat as necessary. Large doses may be required.
3 In severe cases of poisoning, an infusion of atropine 0.02–0.08 mg/kg/hr may be used.
4 Pralidoxime is a cholinesterase activator that is useful if used within 12 hours in severe cases. Seek advice from a poisons unit before using this drug.
5 Measure plasma cholinesterase activity (which is an indicator of the severity of intoxication as well as providing diagnostic evidence). Subsequent measurement of cholinesterase is an indicator of recovery, but is not usually necessary.

Benzodiazepines

Clinical features include ataxia and slurred speech, progressing to cerebral and respiratory depression and possibly hypotension.

Management

1 General supportive measures are all that is necessary.
2 The benzodiazepine antagonist Flumazenil may have a place in the future, but its place in the management of benzodiazepine overdosage is not yet defined. It should be used with caution in patients who have received long-term benzodiazepine therapy: it may cause an acute abstinence syndrome. In mixed overdoses with tricyclics where benzodiazepines may be preventing fitting, this drug is contraindicated.

Barbiturates

Clinical features of barbiturate overdose include cerebral and respiratory depression, hypotension and hypothermia. Cutaneous blisters may be found, but are not pathognomic.

Management

1 General supportive therapy.
2 Forced alkaline diuresis (see above) is only indicated in phenobarbitone poisoning.
3 There is no place for the use of nikethamide as a respiratory stimulant in barbiturate poisoning.

Opiates

Opiate overdosage is common in addicts, but may also be iatrogenic, especially in the elderly and in patients with renal impairment. The usual clinical features are coma, respiratory depression and pinpoint pupils, although the last are not essential for the diagnosis. Hypotension, hypothermia and non-cardiogenic pulmonary oedema are additional complications. Venepuncture marks and thrombosed veins may be found in addicts, although they may be absent when the drug is 'snorted' (i.e taken nasally).

Management

1 Give naloxone 0.1 mg IV every 15 seconds. An improvement in conscious level or respiratory rate should be considered a positive sign. Further IV bolus doses, or an infusion, of naloxone may be necessary to maintain the improvement especially if a long-acting opiate is responsible.
2 The administration of naloxone to addicts may result in an acute withdrawal syndrome, and although this does not contraindicate its use small doses (0.1 mg) should be administered slowly.
3 Non-cardiogenic pulmonary oedema may follow opiate overdose necessitating artificial ventilation with PEEP.

Tricyclic antidepressants

Patients receiving tricyclic antidepressants are depressed and therefore likely to self-administer an overdose. The patient normally goes through a brief excitatory phase, accompanied by restlessness and, occasionally, seizures. This is followed by the development of respiratory depression, hypotension, hypothermia and coma. Anticholinergic features (dilated pupils, dry mouth, urinary retention, tachycardia and other arrhythmias) are also present.

Management

1 Gastric lavage is effective for up to 12 hours since tricyclics delay gastric emptying.
2 Activated charcoal is effective in adsorbing tricylic antidepressants and should always be given.
3 Measure plasma electrolytes and arterial blood gases in all unconscious patients.
4 Cardiodepression and arrhythmias are aggravated by metabolic acidosis, hypokalaemia and hypoxia, which should be detected and treated early.
5 Physostigmine should only be used to treat arrhythmias, hypotension or convulsions that are life-threatening and not responding to other measures. Give an infusion of physostigmine salicylate at a rate of 0.2 mg/min for 10 minutes. It should *never* be used as an alternative to general supportive measures.

Appendix

Poisons Information Service (UK)

Information and advice are available 24 hours a day from the poisons information centres at the following telephone numbers:

London	01-407 7600 or 01-635 9191
Belfast	(0232) 240503
Birmingham	021-554 3801
Cardiff	(0222) 569200
Dublin	(0001) 745588
Edinburgh	031-229 2477
Leeds	(0532) 430715 or (0532) 432799
Newcastle	091-232 5131

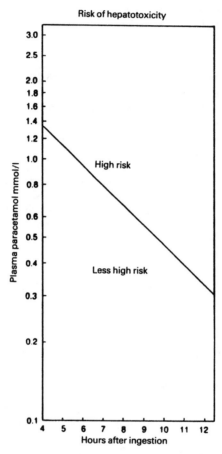

Figure 11.1 The risk of hepatotoxicity following paracetamol ingestion

NOTES

CHAPTER 12

Head Injuries

The number of patients with head injuries admitted to hospital is increasing with the development of high-speed transport. Most head injuries are minor and do not require surgical intervention or intensive care. More severe head injuries may involve destruction of cerebral tissue, cerebral contusion or intracranial haematoma. Intracranial haematomas may be extradural (when a major vessel such as the middle meningeal artery has been torn), subdural (usually an accompaniment of underlying cerebral laceration) or intracerebral. Any injury will produce swelling of the brain (cerebral oedema), the amount depending on the severity of the injury. The importance of these injuries is that the brain is contained in a rigid box (cranium), and any large increase in intracranial volume will lead to a large rise in intracranial pressure (ICP). Any increase in ICP decreases cerebral perfusion pressure (cerebral perfusion pressure = MAP − ICP) leading to further impairment of brain function. If ICP continues to rise, the brain eventually herniates through the tentorium, and death is then inevitable. Haematomas can be removed surgically; the aim of intensive care is to prevent cerebral oedema and other causes of rises in ICP.

Initial Management

Through each phase of the patient's care from the site of the accident onwards, a clear airway is of paramount importance. Coughing and struggling against a partially obstructed airway will cause further cerebral damage, through hypoxia and an increased ICP. Until proved otherwise, a cervical spine injury must be suspected. Other injuries may have been sustained in the accident, necessitating resuscitation. Head injuries do not give rise to shock by themselves, although there may be an associated extensive scalp laceration. If the patient requires vigorous resuscitation, look for other injuries, such as a haemothorax or intra-abdominal bleeding.

Once the airway is secured, the patient should be examined; if he is unconscious, a cranial CT should be performed to exclude surgically remediable lesions, such as intracranial haematomas or skull fractures. If these are found, the patient may require neurosurgical intervention. If surgery is not indicated, therapy should aim either to lower a raised ICP, or to prevent it rising. ICP can be monitored by inserting a small

Table 12.1 Assessment of neurological status. Glasgow 'coma' Scale = E + M + V. Best motor response is scored from the sick with the best response (if there is assymetry). It cannot be applied to preverbal children, patients who are hypoxic, shocked, intoxicated, receiving neuromuscular blocking agents or sedatives or those with a cervical cord lesion.

Response		Pupil size	Limb movements
Eyes open		Right size *(mm)*	Arms
Spontaneously	4		Normal power
To speech	3	Reaction to	Mild weakness
To pain	2 〉E	light	Severe weakness
None	1	Left size *(mm)*	Spastic flexion
			Extension
			No response
Best verbal response		Reaction to	Legs
Orientated	5	light	Normal power
Confused	4		Mild weakness
Inappropriate words	3 〉V		Severe weakness
Incomprehensible	2		Extension
sounds			No response
None	1		
Best motor response			
Obey commands	6		
Localise pain	5		
Withdraws	4 〉M		
Flexion to pain	3		
Extension to pain	2		
None	1		

transducer or monitoring line through the cranium for direct measurement. If this facility is not available, clinical indicators of a changing ICP and changing cerebral function can be used. The best clinical score for this purpose is the Glasgow Coma Score the components of which are shown in Table 12.1.

The classical signs of a rising intracranial pressure are a fall in conscious level, with periods of hypoventilation, a falling heart rate, a rising blood pressure and dilating pupil(s) with a decreased response to light. Some of these signs may be obscured, if the patient is already receiving artificial ventilation and neuromuscular blockers are in use.

When ICP monitoring is in use, treatment should attempt to maintain the ICP at no higher than 25 mmHg. Rising ICP may be indicated not only by an increase in mean ICP but also by exaggerated responses to physiotherapy, tracheal suction and the normal variation seen with respiration and heart beat.

Prevention and Treatment of Cerebral Oedema

Artificial Ventilation

The institution of artificial ventilation with hypocarbia ($PaCo_2$ 3.5kPa) produces cerebral vasoconstriction and reduces the intracranial volume and ICP. This effect lasts four to six hours; the major benefits of early artificial ventilation are the avoidance of hypoxia and hypercarbia, the control of convulsions and, possibly, the prevention of 'steal syndromes' thus improving perfusion of ischaemic areas.

Indications
1 Other injuries (crushed chest).
2 Arterial hypoxaemia when the PaO_2 is <9 kPa on air and does not rise to >13 kPa with oxygen therapy.
3 Abnormalities of the respiratory pattern, resulting in hyper- or hypocarbia ($PaCO_2$ <3.3 or >6 kPa), or hyper- or hypopnoea (respiratory rate <8 or >40 breaths per minute).
4 The presence of flexor or extensor spasms.
5 Persistent hyperpyrexia (>38.5°C).

6 Rise in ICP to >25 mmHg, or >25 per cent of the previous level in a 30-minute period.

7 Early controlled ventilation should be considered in all patients, but young patients (<16 years) in particular respond to this treatment extremely well.

PEEP/CPAP

If these are clinically indicated, up to 10 cmH$_2$O PEEP can be applied without alteration in ICP, as long as the patient is lying at least 10–15° head up.

Chest physiotherapy

In patients with cerebral oedema, this procedure (including tracheal suction) may cause large rises in ICP and should be undertaken only when clinically indicated. If it is not necessary (in the absence of excessive sputum production or clinical signs), it should not be performed on a routine basis (i.e. the usual one or two hourly tracheal suction).

Posture

The patient should lie 10–15° head up, with the head strictly in the midline. Both of these measures allow unimpeded venous drainage. Movement of the patient should be restricted to the minimum. The use of an airbed to lessen the amount the patient needs moving may be desirable.

Endotracheal Tube (ETT)

If the red rubber ETT has been used during the initial resuscitation period, it should be changed for a plastic ETT (preferably via the nasal route, unless a basal skull fracture is present). This should be secured using adhesive tape and not tied in with cotton tape (which may impede cerebral venous drainage).

Sedation/neuromuscular paralysis

No ideal sedative regimen exists. Concomitant bolus administration IV of a muscle relaxant (pancuronium or alcuronium) and a narcotic (phenoperidine) appears to be the most satisfactory regimen currently available. If the patient fails to tolerate controlled ventilation adequately on this regimen, he may have recovered normal cerebral function and the need to continue ventilation should be reviewed. The nursing staff should be instructed to inform the medical staff if sedation or paralysis is needed one-hourly or less. Benzodiazepines should not be used (unless the antagonist is available), as their prolonged effect can make decisions about cerebral function difficult. Rises in ICP may also be treated by the infusion of thiopentone (2–3 mg/kg/hr). This method of treatment is particularly useful if ICP increases following chest physiotherapy or other manoeuvres.

Fluid Balance

Fluid overload and hyponatraemia will make cerebral oedema worse. A moderate degree of dehydration is usually employed; a plasma sodium of 145–155 mmol/l and a plasma osmolality that is greater than normal, but not exceeding 315 mmol/kg, are indicators of this. These aims can be achieved by restricting fluid intake to 1.5–2 l/day, by avoiding dextrose solutions and by using Hartmann's solution or 0.9 per cent sodium chloride instead. In addition, dehydrating agents (mannitol or frusemide) may also be employed.

Mannitol

The use of mannitol, an osmotic diuretic, is controversial. There is no universal agreement on its dose, or method of administration. It is usually administered when the ICP exceeds 25 mmHg, or when clinical signs indicate a rise in ICP. Under such circumstances 0.5–1 g/kg is infused over 15–20 minutes (as the 20 per cent solution) and repeated as necessary. If ICP is being continuously measured, a continuous infusion of mannitol (up to 6 g/kg/day) may be used.

Frusemide

This loop diuretic is employed in a dose of 1 mg/kg IV under similar circumstances to mannitol. In addition to producing a prompt diuresis, it may also lower ICP by decreasing the formation of CSF.

Ventricular drainage

This may be employed in neurosurgical centres. A catheter is inserted into the ventricles and CSF drained off to reduced ICP.

Steroids

The use of corticosteroids (dexamethasone) is only indicated when the patient has a focal lesion (brain tumour). They should not be used indiscriminately for diffuse injuries, lesions such as head injury or hypoxic brain damage.

Cerebral protection

Some centres induce deep barbiturate coma and maintain it for several days in the hope that it will protect against further damage to the brain. This method of treatment is not routinely accepted and has been shown to be of no benefit compared to mannitol.

Duration of treatment

It is usual to continue artificial ventilation for a period of 48–72 hours once it has been instituted. At the end of this period, neuromuscular paralysis and sedation are reversed. If the need for continuing artificial ventilation is demonstrated (as described earlier), a further similar period of artificial ventilation should be undertaken before the patient is re-assessed. Controlled ventilation will no longer be needed by 75 per cent of patients after seven days.

Complications

Stress-induced gastric ulceration should be prevented, as described in Chapter 9. Diabetes insipidus (a urine output of more than 150 ml/hr) usually responds to the use of vaso-pressin (see Chapter 14). Many patients will be unable to eat for some time and will require NG feeding (see Chapter 10).

NOTES

NOTES

CHAPTER 13

Neurological Diseases

Patients may present with neurological disease requiring intensive care, or develop neurological problems during the course of another illness.

Alteration in Conscious Level

This is the most common neurological problem in the intensive care setting. It may result from:

1 A structural lesion: head injury, intracranial haemorrhage.
2 Metabolic abnormalities: hypoxia, hypoglycaemia, diabetic acidosis, hepatic encephalopathy.
3 Drugs (overdose, or abnormal elimination).

To diagnose the cause of an altered state of consciousness, a meticulous neurological examination must be carried out and followed by the appropriate investigations.

Investigations

Further investigations include:

1 Plasma glucose, electrolytes and urea to exclude hypo- or hyperglycaemia, hypo- or hypernatraemia, and uraemia.
2 ABG to exclude hypoxia and hypercapnia.
3 Exclude hyper- and hypocalcaemia.
4 Toxicology screen to exclude drug intoxication.

5 CT scans are not an alternative to a detailed neuro-logical examination. It is indicated when a structural lesion is suspected, or when the diagnosis is uncertain.

6 Ultrasound scanners are portable and may be useful when cranial CT is unavailable. Shifts in midline structures of the brain, by either cerebral oedema or a space-occupying lesion, may be identified.

7 Lumbar puncture is indicated if the above investi-gations do not identify the cause of the coma.

8 A CT scan before lumbar puncture is desirable to exclude raised intracranial pressure. If it is suspected or demonstrated, seek advice before performing a lumbar puncture.

9 Microscopy, Gram-stain, culture, glucose and protein concentrations should be measured in the CSF to exclude intracranial haemorrhage, meningitis and encephalitis.

10 EEG may provide further information:
   (a) Slow rhythms are seen in patients with metabolic coma.
   (b) Seizure activity may be identified in patients without motor manifestations.
   (c) Occasionally a focal lesion not detected by CT may be identified.

Management

The management of an altered state of consciousness depends on the identification of the underlying cause. Iatrogenic or accidental drug poisoning is common in the ICU and should be remembered in all patients whose conscious level deteriorates during their period of illness. It is dealt with elsewhere (see Chapter 17).

Status Epilepticus

This is the rapid, repetitive recurrence of any type of convulsion without recovery of consciousness or baseline neurological function between attacks. It has a mortality of approximately 10 per cent. During the convulsions, cerebral oxygen consumption is increased two- or threefold, while the secondary physiological effects tend to decrease oxygen delivery to the brain.

Aetiology

Neurological

1 Status epilepticus may be the presenting feature of idiopathic epilepsy. It may also occur in a known epileptic, commonly as a result of changes in plasma levels of anticonvulsant (which should always be measured).
2 Tumours in the CNS: primary or secondary neoplasms, vascular malformations.
3 Meningitis or encephalitis.
4 Post-traumatic.
5 Cerebrovascular disease.
6 Acute hypertension.

Metabolic

1 Hypoxia.
2 Uraemia.
3 Drug intoxication.
4 Hepatic encephalopathy.
5 Hypoglycaemia.
6 Hypocalcaemia.
7 Alcohol withdrawal.
8 Pyrexia.

Investigations

1 Plasma glucose, electrolytes and urea.
2 ABG.
3 Plasma anticonvulsant concentrations in known epileptics.
4 Plasma calcium and magnesium.
5 Toxicology screen.
6 Microscopy, Gram-stain, culture, glucose and protein concentrations in cerebrospinal fluid.
7 CT scan if a structural cause is suspected.
8 Measurement of body temperature.

Management

Terminate the convulsions

The convulsions should be stopped as soon as possible to minimise the secondary physiological effects. Correction of the underlying cause may be all that is required to terminate the convulsions, but usually parenteral anticonvulsants are required.

1 Protect the patient from injury.
2 Maintain the airway using an oral airway.
3 Give supplemental oxygen.
4 If the airway cannot be protected, consider inserting an endotracheal tube (see Practical Procedure 1).
5 Establish venous access, take blood for the necessary investigations (see above) and give 50 ml of 50 per cent dextrose IV to exclude hypoglycaemia as a cause.
6 Benzodiazepines are the drugs of choice to stop the convulsions. Give diazepam in increments of 2 mg/min until the fits stop, or 20 mg have been given. This may be followed by an IV infusion to a maximum of 3 mg/kg over 24 hours; it must not be given IM. Clonazepam and lorazepam are suitable alternatives.
7 Phenytoin is additive in effect to diazepam. Give 50 mg/min by slow IV injection, to a maximum of 10–15 mg/kg, until the convulsions are controlled. This may be followed by 100 mg IV six hourly.
8 Paraldehyde (5 ml into each buttock in a glass syringe) may be used intramuscularly if difficulty is experienced with intravenous access.
9 If convulsions are not controlled after 30 minutes:
    (a) Give 40–100 ml of 0.8 per cent chlormethiazole IV and continue with an IV infusion titrated to the patient's response.
    (b) Alternatively, give thiopentone 1–3 mg/kg slowly IV, followed by an IV infusion of 2 g in 500 ml 0.9 per cent saline, at a rate titrated to the response.
10 Muscle relaxants and artificial ventilation will be required if the above measures fail to stop the convulsions, or if respiratory depression (caused either by drugs or cerebral oedema) occurs. Although muscle

relaxants abolish the peripheral manifestations of convulsions, it remains essential to continue anticonvulsants and, if possible, to monitor their effectiveness with EEG.

11 Appropriate chronic anticonvulsant therapy may be required after the convulsions are controlled.

Control the secondary physiological effects

1 Treat hypotension (see Chapter 3), any metabolic acidosis (see Chapter 7) and hypoglycaemia which may be an effect, as well as a cause, of status epilepticus.

2 Patients with hyperthermia should be tepid sponged and fanned.

3 If myoglobinuria is present establish a diuresis with IV fluids and frusemide or mannitol.

4 If cerebral oedema is suspected, it should be treated as described elsewhere (see Chapter 12).

Guillain–Barré Syndrome

This is a polyneuritis that is seen usually, approximately three weeks following a viral infection or immunisation. The patient presents with paraesthesia and numbness, followed by weakness and flaccid paralysis. The neuropathy is mainly motor, and paralysis typically begins in the legs and ascends to cause a symmetrical loss of power in the trunk and the arms. Bilateral facial palsy and bulbar palsy may occur. Sensory loss is usually limited to a reduction in vibration sensation, in a glove and stocking distribution. Sphincter function is usually preserved. Patients require intensive care when respiratory problems and/or bulbar paralysis are present.

Investigations

1 The CSF is acellular and under normal pressure, but the protein content is usually increased. Lymphocytosis occurs in 10 per cent of patients.

2 Nerve conduction studies may reveal reduced conduction velocity and prolonged distal latency.

Management

1 Monitor respiratory function by measuring the vital capacity hourly (initially) and by regular ABG analysis.

2 Endotracheal intubation and artificial ventilation are indicated if respiratory failure occurs (see Chapter 5).

3 The average duration of artificial ventilation is nine weeks, and elective tracheostomy is usually indicated.

4 If bulbar palsy is present, endotracheal intubation or tracheostomy may be required to prevent aspiration of secretions or gastric contents.

5 Regular physiotherapy is essential to prevent the development of contractures.

6 Prescribe subcutaneous heparin (5000 U twice daily) to prevent deep vein thrombosis.

7 Nutrition is normally provided by nasogastric feeding, but parenteral nutrition may be required in patients with autonomic dysfunction involving the gastro-intestinal tract.

8 Manifestations of autonomic dysfunction (tachycardia, sweating, salivation, hypotension, hypertension and ileus) are usually transient. They should be treated only if severe or prolonged and only after excluding other causes of sympathetic overactivity (hypoxia, hypercapnia).

9 Psychological problems may arise, either as a result of the illness or of a prolonged stay in the ICU environment. A tricyclic antidepressant may benefit patients with a reactive depression.

10 Corticosteroids should not be used and the place of plasmaphaeresis has yet to be defined.

Postoperative Care of the Myasthenic Patient

Patients with myasthenia gravis may be admitted to the ICU with a cholinergic or myasthenic crisis. However, they are more commonly admitted for postoperative care.

Bulbar signs, chronic respiratory disease, a low pre-operative forced vital capacity (FVC), a history of myasthenia gravis for over six years, and a requirement of more than 750 mg of oral pyridostigmine daily, all indicate that postoperative artificial ventilation will be required following major surgery. Anticholinesterase medication need not be commenced immediately postoperatively while artificial ventilation is in progress. The timing of weaning from artificial ventilation must be determined individually.

Weaning from artificial ventilation

Indications

A strong cough, to ensure the ability to clear secretions, and an FVC of more than 1500 ml are essential.

Anticholinesterases

The patient's normal daily dose of anticholinergic medication should be recommenced. If it is not possible to administer drugs orally, parenteral administration of a smaller dose is required (see Appendix).

Plasmaphaeresis

This should be considered in patients in whom attempts at weaning persistently fail.

Analgesia

1 Small incremental doses of morphine should be administered under close supervision; normal doses may result in respiratory depression.
2 Local analgesic techniques using a small dose of local anaesthetic (bupivacaine) are useful.

Other measures

1 Maintain normokalaemia and normocalcaemia; electrolyte imbalance can cause muscle weakness.
2 Certain drugs can worsen myasthenia gravis and should be avoided. These include:
   (a) Antibiotics – aminoglycosides, polymyxin, colistin, bacitracin.

(b) Antiarrhythmics – lignocaine, quinidine, propranolol, procainamide.

(c) Non-depolarising neuromuscular-blocking agents.

Myasthenic and cholinergic crisis

1 Myasthenic and cholinergic crises may be difficult to tell apart clinically and both may occur either as isolated events or postoperatively.

2 A myasthenic crisis occurs when there is an acute deterioration in the disease process. It may be precipitated by drugs (see above), infection or pregnancy. Precipitating drugs should be stopped and infection treated.

3 Overdosage with anticholinesterases can cause a cholinergic crisis due to a depolarising-type neuromuscular blockade, resulting from the accumulation of acetylcholine. The patient complains of weakness, excessive salivation, bronchosecretion, abdominal cramps and sweating; bradycardia and hypotension may be found on examination.

4 To differentiate between the two conditions, a Tensilon (edrophonium) test may be performed:

(a) Give a test dose of 1 mg of edrophonium.

(b) If there is no effect give a further 1–4 mg IV.

(c) Failure to improve, or a deterioration in muscle power, indicates anticholinesterase overdosage is likely.

(d) Atropine should be available to reverse any unwanted muscarinic effects.

5 In both conditions, anticholinergics should be stopped and artificial ventilation instituted if necessary (FVC less than 1000 ml), until improvement in the FVC occurs.

6 In a cholinergic crisis it may be necessary to ventilate the patient artificially for several days, until the anticholinesterase is cleared.

7 The advice of an experienced neurologist is invaluable in the management of these conditions.

Tetanus

Tetanus is caused by the Gram-positive, spore-producing rod *Clostridium tetani.* The organism is strictly anaerobic and tends to grow only in areas of necrotic, infected or extensively damaged tissue, or in the vicinity of foreign bodies. The incubation period of tetanus is usually four to 21 days, but may range from one day to several months. The clinical manifestations are due to the toxin tetanospasmin, which travels via the peripheral nerves to the central nervous system; there it interferes with the inhibition of spinal reflexes and, occasionally, with the autonomic nervous system.

Presentation

Patients usually present with dysphagia and stiffness and pain in the muscles of the neck, back and abdominal wall. Examination reveals hypertonus (legs more than arms) and trismus. Sustained contraction of the facial muscles produces the characteristic expression – risus sardonicus. Paroxysms of painful spasms result in extension of the neck, back and legs, and flexion of the shoulders and arms. In contrast to rabies, the rigidity persists between spasms.

Tetanus may be classified as shown below:

Grade 1. No dysphagia or respiratory difficulty.
Grade 2. Pronounced spasticity; some dysphagia or respiratory difficulty.
Grade 3a. Gross spasticity and major spasms requiring muscle relaxants and artificial ventilation.
Grade 3b. As in Grade 3a, but with evidence of autonomic dysfunction.

Partial immunisation may result in localised tetanus, in which rigidity is confined to the muscle groups near the site of infection. The onset time is the time between the first symptoms and the first spasm. The shorter the incubation period or the onset time, the worse the prognosis. The differential diagnosis of tetanus includes dental abscesses causing trismus, dystonic reactions to phenothiazines or metoclopramide, and tetany due to hypocalcaemia or hysterical hyperventilation. These may need to be excluded with X-rays, serum calcium and a toxicology screen.

Tetanus is a notifiable disease (see Chapter 19).

Management of established tetanus

Inactivation of the organism and its toxin

1 Passive immunisation. Given human tetanus immuno-globulin (HTIG) 30–300 U/kg IM. This only inactivates toxin in the wound and bloodstream. It is ineffective against toxin that has already entered the central nervous system.

2 Prescribe benzylpenicillin 1 MU six hourly IV for 10 days to eradicate remaining clostridia. Erythromycin may be used in patients allergic to penicillin.

Wound care

1 Debride and excise all dead tissues and send excised material for culture.

2 Wait at least one hour after the administration of HTIG before debriding the wound.

3 Leave the wound open and irrigate three times a day with hydrogen peroxide.

4 Tetanus may be caused by a trivial injury; the entry wound is not found in many patients.

Reduction of rigidity

1 Diazepam is titrated to the effect, and dose varies from 3 to 10 mg/kg/day orally or via NG tube.

2 Chlorpromazine 75 mg four hourly orally or via NG tube.

3 Meprobamate 400 mg six hourly orally or via NG tube.

Prevention of spasms

Spasms are painful and may cause hypoxia or crush fractures. They may be precipitated by afferent stimulation such as noise, bright light, a full bladder, swallowing or faecal impaction. Patients should be nursed in a quiet room and disturbed as little as possible.

Indications for muscle relaxants and artificial ventilation

1 Generalised spasms.

2 Laryngospasm.

3 Uncontrolled rigidity interfering with respiration.

4 Tracheostomy is indicated for long-term artificial ventilation, and may be needed earlier, if dysphagia or laryngeal spasm are prominent features.

Nutrition

1 Patients with severe tetanus are in an intense catabolic state and have increased fluid and nutritional requirements.

2 Spasms may be precipitated by swallowing.

3 Pass a NG tube early in the disease, especially if dysphagia is a prominent feature.

4 Parenteral nutrition may be required.

Autonomic instability

1 This may result in tachycardia or bradycardia, a labile blood pressure, sweating, hyperpyrexia and dysrhythmias.

2 Bradycardia usually responds to atropine 0.3–0.6 mg IV but temporary pacing may be required.

3 Severe hypertension is best treated with labetalol.

4 Hypotension usually responds to simple measures, such as positioning the patient head down.

Appendix

Drug	Therapeutic range ($\mu mol/l$)
Phenytoin	25–70
Phenobarbitone	40–170
Valproate	400–600
Carbamazepine	30–50
Ethosuximide	280–700

CSF	*Normal volumes and values*
Volume	100–160 ml
Glucose	2.5–4.5 mmol/l
Protein	0.15–0.45 g/l
Pressure	7–18 cmH$_2$O
pH	7.33–7.37
Osmolality	306 mmol/kg
Cell count	0–5 mosm/kg

Equivalent doses of anticholinesterases

15 mg oral neostigmine is equivalent to 0.5 mg parenteral neostigmine

60 mg oral pyridostigmine is equivalent to 2 mg parenteral pyridostigmine

60 mg oral pyridostigmine is equivalent to 15 mg oral neostigmine

1 mg parenteral pyridostigmine is equivalent to 0.5 mg parenteral neostigmine

NOTES

NOTES

CHAPTER 14

Endocrine Emergencies

Diabetes Mellitus

Diabetic ketoacidosis

Diabetic ketoacidosis usually occurs in insulin-dependent diabetics. It may be the first manifestation of diabetes in a previously undiagnosed diabetic, or it may be precipitated in a known diabetic by infection, pregnancy, myocardial infarction or failure to comply with insulin therapy.

Clinical features

The patient may complain of increasing lethargy, fatigue and nausea. Abdominal pain may be present and may be mistaken for an acute abdominal problem. In addition there may be the symptoms and signs of hyperglycaemia (polydipsia and polyuria), dehydration, acidosis and infection.

Management

Dehydration

1　Haematocrit and plasma urea are raised.
2　The average deficit is 6 litres.
3　Give 0.9 per cent sodium chloride: the first litre in 30 minutes; the second litre in one hour; the next litre in two hours. (Use 0.45% sodium chloride if the plasma sodium is >150 mmol/l.)
4　Subsequent fluid therapy should be guided by

measurement of the urine output, the CVP and the patient's clinical condition.

5 An ileus is common; a NG tube should be passed in all patients with a depressed level of consciousness.

Hyperglycaemia

1 Measure blood glucose hourly with a reflectance meter.
2 Give insulin by IV infusion starting at a rate of 10 U/hr and adjusting the rate according to plasma glucose measurements.
3 Aim for a fall in blood glucose of 5–10 mmol/hr.
4 Plasma glucose normally falls faster than plasma ketones; when the plasma glucose is less than 15 mmol/l, a 5 per cent dextrose infusion should be started and the insulin infusion continued at reduced dosage.
5 Start subcutaneous insulin once the patient is eating again.

Potassium

1 Measure plasma potassium one to two hourly until the blood glucose is less than 15 mmol/l and then four hourly.
2 Although the plasma potassium may be high initially, there is a large potassium deficit. The plasma concentration will fall rapidly when insulin is started, as the potassium moves intracellularly.
3 Monitor the ECG for the changes of hypo- or hyperkalaemia.
4 Potassium should be replaced at a rate of approximately 20 mmol/hr, but replacement should be guided by the plasma potassium measurements.
5 Give some of the potassium as potassium phosphate, since there is usually a deficiency of phosphate.
6 Aim for a plasma potassium of 4–5 mmol/l.

Acidosis

1 The severity of acidosis and its response to therapy should be assessed by measuring ABG at two hourly intervals initially. Ketostix and Acetest tablets are not reliable for this purpose.
2 The acidosis is reversed with insulin and fluid therapy. Do not give sodium bicarbonate routinely, since its use

may lead to cerebral oedema, a shift in the oxygen dissociation curve to the left and an exacerbation of hypokalaemia.

3 Consider sodium bicarbonate only if the hydrogen ion concentration is >100 nmol/l. If indicated, give 250–500 ml of the 1.4 per cent solution over one hour.

4 Give extra potassium if sodium bicarbonate is used.

Precipitating factors

1 Look for evidence of infection: send blood, urine and sputum for culture and obtain chest X-ray.
   (a) The WCC is usually elevated in ketoacidosis and is not a reliable indicator of infection.
   (b) Pyrexia may be absent in ketoacidosis.
   (c) Antibiotics should only be used in the presence of proven infection.

2 Perform serial ECG and cardiac enzymes, if myocardial infarction is suspected (see Chapter 4).

Hyperosmolar non-ketotic hyperglycaemic coma

Hyperosmolar non-ketotic coma occurs in both diagnosed and undiagnosed non-insulin-dependent diabetics. The condition may be precipitated by infection, drugs (thiazides), myocardial infarction, a cerebrovascular accident or subarachnoid haemorrhage.

Clinical features

The patients are usually older than those with ketoacidosis. The symptoms and signs are those of hyperglycaemia and dehydration. In addition:

1 Fever is common, even in the absence of infection.

2 Neurological signs, including coma and convulsions, are common. They do not necessarily indicate intra-cranial disease and improve with treatment.

Management

The management of this condition is similar to that of ketoacidosis, with the following differences:

1 The plasma sodium, glucose and osmolality are usually markedly elevated; there is no acidosis and the plasma

bicarbonate is normal. Plasma sodium and osmolality should be measured regularly during the period of rehydration.

2 If the plasma sodium is above 150 mmol/l, rehydration should start with 0.45 per cent sodium chloride and be followed with 0.9 per cent saline.

3 Fluid overload and pulmonary oedema are easily precipitated.

4 Too rapid a reduction in plasma osmolality can cause, or exacerbate, cerebral oedema.

5 These patients are sensitive to insulin and smaller doses should be used. Start with an IV infusion of 5 U/hr and adjust the rate as necessary.

6 Give subcutaneous heparin 5000 IU 12 hourly, as there is a high incidence of thrombosis in this condition. Do not give heparin to patients with focal neurological signs or subarachnoid haemorrhage.

7 Treat any precipitating factors.

Hypoglycaemia

Aetiology

The most common cause of hypoglycaemia is excess insulin administration, but it may also be drug-induced (salicylates, alcohol), or complicate liver failure, hypoadrenalism, hypothyroidism, septicaemia and end-stage renal failure.

Clinical features

Patients will initially be confused and exhibit abnormal behaviour. Later seizures and coma may occur possibly, with focal neurological signs. Signs of catecholamine release, pallor, tachycardia and sweating are usually present; they may be absent in patients receiving beta-blockers, or who have an autonomic neuropathy.

Management

1 The blood glucose concentration should be monitored regularly, using a reflectance meter, in all patients at risk.

2 Hypoglycaemia is treated by the infusion of 25–50 ml of 50 per cent dextrose into a large peripheral or central vein.

3 Subsequently maintain the blood glucose between 6–10 mmol/l by the infusion of 5 or 10 per cent dextrose.

4 Give glucagon (1 mg IM) if difficulty is experienced in establishing venous access. Glucagon raises the blood glucose concentration within five to 20 minutes.

5 Glucagon is not effective in treating the hypoglycaemia associated with hepatic disease.

Thyroid Diseases

Myxoedema coma

This may occur following autoimmune thyroiditis, total thyroidectomy, or radioactive iodine treatment, or be secondary to hypopituitarism. The condition is rare nowadays, but may still occur in patients who do not take their thyroxine, or in previously undiagnosed hypothyroid patients. It may be precipitated in hypothyroid patients by stress, trauma, surgery, infection, sedatives and opioids.

Clinical features

The patient may be psychotic (myxoedema madness) before becoming comatose. The features of severe hypothyroidism are present, but in addition hypothermia, respiratory depression, hypotension and bradycardia are present. If a hypothyroid patient is comatose, but is normothermic and normotensive, then the coma has some other aetiology.

Management

Hypoglycaemia

1 Measure plasma glucose regularly and treat hypoglycaemia.

Thyroid hormone replacement

1 Take blood for thyroid function tests and random cortisol.

2 Do not wait for the results before initiating treatment.

3 Monitor the ECG to observe the effects of thyroxine and hypothermia. Thyroxine may precipitate angina or myocardial infarction.

4 *Always* give 300 mg hydrocortisone IV before starting thyroxine, since an adrenal crisis may be precipitated by the increase in metabolic rate. Continue steroid therapy until the patient has recovered and hypoadrenalism is excluded.

5 Comatose patients who are hypothermic and hypotensive should receive 200 mcg of thyroxine, preferably down the NG tube (if an ileus is present IV may be necessary) depending on the severity of the hypothermia and hypotension. A response is seen within 24 hours of the first dose.

6 Thyroxine 50–100 mcg IV or orally should be given 24 hours after the first dose and then daily.

Hypotension

1 Hypotension usually responds to thyroid replacement.

2 Fluids and inotropes may also be required (see Chapter 3).

Hypoventilation

1 Measure ABG regularly. If necessary, give supplemental oxygen by face mask.

2 A rising $PaCO_2$ is an indication for artificial ventilation (see Chapter 5).

Hypothermia

1 The patient should be rewarmed in a warm room using warm blankets.

2 Active rewarming can cause cardiovascular collapse.

Hyponatraemia

This is common and is due to impaired water excretion and inappropriate ADH secretion (see Chapter 7).

Thyroid crisis

This is rare nowadays, but may occur in patients with poorly controlled or undiagnosed hyperthyroidism, in which case it may be precipitated by infection, surgery or labour.

Clinical features

The diagnosis is made on clinical findings. The degree of elevation of thyroid hormone level cannot be used to differentiate severe thyrotoxicosis from a thyroid crisis. The plasma T_3, free T_4 and free thyroxine index are raised. There is a marked increase in all the symptoms and signs of thyrotoxicosis, including:

1 Pyrexia. This is almost invariable and may rise to above 40°C.
2 Cardiac signs. There is a hyperdynamic circulation, with hot extremities and a wide pulse pressure. Sinus tachycardia or tachyarrhythmias (fast atrial fibrillation) are present and out of proportion to the pyrexia. Congestive cardiac failure, hypotension and vascular collapse may follow.
3 CNS signs. The patient is irritable and this progresses to confusion, restlessness and coma.
4 Signs of hepatic dysfunction. Jaundice indicates a poor prognosis.

Management

Cool the patient

Cooling blankets, fanning and sponging may be used. Salicylates are contraindicated.

Beta-blockers

These are given to reduce catecholamine effects.

1 Give propranolol in increments of 0.5 mg IV, to a maximum of 5 mg. Alternatively give oral propranolol 40 mg eight hourly.
2 If the patient is in heart failure or atrial fibrillation, then he should be digitalised.

Reduce the formation and release of thyroid hormone

1 Lugol's iodine reduces thyroid hormone release. Give 0.1–0.3 ml eight hourly orally.
2 Give propylthiouracil 100–300 mg eight hourly orally, or carbimazole 10 mg six hourly orally.
3 The dose of drugs is decreased as the patient's condition improves.

Fluids

Fluids and electrolytes need replacement, preferably under CVP guidance.

1 Monitor plasma potassium and correct hypokalaemia.
2 Pay attention to nutritional needs, as these patients have a very high metabolic rate. Extra calories and vitamins may be necessary.

Steroids

A relative deficiency of steroids may exist due to increased hepatic metabolism and increased stress. Steroids may also inhibit peripheral conversion of T_4 to T_3. Give hydrocortisone 100 mg IV six hourly.

Hypoadrenalism

Hypoadrenalism must be suspected in all patients if this easily treatable and potentially fatal disease is not to be missed. It occurs most commonly in patients who receive them as part of their treatment for a pre-existing disease following withdrawal or failure to increase the dose of glucocorticoids during periods of stress. Shock may also lead to its development and in all patients receiving large doses of catecholamines with little effect, a short ACTH (tetracosactrin Synacthen) test should be performed and followed by treatment. Additional causes are idiopathic hypoadrenalism, septicaemia, tuberculosis, metastastic disease and hypopituitarism.

Clinical features

Patients present with hypotension, dehydration and possibly coma. The signs of chronic hypoadrenalism are not necessarily present (pigmentation of the hands, feet and buccal mucosa). Hypoadrenalism may be associated with features of other organ-specific autoimmune diseases. In patients with chronic adrenal insufficiency, an adrenal crisis may be precipitated by trauma, surgery, sepsis and myocardial infarction.

Management

Hypoglycaemia

1 Hypoglycaemia is usually present. The plasma glucose should be measured regularly, using a reflectance meter.
2 Treat with 25 g IV glucose.

Steroids

1 Perform a short ACTH (tetracosactrin Synacthen) test before giving steroids. This can be performed at any time.
   (a) Take a baseline sample for plasma cortisol, give 250 mcg tetracosactrin IV and take a second sample 30 minutes later.
   (b) The normal response to tetracosactrin is a rise in plasma cortisol by at least 200 nmol/l over the baseline value, with a final value over 500 nmol/l.
2 Give hydrocortisone 200 mg IV.
3 Give hydrocortisone 100 mg six hourly IV on day 1, 50 mg six hourly IV on day 3 and 25 mg eight to 12 hourly IV on day 5.
4 More hydrocortisone may be required if hypotension or vomiting persists or recurs.
5 Mineralocorticoid replacement (fludrocortisone) is not necessary when large doses of hydrocortisone are being used but may be necessary when the dose of hydrocortisone is lessened to maintenance levels.

Fluid balance

1 Hyponatraemia and hyperkalaemia may be present.
2 The ECF volume may be 20 per cent depleted. Salt and water replacement is best guided by measurement of the CVP.

Precipitating causes

These need to be identified and treated.

1 Exclude infection. Antibiotics should only be used when an infection is demonstrated.
2 Perform an ECG to exclude myocardial infarction.

Diabetes Insipidus (DI)

This results from inadequate reabsorption of filtered water by the renal tubules. DI may be caused by:

1 Central failure to secrete antidiuretic hormone (ADH) following intracerebral injury (trauma, infection, surgery, hypoxia or aneurysms).

2 The renal tubules may fail to respond to ADH (nephrogenic DI) in hypokalaemia, hypercalcaemia, multiple myeloma, or following acute tubular necrosis or renal transplantation.

Clinical features

The sudden onset of polyuria is usually the only sign in a critically ill patient; dehydration will occur quickly if urinary losses are not replaced and the diuresis slowed.

Management

1 Measure plasma and urine electrolytes and osmolality. The plasma sodium and osmolality are raised, with an inappropriately low urine osmolality. In central DI, the urine osmolality rises at least 10 per cent after the injection of vasopressin (5 U IV). In patients with nephrogenic DI, the urinary osmolality does not rise.
2 Urinary losses should be replaced with a solution similar to the composition of urine.
3 Central DI is treated with vasopressin (5 U IV). The duration of action of vasopressin is three to six hours.
4 Fluid balance should be carefully monitored to avoid water intoxication.
5 DI in conscious patients is controlled with intranasal desmopressin 10–20 mcg once or twice daily.
6 In nephrogenic DI, underlying causes should be treated if possible and fluid losses replaced. Only thiazide diuretics and salt restriction are of value in reducing the urine output.

NOTES

NOTES

CHAPTER 15

Haematology

Anaemia

Anaemia (Hb <10 g/dl) is common in patients requiring intensive care. It may be due to one or more factors including:

1 Blood loss. Continuing blood loss from injuries or other sites (especially the GI tract) replaced by fluids other than blood.

2 Chronic disease. Chronic renal failure, rheumatoid arthritis, malignancy and liver disease.

3 Haemolysis. Infection (streptococcal, clostridial, malaria), drugs (sulphonamides, methyldopa), enzyme deficiencies (G-6-P deficiency), congenital abnormalities (spherocytosis, haemoglobinopathies) or mechanical damage (prosthetic heart valves).

4 Deficiency anaemias. Iron, vitamin B_{12}, folic acid or vitamin C.

5 Bone marrow aplasia. Drugs (chloramphenicol).

Presentation

Patients may present in an ICU with a condition that is exacerbated by anaemia (myocardial ischaemia), or it may be found as a coincidental finding on routine laboratory investigation during the course of an illness. Physical signs may be variable and include dyspnoea, signs of a hyperdynamic circulation and pallor. Cardiac failure may be precipitated by anaemia.

Investigations

Haemoglobin

This should be performed daily in all critically ill patients. A sudden fall usually indicates bleeding often from the GI tract. The haematology laboratory usually reports, in addition to Hb, mean cell volume (MCV), mean cell haemoglobin (MCH) and red cell count (RCC). From these parameters it is possible to identify the different types of anaemias (see Table 15.1).

Table 15.1 Parameters in different types of anaemia

Type	MCV	MCH	RCC
Iron deficiency	↓	↓	↓
Thalassaemia trait	↓	↓	↑
Chronic infection or malignancy	N	N	↓
Megaloblastic (folate, B deficiency, cirrhosis, alcoholism)	↑	↑	↓

Reticulocyte count

If raised, this indicates an increase in the formation of red cells. It is seen in haemolysis, haemorrhage and when treatment is started for haematinic deficiency anaemias.

Haematocrit (PCV)

This is the percentage of a blood volume occupied by the red cells. It can be easily and accurately measured at the bedside using a centrifuge and therefore is often used during resuscitation in preference to Hb concentration. A PCV of 0.3–0.35 is aimed for during resuscitation offering good oxygen carriage with a low viscosity, improving flow in and oxygen delivery to the microcirculation.

Blood film

Further information about the morphology of red cells can be obtained from examination of a blood film (e.g., fragmentation reticulocytes, thrombocytopenia, neutropenia, etc.).

White cell and platelet count

These may be decreased in marrow aplasia and megaloblastic anaemias.

Haemolysis screen

If this is suspected, the following additional tests should be performed:

(a) *Direct Coombs Test.* To detect the presence of antibodies on the red cell surface.

(b) *Plasma haemoglobin.* This is increased when intravascular haemolysis is present.

(c) *Serum haptoglobin.* This falls in haemolysis, but may also be low in patients with liver disease.

(d) *Reticulocyte count.* See above.

(e) *Plasma bilirubin.* As the red cells are broken down the haem released is metabolised to bilirubin.

(f) *Urobilinogen.* Excess conjugated bilirubin is excreted in the urine.

Bone marrow aspiration

This is useful in the diagnosis of megaloblastic anaemia and marrow aplasia.

Haemoglobin electrophoresis (sickle cell disease)

All dark-skinned and southern mediterranean patients must be screened for sickle cell disease. Sickling crises can be precipitated by severe illness or injury even in heterozygous patients. Other haemoglobinopathies may be found.

Other investigations

These include serum B_{12}, red cell folate and iron studies.

Management

Whenever possible all appropriate investigations should be performed before treatment is started.

Acute anaemia

This usually requires prompt treatment if the haemoglobin is less than 10 g/dl by:

1 Resuscitation.

2 Blood transfusion. Concentrated red cells (CRC) should be used (unless the patient is hypovolaemic when whole blood should be used). Each unit will increase the Hb concentration by approximately 1 g/dl in an adult. The volume of each unit is approximately 250 ml and in patients with heart failure a diuretic (frusemide 10 mg IV) may need to be administered with each one.

Chronic anaemias

This is a particular problem in patients with chronic renal failure who normally have an Hb concentration of 6–7 g/dl. Various compensatory mechanisms in the red cell allow increased oxygen delivery to the tissues and enable the patient to lead a normal life. When patients become acutely ill these mechanisms may become upset or their own blood replaced by transfused blood. It is, therefore, usual if these patients become critically ill (especially if they require artificial ventilation) to maintain a higher Hb concentration of 8–10 g/dl. Similar arguments apply to other patients with a chronic anaemia associated with other diseases.

Bleeding Disorders

Disorders of coagulation are common in patients requiring intensive care.

Coagulation cascade

The extrinsic pathway, intrinsic pathway and common pathway of blood coagulation are shown in Figure 15.1.

Investigations

1 *Platelet count.* Significant if below 80 000 × 10^9/l.
2 *Prothrombin time* (PT). Assesses the extrinsic and common pathway. Also used to guide warfarin dose.
3 *Kaolin partial thromboplastin time* (KPTT). Assesses the intrinsic and common pathway. Used to guide heparin dosage.
4 *Thrombin time* (TT). Assesses the conversion of fibrinogen to fibrin.

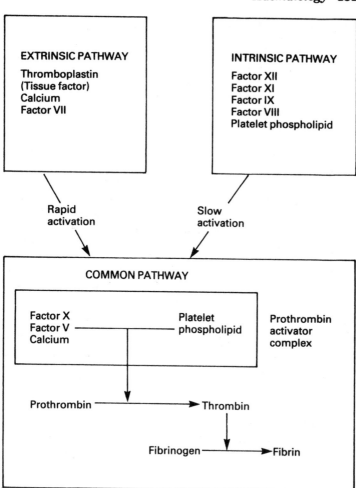

Figure 15.1   Coagulation cascade

5 *Plasma fibrinogen.* Assay of this factor.
6 *Fibrin degradation products* (FDP). Increased when excessive fibrin is being broken down.
7 *Bleeding time.* This measures the effectiveness of platelet clots and its interaction with the vessel wall.

The approach to the bleeding patient

The following points should be asked:

1 Is the patient resuscitated?
2 During massive transfusion have coagulation factors been replaced adequately (see below)?
3 Has the underlying cause been treated adequately, for example:
  Surgically correctable bleeding?
  Sepsis?
4 Have any drugs that alter coagulation been administered within, or outside, the hospital (aspirin, heparin for monitoring lines)?
5 Is there a past history or a family history of abnormal bleeding (haemophilia)? Has the patient a warning bracelet or card about drug therapy (oral anticoagulants) or disease?
6 Does the patient suffer from a condition that interferes with vitamin K absorption (jaundice, malabsorption)?

Specific coagulation problems

Obtain assistance from a haematologist with all coagulation problems. If coagulation is deranged, remove heparin from the monitoring flush lines.

Massive blood transfusion

Platelet count reduced; PT and KPTT increased; TT, fibrinogen and FDP normal. This occurs when more than one blood volume (5 l) has been replaced rapidly. In addition to the loss of platelets and clotting factors, citrate (part of the anticoagulant in stored blood) binds calcium and renders it inactive.

Treat on the basis of coagulation results. If these are not available: give 2 U of fresh frozen plasma (FFP) for each 10 U of blood and also calcium gluconate (2.2 mmol IV) for every 4 U of blood transfused. Platelet administration is based on the platelet count.

Disseminated intravascular coagulation (DIC)

Platelet count reduced; PT, KPTT and TT increased; fibrinogen decreased; FDP increased. Widespread intravascular coagulation and subsequent lysis of the clot occur. All clotting factors and platelets are consumed. DIC may be precipitated by many causes including sepsis, anaphylaxis, obstetric problems, malignant disease and transfusion reactions. Expert haematological help is essential with the management of this condition.

Malabsorption of vitamin K

Platelet count normal; PT increased; KPTT and TT normal; fibrinogen and FDP normal. Give vitamin K (10 mg/day IV slowly for three days) and then assess the effect. Rapid correction, if necessary, can be achieved with FFP.

Severe liver disease

Platelets reduced; PT, KPTT and TT increased; fibrinogen reduced; FDP increased. Failure to synthetise clotting factors (due to deranged liver function, malabsorption of vitamin K and hypersplenism) leads to a coagulopathy. It may be corrected by the administration of vitamin K, FFP and platelets.

Renal failure

Platelet count increased or decreased; PT and KPTT normal; TT may be increased; fibrinogen normal; FDP slightly increased. The bleeding time is prolonged because uraemia interferes with platelet function. FDP are retained in the body, prolonging thrombin time. When treatment is required correct the anaemia, consider haemodialysis, administer cryoprecipitate. Platelet concentrate may also be of use.

Transfusion Reactions

Clinical features

The most common cause for a major transfusion reaction is a clerical error. Mild allergic transfusion reactions are common and consist of itching, urticaria and flushing. ABO incompatibility usually causes more serious reactions than those due to Rhesus factor. The conscious patient may complain of nausea, pain in the loins, in the precordium and in the limb being infused. Tremor, rigors and pyrexia may be present. Later signs include bronchospasm, shock, haemoglobinaemia and haemoglobinuria. In the unconscious patient, a transfusion reaction may manifest itself as hypotension, tachycardia, shock, renal failure and unexplained bleeding.

Management

1 Blood transfusion procedures should be rigorously followed.
2 In mild allergic reactions, continue the transfusion and prescribe an antihistamine (chlorpheniramine 10 mg IV over one minute).
3 If the patient develops hypotension (not due to hypovolaemia), bronchospasm, or signs of anaphylaxis, stop the blood transfusion immediately and treat as for anaphylactic shock (see Chapter 3).
4 Send the remainder of the blood in the bag and a specimen of the patient's blood and urine to the laboratory for further compatibility studies.

Nitrous Oxide

The administration of nitrous oxide in anaesthetic concentrations for a period in excess of two hours inactivates vitamin B_{12} and may lead to impaired DNA synthesis and the development of megaloblastic bone marrow haemopoiesis. In fit patients this is of little significance, but in critically ill patients it may increase mortality.

Management

1 Haemopoietic changes induced by nitrous oxide can be reversed with folinic acid.
2 Give folinic acid (30 mg IV twice daily for two days) to all patients requiring intensive care following surgery in which nitrous oxide was used as part of the anaesthetic for more than two hours.
3 Vitamin B_{12} (1 mg IV daily for two days) may replace that which has been inactivated.

NOTES

CHAPTER 16

Brain Death and Organ Transplantation

Brain Death

Brain death exists when there is no demonstrable brain stem function in the presence of a diagnosis compatible with irreversible structural brain damage. The definition is accepted by many countries in the world. The patient will be totally dependent on intensive support, including artificial ventilation. There are no published episodes of recovery from this condition. The common causes of brain death include:

Cerebral trauma
Cerebrovascular accident
Cerebral tumours
Hypoxic brain damage

The Royal Colleges of the United Kingdom have agreed a system of formalised clinical testing, by two doctors, to enable the diagnosis of brain death to be made. These tests are shown in the Appendix to this Chapter. The following points should be noted:

1 There should be no doubt that severe irremediable *structural* brain damage has occurred to that patient. Reversible causes, including poisoning, prolonged response to drugs (muscle relaxants, benzodiazepines, opioids, etc.), hypothermia (<35°C), metabolic and endocrinological disorders, must have been excluded.

2 Two doctors are needed to certify brain death. The first should be the consultant in charge of the patient or his deputy (who must have been registered for five years or more and be adequately experienced). The second doctor must be suitably experienced and clinically independent of the first. Neither doctor must be a member of the transplant team.

3 The tests should be recorded on a suitable form.

4 The diagnostic tests should be performed on at least two occasions, separated by several hours. The exact time interval will depend upon the patient's condition.

5 Tests other than those described in the Appendix, such as EEG, are unnecessary.

6 The time of the patient's death is the time of completion of the second set of brain death tests. It is important that this is the time of death which is both recorded in the notes and written on the death certificate.

7 If organ transplantation is not to be carried out, on completion of the second set of tests the patient may be left disconnected from the ventilator.

8 Caring for the relatives at this time requires tact and understanding. If organ transplantation is not to take place, they may wish to remain in the room until the heart stops beating.

Consent for Organ Donation

When the first set of brain death criteria has been fulfilled the question of organ suitability for donation should be raised. This question should only be raised with the relatives by a senior member of the medical team. If the patient carried a donor card, there is no legal need to request consent for organ donation from the relatives, but it is still wise and humane to discuss it with them. If there are no relatives, the Hospital Administrator (as the legal possessor of the body) has the authority to grant permission for organ transplantation. If the events surrounding brain death require that the Coroner or Procurator Fiscal be informed, this should be undertaken at an early stage and consent sought from him for the removal of organs. In some hospitals, the Hospital Pathologist has been delegated this authority.

The Organ Donor

Recent advances in anaesthetic, surgical and immuno-suppressive techniques have now made it possible to transplant many organs from one brain dead donor into different recipients. This may result in an improvement in the quality and length of life for the recipients. The following organs may be transplanted:

Heart (or heart–lungs)
Kidneys
Pancreas
Liver
Corneas

It is important to realise that, if it was the wish of the patient when he was alive, or of the relatives following his death, to allow organs to be removed for transplantation, it is the duty of the ICU staff to ensure that these organs are maintained in a good condition. Failure to do so not only results in the wishes of the patient being disregarded, but also exposes the recipients to unnecessary risk.

Once the criteria for the first set of brain death tests have been fulfilled and consent has been obtained, the Regional Transplant Co-ordinator should be informed. It is imperative that he or she is informed as early as possible after the first set of tests, to avoid wastage of time and effort in the ICU. Suitability for organ transplantation should be considered in any patients satisfying the following:

1 Aged four months to 70 years (corneas up to 90 years).
2 Free of transmissable infection.
3 Free of overt bacterial, fungal or viral infection (septicaemia, perforated gastrointestinal tract, etc.).
4 No widespread atherosclerosis.
5 No trauma, infection or chronic disease of any organ that may be transplanted.

6 Hepatitis B antigen negative.

7 HIV negative.

8 Free of malignant disease (except primary cerebral tumours).

Donor Maintenance in the ICU

When brain death is confirmed and consent for organ donation obtained, patient care becomes donor maintenance. Changes in treatment may result including alteration of artificial ventilation, plasma volume expansion and freer changes of posture.

1 Establish two reliable IV lines; one may be a central venous line.

2 Try to maintain a systolic pressure above 90–100 mmHg, to ensure adequate renal blood flow and urine output, by:

(a) Giving a volume expander (gelatin solution, HAS, etc.) rapidly to restore blood pressure and maintain a CVP of 8–10 mmHg. Patients who have been dehydrated should receive 5 per cent dextrose or Hartmann's solution, according to the plasma electrolyte results.

(b) If the blood pressure fails to respond, start an infusion of dopamine at a rate of 2–10 mcg/kg/min. Noradrenaline, metaraminol and methoxamine are potent vasoconstrictors and, although they raise the blood pressure, they decrease organ perfusion and should not be used.

3 Insert a urinary catheter, if one is not already in place. Maintain a urine output of at least 1.0 ml/kg/hr.

(a) If urine output does not respond to fluid replacement, give 10 per cent mannitol (0.5 gm/kg/hr IV).

(b) If there is no response to the above measures, give frusemide (0.2 mg/kg IV) repeated at 30-minute intervals.

4 If diabetes insipidus develops (urine output more than 4 ml/kg/hr) give 5–20 U pitressin IV over four hours, repeated if necessary. Replace the urinary losses with

0.45 per cent sodium chloride/2.5 per cent dextrose with 15 mmol potassium chloride per 500 ml added.

5 Monitor arterial blood gases.
   (a) Adjust the inspired oxygen concentration to give a $PaO_2 > 10$ kPa.
   (b) Adjust ventilation to give a $PaCO_2$ of 5 kPa. Low minute volumes may be necessary because of the low metabolic rate.

6 Monitor blood glucose levels at hourly intervals with a reflectance meter. If the level rises above 10 mmol/l, infuse insulin via a syringe pump at 2 U/hr; this dose may have to be adjusted in the light of further readings. (See Chapter 10.)

7 Monitor body core temperature (rectal); aim to keep it at 34–6°C by using a reflective foil blanket, or warming blanket, as necessary.

8 The following investigations may be requested by the transplant co-ordinator:
   (a) ABO blood group.
   (b) Plasma U&E.
   (c) Hepatitis B surface antigen status.
   (d) Arterial blood gases.
   (e) Liver function tests.
   (f) Tissue type.
   Additional investigations may be requested in certain patients, including:
   (a) HIV serology.
   (b) 12-lead ECG (heart/heart–lung donors).
   (c) Chest X-ray (heart/heart–lung donors).
   (d) Serum amylase (pancreas donors).

Appendix

Checklist of criteria for diagnosis of brain death

Diagnosis to be made by two independent doctors, one a consultant and the other a consultant or senior registrar. Diagnosis should not normally be considered until at least six hours after the onset of coma or, if cardiac arrest was the cause of the coma, until 24 hours after the circulation has been restored.

Name .... Unit No. ....

PRECONDITIONS

Are you satisfied that the patient suffers from a condition that has led to irremediable brain damage? Specify the condition:	Time of onset of unresponsive coma:
Dr A	
Dr B	....

Are you satisfied that potentially reversible causes for the patient's condition have been adequately excluded, in particular:

	Dr A	Dr B
Depressant drugs		
Neuromuscular blocking (relaxant) drugs		

Appendix — *contd*

Hypothermia

Metabolic or endocrine disturbances

TESTS FOR ABSENCE OF BRAIN-STEM FUNCTION

	Dr A		Dr B	
	1st testing	2nd testing	1st testing	2nd testing
Do the pupils react to light?				
Are there corneal reflexes?				
Is there eye movement on caloric testing?				
Are there motor responses in the cranial nerve distribution, in response to stimulation of face, limbs or trunk?				

	Dr A		Dr B	
	1st testing	2nd testing	1st testing	2nd testing
Is there a gag reflex? (If the test is practicable)				
Is there a cough reflex?				
Have the recommendations concerning testing for apnoea been followed?*				

Appendix — *contd*

Were any respiratory movements seen?

	Dr A	Dr B
Date and time of first testing	....	....
Date and time of second testing	....	....

(As stated in paragraph 30 of the Code of Practice the two doctors may carry out the tests separately or together.)

Dr A Signature ....   Dr B Signature ....

Status ....   Status ....

* Diagnosis of Brain Death, *Br. Med. J.*, 1976, ii, 1187–8. See note (b) on page 35 of the Code of Practice.

Reproduced with the permission of the Controller of Her Majesty's Stationery Office from *The Removal of Cadaveric Organs for Transplantation: A Code of Practice*, DHSS, London, 1979.

NOTES

CHAPTER 17

Sedation and Analgesia

Failure to provide adequate sedation and/or analgesia for patients receiving artificial ventilation will result not only in distress to the patient, but also in inadequate gas exchange, if the patient fails to synchronise with (fights against) the ventilator. In spontaneously breathing patients, failure to provide analgesia, especially after thoracic or abdominal operations, will result in respiratory impairment due to pain and inability to cough and to take deep breaths. The necessary level of sedation and analgesia, and response to drugs, varies enormously between patients. Careful administration of sedative and analgesic drugs is necessary, together with individual assessment of the patient's response.

The aim, for a patient receiving assisted ventilation, is that he should not be distressed by his surroundings, or by the procedures that are being undertaken, yet that he can be woken. For the spontaneously breathing patient, the aim should be effective analgesia, with minimal sedation.

Sedation

Sedation may be achieved by many drugs, and many of the parenteral analgesics (especially morphine) have sedative properties, making additional sedative drugs unnecessary. It should be remembered that although analgesics may provide sedation, sedatives *do not* provide analgesia; agitation caused by pain should be treated with an analgesic and not by increasing the dose of the sedative. The ideal sedative agent should be rapidly acting, safe and non-cumulative, should allow rapid awakening and should be contained in a small volume. Several agents are currently available to produce sedation; none is ideal.

Benzodiazepines

Intermittent injection. Lorazepam (2–4 mg six hourly IV) or diazepam (5–10 mg four hourly IV) has been used with success.

Continuous infusion. The use of the short half-life benzodiazepine midazolam by continuous infusion, in the dose range 3–5 mg/hr, has become popular. Larger doses may be necessary, in some patients. It is usually prescribed as 50 mg of midazolam in 50 ml of 5 per cent dextrose and given by syringe pump.

Before starting a midazolam infusion, the patient's response to boluses of 2.5–5 mg should be ascertained. Only if repeated bolus doses are necessary at frequent intervals, should a midazolam infusion be started. Once an infusion is started, it should be stopped (or the dose halved) at least daily until the patient awakes when it is restarted. If patients are not assessed in this way, difficulties with delayed awakening will be encountered when the infusion is stopped.

During recovery from a midazolam infusion, a period of agitation is common. This should not be treated by further midazolam administration and will spontaneously resolve in a few hours.

Chlormethiazole

Although chlormethiazole is effective and controllable, it is available only in a dilute solution (0.8 per cent) and imposes a considerable water load. It is usually administered in the dose range of approximately 1 ml/min, although a higher starting rate may be necessary (4 ml/min).

Barbiturates

Methohexitone, thiopentone. This group of drugs can be used to give sedation, but they can be cumulative and cause delayed awakening. They are not frequently used.

New agents

Several are currently under evaluation including propofol (a short-acting anaesthetic induction agent, given by infusion at a rate of 30–60 mg/hr) and isoflurane (a volatile anaesthetic agent given at low concentrations for prolonged periods). However, for neither drug is this currently an approved indication.

Before agitation is treated pharmacologically in the spontaneously breathing patient, other causes such as hypoxia, hypoglycaemia and a full bladder, should be excluded.

1 Benzodiazepines in small doses (midazolam, 2.5–5 mg IV), titrated to produce the desired effect, are useful. They do carry the risk of producing respiratory depression.
2 Haloperidol (5–10 mg IV) may be useful in the acutely agitated patient in whom respiratory depression is undesirable.
3 Routine recording of sedation level on the 24-hour chart is a valuable asset.

Analgesia

Parenteral analgesics

This is the most popular method of providing analgesia for patients needing intensive care. Most postoperative patients will suffer severe pain, unless an appropriate analgesic is administered in an effective dose, at suitable intervals.

1 Morphine sulphate (2–5 mg IV as necessary) is effective. Many of its disadvantages, in patients breathing spontaneously, become advantages, when artificial ventilation is necessary; it is a sedative, an antitussive and a respiratory depressant. The advantages of newer opiates (e.g., fentanyl), with their lesser effects on the cardiovascular system and histamine release, may be of use in certain circumstances, such as in the shocked patient or the asthmatic.
2 The frequency of administration should be assessed and

the patient given an IV dose of morphine (2–5 mg), repeated as necessary, to relieve pain. When pain recurs, a further IV injection of an opiate should be given and repeated as necessary. If the time interval between repeated injections is short, consider starting a continuous morphine infusion at a rate of 2–5 mg/hr. The infusion should be stopped or decreased each day and restarted when the first signs of discomfort appear. Failure to assess the patient's needs will result in over-dosage and difficulty in weaning the patient from ventilation. In particular, patients with renal failure do not eliminate morphine normally, and accumulation can occur very rapidly with a morphine infusion. When a patient is being weaned from assisted ventilation, it is usually necessary to decrease, or stop, an analgesic infusion, so avoiding respiratory depression and sedation.

The level of analgesia produced should be sufficient to keep the patient comfortable during normal medical and nursing procedures. Physiotherapy and some other procedures may be extremely painful, and the level of analgesia maintained throughout the 24-hour period should not be such as to remove these peaks of pain. These painful procedures necessitate a transient increase in the level of analgesia, and this can be achieved by one of these means:

1 Increasing the rate of the morphine infusion.
2 By the bolus administration of a short-acting opiate, such as alfentanil (500–1000 mcg).
3 Using 50 per cent nitrous oxide in oxygen (Entonox) as the inspired gas so long as:
   (a) The daily exposure time to nitrous oxide is brief.
   (b) The patient does not have an abnormal gas-filled cavity in his body, expansion of which would cause clinical deterioration (pneumothorax, air embolus, etc.).
   (c) The patient can tolerate an F_1O_2 of 0.5.
4 As soon as the gastrointestinal tract is working, orally administered analgesics may be used, including di-hydrocodeine (30–60 mg four to six hourly) and controlled release morphine (20–30 mg eight hourly),

in addition to the less-potent analgesics such as paracetamol.

Morphine is the standard analgesic agent in this section, but other opiates (papavaretum, pethidine) may be used according to local preference.

Epidural opiates

Small doses of opiates can be very effective at relieving pain when given by this route; they can be particularly useful in the management of patients with fractured ribs and following chest and abdominal surgery. Prolonged analgesia without adverse effects on the cardiovascular system is possible, using this technique.

1 An epidural catheter is inserted at the appropriate level (see Practical Procedure 10).
2 Preservative-free opiate, usually morphine (2 mg in 10 ml 0.9 per cent saline), is administered through a bacterial filter into the epidural catheter.
3 Further epidural boluses of analgesic may only be required at eight to 12 hourly intervals.
4 Some ICU prefer to infuse continuously a short-acting opiate such as fentanyl.
5 Pruritus may be a problem, but this can be resolved by the administration of 0.1–0.2 mg naloxone SC, without reversal of the analgesia.
6 Rarely, late respiratory depression may occur (up to 16 hours after the last dose) if the patient is breathing spontaneously, or on a weaning mode.

Spinal opiates

When performing spinal anaesthesia, some anaesthetists inject opiate along with the local anaesthetic. This is not usually repeated in the postoperative period during intensive care, but may produce problems with late respiratory depression and pruritus.

Respiratory depression

1 Patients may develop respiratory depression following administration of opiates by any route.

2 This can be reversed by naloxone, but great care is necessary in the administration of this drug to patients who are in pain. The injection of a large dose of naloxone will not only reverse respiratory depression, but will also reverse analgesia, with the patient experiencing severe pain.

3 Reversal of respiratory depression should be undertaken, with small doses of naloxone. Dissolve 0.4 mg of naloxone in 10 ml of 0.9 per cent saline and inject slowly.

4 Sudden reversal of analgesia with naloxone, in addition to producing pain may lead to haemodynamic changes, including cardiac arrest.

Regional analgesia

Use of local anaesthesia may be advantageous, obviating or diminishing the need for opiate analgesia for painful injuries.

Epidural analgesia

1 An epidural catheter with an attached microbial filter is inserted into a lumbar or thoracic interspace (see Practical Procedure 10).

2 Bupivacaine hydrochloride is the only long-acting local analgesic available at the moment. The maximum dose should not exceed 2 mg/kg per four hours.

3 Approximate doses of bupivacaine by this route are:
   (a) *Lumbar epidural.* Approximately 7–10 ml of 0.25 or 0.5 per cent bupivacaine plain.
   (b) *Thoracic epidural.* 4–5 ml of 0.25 or 0.5 per cent bupivacaine.

4 Bupivacaine can be infused into an epidural catheter in either region at a rate of 3–5 ml/hr. Supplemental top-up doses may be necessary, but at longer time intervals; they should be approximately two-thirds of the bolus doses above.

5 The lower concentration is usually used first, and if an inadequate block is obtained a higher concentration is used.

6 If when the higher concentration is used the block is still inadequate, pin-pricking should be used to establish the extent of the block. If it does not extend high

enough, the volume of solution should be increased. It may then be possible to decrease the concentration of the bupivacaine used.

7 Failure to obtain pain relief, after increasing both the concentration and the volume of bupivacaine, should raise the suspicion of a misplaced catheter.

Side effects

1 Systemic hypotension due to sympathetic vasodilation. This should be treated by the rapid infusion of a volume expander (500 ml), and if this fails to produce an improvement a further 500 ml of fluid should be administered (assuming the patient's condition permits). If this also fails, or if the patient's condition (renal failure, pulmonary oedema or confusion) does not permit the administration of large amounts of fluid, then ephedrine 5–10 mg IV (an alpha- and beta-agonist) should be used and repeated if necessary.

2 Sinus bradycardia. This may occur, due to blockade of the sympathetic cardiac nerves in the thoracic region. If hypotension has not occurred, then atropine (0.3–0.6 mg IV) should be injected. If hypotension has occurred, then the use of ephedrine will usually resolve this problem.

3 Total spinal anaesthesia. If the epidural catheter penetrates the dura, then any bupivacaine administered will result in spinal anaesthesia. Since relatively large volumes are being given, an extensive block will result. Full supportive treatment should be given; fluid, vasopressors and respiratory support may be needed until the local anaesthetic wears off (about two hours), when recovery occurs.

Intercostal nerve blockade

This is a useful, simple technique that can provide good analgesia following upper abdominal operations and is especially useful during weaning from artificial ventilation. The anterior abdominal wall is innervated by the thoracic nerves T7 (xiphisternum) to T10 (umbilicus). These nerves can readily be blocked in the subcostal groove (see Practical Procedures 11). The major hazard is the risk of pneumothorax, and the routine use of this technique on patients receiving artificial ventilation is not advised, because of the risk of a tension pneumothorax.

Other regional anaesthetic techniques

Appropriate techniques may be used for nerve blockade of limb injuries. Catheters may be introduced into many different sites, such as the paravertebral space or brachial plexus, permitting top-up doses of local anaesthesia to be given for long periods. These techniques are described in some of the references recommended in the suggested further reading section at the end of this book.

Neuromuscular Blockade

Neuromuscular-blocking drugs (pancuronium, alcuronium, curare, etc.) act by preventing neuromuscular transmission. They do not produce sedation or analgesia and *must not* be used as a substitute for drugs that do. Following administration of these drugs, the patient will lie still and tolerate assisted ventilation but, unless adequately sedated and analgesed, may be awake and in pain.

1 They must only be used on patients who are receiving assisted ventilation.
2 The prescription must state that they are only to be administered while the patient is receiving artificial ventilation.

They should be used in specified situations such as:

1 To prevent a further rise in intracranial pressure in a patient whose intracranial pressure is already high.
2 To prevent barotrauma to the lungs in patients with poorly compliant lungs.
3 To facilitate ventilation in certain patients in whom the following have been excluded:
   (a) Pain.
   (b) Inadequate sedation and analgesia.
   (c) Hypercarbia (check ABG).
   (d) Hypoxia (check ABG).

(e) Endotracheal tube irritating the carina (ETT too far down on CXR).
(f) General discomfort (full bladder, constipation).
(g) Bronchospasm.

Only when these remediable conditions have been treated, should patients receive neuromuscular-blocking drugs.

NOTES

CHAPTER 18

Paediatric Intensive Care

The principles of intensive care described in this book apply to paediatric patients as well as to adults. This chapter attempts to highlight essential differences between adult and paediatric practice; it must, however, be seen only as a guide to this area. It is not intended to replace help from experts, which should be obtained early, as children can deteriorate much more rapidly than adults.

Children should not be treated as small adults; they have certain important physiological differences. The cardio-vascular system is different, the systolic blood pressure being 60–70 mmHg at birth, and increasing to 100 mmHg by two years. The resting heart rate is 130 beats per minute at birth and does not fall to less than 100 beats per minute until after the age of five years. In the lungs, most of the resistance to air flow in small children is due to the small airways, the number of alveoli increasing eightfold up to the age of eight years. The respiratory rate is faster than in adults, and the amount of work performed during breathing is therefore much greater than in adults. The glomerular filtration rate is equal to that of an adult by the age of one year. The surface area/body weight ratio is much higher at birth than in an adult and gradually falls thereafter; heat loss can be a major problem because of this.

Fluid and Electrolyte Balance

Requirements

The daily requirements for children of different ages are shown below:

1 The child weighing less than 10 kg will require 85–120 ml/kg/day water and 3 mmol/kg/day sodium and potassium.
2 Children weighing 10–30 kg will need 60–90 ml/kg/day water and 2 mmol/kg/day sodium and potassium.
3 Children more than 30 kg will need 40–90 ml/kg/day water and 1.5 mmol/kg/day sodium and potassium.
4 Water and electrolyte needs will vary widely and the stated requirements should be reviewed frequently.

Assessing fluid balance

This can be difficult in children, because small inaccuracies in measurement may be significant. Furthermore, assumptions about insensible losses, intra-abdominal losses, etc., may be inaccurate. Three measurements can be used to help with this:

1 A urine output of 0.5–1 ml/kg/hr and the presence of normal plasma electrolyte values indicate that dehydration is unlikely.
2 The haematocrit is a useful indicator of dehydration and can be used to guide treatment. As rehydration proceeds the haematocrit will fall.
3 Daily weighing of a patient will often be helpful in assessing fluid balance status.

Blood volume and transfusion

Blood volume of a child (ml) = body weight (kg) × 80

The amount of red cell concentrate required in millilitres to increase haemoglobin concentration can be calculated from

Weight (kg) × 3 × desired rise in Hb (g/dl).

General points

1 Laboratory analyses are performed on smaller samples than for adults, because of the child's smaller cir-

culating blood volume. You should obtain the correct specimen tubes. If frequent or multiple tests are required, contact the laboratory with the list of tests and ask them the minimum quantity of blood required. It is usually much less than the individual volumes for each test added together.

2 Flushing solutions for the monitoring lines must be given using a syringe driver, set to deliver 1 ml/hr or less. Do not use adult flushing devices, which deliver 3 ml/hr, as this volume is too large, especially when multiple monitoring lines are used.

3 Record the volume of blood removed for each laboratory test and the volume of flushing solution used to clear the monitoring lines afterwards. Accurate fluid balance is important.

Airway and Artificial Ventilation

Endotracheal tube (ETT)

The child's airway differs from the adult's in that its narrowest part is not at the level of the vocal cords, but below the glottis at the level of the cricoid cartilage. It is possible to pass an ETT, in a child, through the vocal cords, which is too big for the subglottic area. Do not force the ETT through this area; this will result in damage to the area, causing both long-term problems (tracheal stenosis) and short-term difficulties in extubating the child (laryngeal oedema). In children aged less than eight to 10 years, it is usual to use an uncuffed ETT, due to the dangers of producing laryngeal/tracheal damage. All uncuffed tubes should therefore be of a sufficiently tight fit to allow a slight, but not excessive, leak around them. If rising inflation pressures during artificial ventilation increase the leak to an unacceptable level and minute volume falls, either change the ETT or, as a short-term measure, place a throat pack around the tube, taking care not to dislodge the tube during this manoeuvre. An approximate guide to the diameter of an ETT required for a child is

$$\frac{\text{age}}{4} + 4.5$$

Thus 2 years = 5 mm, 4 years = 5.5 mm, 6 years = 6 mm, 8 years = 6.5 mm, 10 years = 7 mm. The length of the tube, if inserted orally, is equal approximately to one and a half times the nose-to-ear distance.

Nasal intubation is preferable for children requiring an artificial airway. It is easier to fix in place and more comfortable.

Artificial ventilation

Children require smaller tidal volumes and higher frequencies than adults. The compressibility of the internal volume of the ventilator can become an important factor. Adult ventilator tubing should be replaced by small-bore rigid tubing of the shortest possible length to overcome this problem.

Certain ventilators (e.g. Siemens–Servo) require their patient trigger level to be set at a more negative value than in adults, if children are being artificially ventilated with uncuffed ETT. Failure to do this will result in a false respiratory effort being detected and high minute volumes being generated, in response, by the ventilator.

Humidification

Humidification can be provided by small heat and moisture exchanging humidifiers or by low-dead-space water bath humidifiers.

Stridor

The development of stridor in a small child is a serious and possibly life-threatening problem. It develops, in an otherwise healthy child, following a coryza or other infection. The child may have laryngotracheobronchitis or epiglottitis, or a foreign body. Irrespective of the aetiology, do not attempt endotracheal intubation. Do not take the child to the X-ray department. Summon help from an experienced anaesthetist (who should stay with the child) and an ENT surgeon. The child should be assessed by this team. Clumsy attempts at endotracheal intubation may precipitate complete airway obstruction.

Table 18.1 Drug dosages for paediatric use

Drug	Dose
Analgesics	
Fentanyl	1–5 mcg/kg
Morphine	0.1 mg/kg RH
Papaveretum	0.3 mg/kg (IM) RH
Pethidine	1 mg/kg (IM) R
Naloxone	10 mcg/kg (IM/IV/SC)
Sedatives	
Diazepam	100–200 mcg/kg (titrated to response)
Midazolam	50–100 mcg/kg* (titrated to response)
Muscle Relaxants	
Alcuronium	0.2 mg/kg R
Atracurium	0.3–0.6 mg/kg
Pancuronium	0.05–0.1 mg/kg R
Suxamethonium	1.0 mg/kg
Vecuronium	0.05 mg/kg
Antibiotics	
Ampicillin	10 mg/kg 6 hourly (IV/IM)
Benzyl Penicillin	2.5–5 mg/kg 6 hourly (IV/IM)
Ceftizoxime	7.5–15 mg/kg 6 hourly (IV/IM) R
Erythromycin	6–12 mg/kg 6 hourly (IV infusion) H
Flucloxacillin >2 yrs	125–250 mg 6 hourly (IV/IM)
<2 yrs	62.5–125 mg 6 hourly (IV/IM)
Gentamicin	2.0 mg/kg 8 hourly R
Metronidazole	7.5 mg/kg 8 hourly (IV infusion)
Tobramycin	2 mg/kg 8 hourly R
Miscellaneous	
Aminophylline	4 mg/kg (slow IV) then 1 mg/kg/hr (IV infusion) H
Cimetidine	5–10 mg/kg 6 hourly R
Frusemide	1.0 mg/kg
Hydrocortisone	1–5 yrs 50 mg 6 hourly (IV/IM)
	6–12 yrs 100 mg 6 hourly (IV/IM)
Loperamide	4–8 yrs 5 mg 6 hourly (oral)
	9–12 yrs 10 mg 6 hourly (oral)
Metoclopramide	<3 yrs 1 mg 8 hourly (IV/IM)
	3–5 yrs 2 mg 8 hourly (IV/IM)
	5–14 yrs 2.5–5 mg 8 hourly (IV/IM)
Salbutamol	2.5 mg nebulised

*No product licence for use in children. R = Dose adjustment necessary in renal failure. H = Dose adjustment necessary in hepatic insufficiency.

Pharmacology

The doses of some of the drugs used commonly in intensive care for paediatric patients are in Table 18.1. These do not apply to neonates. All drug dosages are for the IV route unless otherwise stated.

Resuscitation

Drug doses used during resuscitation of paediatric patients are given in Table 18.2. External DC shock is started at 2 J/kg body weight.

Table 18.2   Paediatric resuscitation drugs

Drug	IV Dose
Antiarrhythmics	
Adrenaline	10 mcg/kg (slow IV)
Atropine	0.02 mg/kg
Digoxin	10–20 mcg/kg/day R
Verapamil	
1–5 yr	2–3 mg H
6–15 yr	2.5–5 mg H
Calcium chloride (10%)	0.15 mg/kg
Sodium bicarbonate $\neq$ 0.5 mmol/kg (or as guided by ABG estimation)	

R = dose adjustment necessary in renal failure.
H = dose adjustment necessary in hepatic insufficiency.

Child Abuse

Child abuse should be suspected in any child who has recurrent episodes of injury, in whom coexist different types of injury (burns or fractures, etc.), or in a child for whom the explanation of the injury is inadequate. It should also be considered if the parents exhibit either an unusual reaction to the child's injury, or disturbed behaviour. The child should be carefully examined; look for small, apparently insignificant, injuries such as bruising or small cuts. The child must be completely examined and a skeletal survey performed. If you suspect this, inform a senior member of staff.

NOTES

CHAPTER 19

Microbiology

Microbiological Sampling

Prior to the administration of an antibiotic, samples of urine, sputum and blood should be sent to the laboratory for culture, together with wound swabs. Once an antibiotic is started, it is very difficult to culture a susceptible organism and thus obtain assistance from the laboratory. Routine surveillance should include regular culture of the above samples (excluding blood cultures) and swabs from sites where monitoring and drug administration lines penetrate the skin. The frequency with which these samples are sent should depend on the severity of illness; in some immunosuppressed, critically ill patients, they may be sent daily, whereas in patients recovering from a long illness, twice-weekly specimens may suffice. Whenever a line or tube is removed from a patient, the tip should be cut off and sent to the laboratory for culture and sensitivity.

All specimens must be sent promptly and not left sitting on a bench or specimen tray overnight. Swabs may need to be sent in special transport medium.

Blood cultures

These should be sent whenever a patient has a pyrexia. Two or three samples may need to be sent on the day when the initial pyrexia presents. Routine blood cultures are rarely useful.

Indications for Antibiotic Prophylaxis

Indiscriminate use of antibiotics leads to superinfection with resistant organisms. Few indications exist for antibiotic prophylaxis, the common ones including:

211

Surgical operations

Those that risk septicaemia (common bile duct obstruction).

Implantation of foreign materials or prosthesis into the body (aortic grafts, etc.).

Surgery in areas where postoperative infection is common (e.g. colorectal surgery).

Prevention of cross-infection

Household contacts of meningococcal meningitis infection.

At-risk patients

Splenectomy or sickle cell (pneumococcus).

Suggested Antibiotics Regimens

Whenever possible seek expert advice from a microbiologist before starting antibiotics.

Septic shock

Benzylpenicillin. 2 MU IV four hourly for 24 hours, then reduce dose.

Gentamicin. Patients more than 60 kg 80 mg eight hourly, less than 60 kg 60 mg eight hourly. Check levels after 24 hours. Increase dose interval in renal failure.

Metronidazole. 500 mg eight hourly IV (covers anaerobes).

Pneumonia

Erythromycin. 1 g six hourly IV (covers atypical pneumonias).

Cefotaxime. 2 g eight hourly IV.

Chest infection

Ampicillin. 500 mg–1 g six hourly oral/IM/IV.

Meningitis

    (a) Adults—first dose

Benzylpenicillin. 2 MU IV.

    (b) Children—first dose

Chloramphenicol. 1 g six hourly IV.

Consult a microbiologist after the first dose and follow his advice.

Aspiration pneumonia

Benzylpenicillin. 1 MU IV four hourly.
Gentamicin. Dose as above.
Metronidazole. Dose as above.

Hepatitis B

Infection with the hepatitis B virus may result in an acute infective hepatitis, which usually resolves, but can progress to the chronic carrier state. The chronic carrier state predisposes to the late development of hepatocellular carcinoma and chronic active, or persistent, hepatitis. Infection and carriage of the hepatitis B virus are common in certain groups, including:

1 Jaundiced patients.
2 Drug abusers.
3 Homosexuals.
4 Prostitutes.
5 Certain ethnic groups have a high incidence of this virus, including those from Asia, Africa and central Mediterranean countries.
6 Tattooed patients.
7 In countries where routine screening of patients is not available, patients requiring haemodialysis and frequent blood products may also be carriers.

The importance of hepatitis B infection or carriage lies in the risk of infection to the medical and nursing staff caring for that patient and in transmission to other patients in the ICU. Although vaccination against this virus is now feasible, the duration of immunity is uncertain. Complacency among the staff in an ICU can pose an unnecessary risk to themselves and others.

Serology

1 This should be performed in the above, high-risk, patients and in other patients with liver dysfunction of unknown aetiology.

2 Patients carrying the surface antigen (HBsAg), and particularly the e antigen (HBeAg), are highly infectious.

3 HBeAg always occurs in recent infection; it is usually later replaced by antibody to the e antigen (anti-HBe).

4 Patients with anti-HBe and HBsAg are less infectious.

5 During recovery, antibody to the surface (anti-HBs) and core antigen is formed (anti-HBc) and indicates past infection.

6 The chronic carrier state is associated with HBsAg, and either HBeAg or anti-HBe.

Hepatitis B is usually not specifically treated apart from supportive therapy. Due to its infectivity, it is usual in the UK to isolate these patients and to apply precautions to prevent others becoming infected. In some countries, infection with this virus is so common that few special precautions are taken. If there is doubt over the need to isolate such a patient, specialist advice should be sought. Patients with other acute viral causes of hepatitis may require isolation in a similar manner.

Acquired Immune Deficiency Syndrome (AIDS)

Presentation

A patient suffering from AIDS may present with a rare dermatological malignancy (Kaposi's sarcoma) or with an interstitial pneumonia, pneumocystitis carinii or a neurological illness (toxoplasmosis). In addition, both known and undiagnosed AIDS sufferers may be admitted to an ICU suffering from an unrelated condition, such as trauma. A severe pneumonia may be the initial presentation.

AIDS is caused by a retrovirus (known as human immunodeficiency virus, HIV). Transmission of this agent is mainly by sexual contact, infected blood and blood products, and by the sharing of syringes and needles by drug abusers. The virus is not, however, as infective as that causing hepatitis B infection, and transmission by needle stick injury is rare in medical and nursing attendants. The virus is not transmitted by droplet or airborne spread. Although all patients with AIDS are infected with HIV, not all of patients infected with HIV have AIDS when the antibody is discovered. All patients with HIV antibodies are currently thought to be an infection risk.

AIDS should be suspected in the following group of patients:

1 Homosexual and bisexual males.
2 Intravenous drug abusers.
3 Haemophiliacs.
4 Patients who have had sexual partners resident in or have received blood transfusion in the West Indies and the sub-Saharan African continent since 1981.
5 Sexual partners and babies of the above groups.

Investigation

Serology confirms the presence of HIV antibodies (new tests are soon to become available for HIV antigen). False positives may occur in patients requiring chronic haemodialysis. In the UK, it is recommended that this test should not be undertaken without the patient first being counselled about the implications of a positive test. The diagnosis of AIDS (or HIV infection) has a major impact on all aspects of a patient's life. If the patient is unconscious and unable to give consent, advice must be sought from a consultant before testing is done.

If permission for the test is refused, or the test is unavailable, then the patient should be treated as if they are infective.

Treatment

There is no specific treatment to reverse immunodeficiency that has already arisen from AIDS.

Pneumocystitis carinii infection may be treated with trimethoprim or other agents, but survival following assisted ventilation, if respiratory failure supervenes, is uncommon. Many sufferers from AIDS have expressed a wish not to receive intensive care for their pneumonias.

Patients who have AIDS, but who are admitted to the ICU for other reasons, should be treated normally, apart from precautions to prevent cross-infection. No medical or nursing attendants with herpes, or sores, should be allowed to care for these, or for other immunosuppressed patients.

Prevention of Cross-infection from Patients with Viral Hepatitis and AIDS

1 Although not essential, it is desirable to isolate initially the patient in a single room.
2 All cuts and abrasions on the hands of medical and nursing attendants should be covered with waterproof plasters.
3 If any contact with body fluids is likely, gloves should be worn.
4 If a procedure involves a more considerable exposure to body fluid, waterproof plastic aprons and eye protection may be necessary.
5 Restrict the number of venepunctures; an arterial line greatly reduces the number necessary.
6 Never resheath needles.
7 Never overfill blood containers.
8 Great care must be taken over labelling and packaging specimens for laboratory tests.

Spillages of body fluids should be washed up with strong hypochlorite (10 000 ppm) solution.

Needle Stick Injuries

These pose a risk of transmission of viruses, primarily those causing hepatitis. HIV transmission by this route is extremely rare in health care personnel. These injuries can be prevented by never resheathing needles and taking care to dispose of all needles and other sharps promptly into a proper container, which is later incinerated.

In the event of a needle stick injury:

1 Make the lesion bleed by squeezing it.
2 Wash it thoroughly with running water.
3 Apply iodine in 70 per cent alcohol.
4 Dress the wound.
5 Document the accident either in the patient's notes or on a suitable form.
6 Take blood from the patient to see if he has HBsAg.
7 If the patient is infected and the person who has suffered the needle stick injury has not been vaccinated, the use of hyperimmune globulin should be considered, usually with a course of hepatitis B vaccine.

Other Viral Diseases

There are many other viral illnesses that may present in the ICU. Some, such as chickenpox, are easy to recognise, but others may present in a more insidious manner, with the patient just being generally unwell. Usually these can be diagnosed only with the assistance of serology, culture or electronmicroscopy. (These include cytomegalovirus, coxsackie virus, rabies and herpes.)

Diagnosis may depend on the demonstration of rising titres. It is worth sending blood for serology to microbiology when critically ill patients are first admitted to the ICU and subsequently at weekly intervals. Specific treatment (acyclovir) is available for herpes.

Fungal Infections

With the widespread use of broad-spectrum antibiotics, fungal colonisation and infection are becoming increasingly common. The two most common infections are *Candida* and *Aspergillus*. Both may be cultured; *Aspergillus* infection can also be demonstrated by seroconversion. The use of amphotericin for both infections should be augmented by stopping antibiotics when possible. Advice on the dosage and rate of infusion must be sought before they are started.

Notification of Infectious Diseases

Table 19.1   Notifiable infectious diseases

Anthrax	Meningitis
Cholera	Plague
Diphtheria	Poliomyelitis
Dysentery (amoebic or	Rabies
bacillary)	Relapsing fever
Ebola	Scarlet fever
Encephalitis	Smallpox
Food poisoning	Tetanus
Infective hepatitis	Tuberculosis
Lassa fever	Typhoid
Leprosy	Typhus
Leptospirosis	Whooping cough
Malaria	Yellow fever
Marburg disease	
Measles	

The infectious diseases notifiable (in Britain) to the Medical Officer for Environmental Health are listed in Table 19.1.

Diseases Contracted Abroad

With the advent of high-speed jet travel, highly infectious diseases that are contracted in remote parts of the world cannot be incubated during the period of travel. The patient thus only becomes unwell after several days in this country. The patient may be seen in an accident and emergency department with a severe illness necessitating intensive care. If he has recently returned from Africa or South America, seek advice before admitting him to the ICU. If already in the ICU when a history of foreign travel becomes available, isolate the patient and seek immediate advice. Possible diseases that may be contracted abroad include rabies, acute haemorrhagic fevers (lassa fever, Marburg disease and ebola). These are all highly infectious and pose a serious risk not only to the patient, but also to the staff in the ICU, and are usually sent to special units. Acute diarrhoeal illnesses are common after foreign visits; most are self-limiting illnesses, but occasionally typhoid and paratyphoid may present in this way.

Malaria

This results from infection by *Plasmodium falciparum*, *P. vivax*, *P. ovale* or *P. malariae*. Malaria is endemic or sporadic throughout most of the tropics and subtropics, below an altitude of 1500 metres. The patient presents with fever, sweating and vomiting, often with a headache. Cerebral malaria may develop; the patient becomes comatose without localising signs or with acute hyperpyrexia. Acute renal and hepatic failure, haemolysis and dehydration may also occur.

Diagnosis

The blood film (both thick and thin) should be examined repeatedly, if necessary, for plasmodium parasites. Malaria may coexist with other diseases.

Treatment

Specialist advice is now needed in the seriously ill patient because of the presence of chloroquine resistance. In the less ill patient give chloroquine or amodiaquine in the following dose regimen: if the patient can take oral drugs, 600 mg followed by 300 mg six hours later, then 150 mg bd for up to seven days. If the patient is unable to take oral medication, give 5 mg/kg of chloroquine IV or 10 mg/kg quinine IV both infused over 2–4 hours. Repeat at eight hourly intervals, until the patient can take drugs orally.

Antibiotic Assays

Gentamicin, tobramycin, amikacin, vancomycin, 5-fluorocytosine, streptomycin and sometimes trimethoprim or ciprofloxacins are commonly assayed. Concomitant treatment with several antibiotics may cause assay difficulties and must be discussed with the microbiologist.

Aminoglycosides

These are the most commonly assayed antibiotics, because of their potential for nephro- and ototoxicity. If treatment for 48 hours or less is required, no assays are necessary. In treatment for longer periods than this, the drug must be assayed in the second 24-hour period of its administration.

Take 5 ml of clotted blood immediately before the injection (trough level); then take a second similar sample either 15 minutes after an IV injection (the time interval differs between laboratories), or 60 minutes after an IM injection (peak level). High trough levels indicate that accumulation is occurring and the interval between doses should be increased; whereas a high peak level and a high trough level indicate excessive dosage.

Table 19.2 Normal ranges for antibiotic levels

Antibiotic	Level	
	Trough (mg/l)	*Peak (mg/l)*
Gentamicin	<1.5	5–10
Tobramycin	<1.5	5–10
Streptomycin	<3	20–30
Vancomycin	<8	20–30
Amikacin	<8	30

NOTES

NOTES

CHAPTER 20

Communication in the Intensive Care Unit

Good communication within the ICU is essential for it to run smoothly. Communication with the patient is an important and often forgotten problem. Attendants may talk thoughtlessly about a critically ill patient without realising that he is awake and listening. Whenever a patient's prognosis is being discussed always ensure the conversation cannot be heard by the patient even if they appear comatose. The ICU doctors and nurses must communicate effectively among themselves about changes in the patient's condition and treatment. Salient points about the patient must also be passed on to other clinicians involved in the patient's care. In addition, relatives need special consideration. Various authorities and the press may also require or request information about the patients.

Talking to Relatives

Discussing a patient's condition with relatives can be a difficult task. Relatives are often bewildered; they are worried about the patient, they may be tired, and they may find themselves in a strange environment. They require clear, concise information in small amounts, given by either the medical or nursing staff. When discussing the patient with his relatives, the following points should be remembered:

1 Do not talk to the relatives alone; always have a member of the nursing staff with you. This not only

allows the nursing staff to comfort the relatives, but ensures that the same information is given to the relatives by all members of the intensive care team. Remember that the nurses probably know the relatives much better than you do.

2 Discussions with the relatives at the bedside should be limited to brief exchanges of information. Longer discussions should not take place at the patient's bedside, but in another area.

3 Most relatives require a more formal, prearranged, period of discussion to allow a two-way exchange of information from time to time. The frequency of such a meeting will depend on the progress of the patient (as he improves, this will become less frequent), how long the patient has been in the ICU and the relatives' rapport with the nurses. Most relatives will require such a meeting once or twice per week.

4 Personal difficulties may arise between relatives who may not have seen each other for many years. These need handling with tact and sympathy.

5 Anger and guilt are very common emotions experienced by relatives. They may be directed at themselves, other relatives or, sometimes, at members of the medical profession. Whenever medical treatment prior to admission to the ICU is involved, the merits, or otherwise, of such treatment should not be discussed.

6 The involvement of outside assistance in the management of relatives is sometimes useful. The hospital chaplain, or the patient's general practitioner, may be of great help to some relatives as a person in whom they can confide, but who has no direct connection with the patient's current management. Not all relatives appreciate religious intervention, and the introduction of this sort of help requires caution.

7 Accommodation for the relatives can be difficult to provide in some hospitals, but strenuous efforts must be made to obtain it. Relatives often travel long distances to see a patient during the acute phase of his illness. They should not be expected to sleep on the floor, in chairs or on couches. Private telephone facilities should be made available to them. The use of a ward telephone in a busy corridor is unacceptable.

8 Relatives will often enquire how long the patient is expected to be in the ICU, so that they can make necessary arrangements with their place of work or children. This can be extremely difficult in the case of the more seriously ill patient, who may die in the immediate future, or remain in the ICU for some time in a critical condition. A realistic estimate should be attempted, but the relatives cautioned about the difficulties of providing it. If you are unsure, seek guidance from a more senior member of staff; inaccurate estimates made as a result of inexperience may result in unnecessary, or inappropriate, degrees of concern and the expenditure of large sums of money by the patient's relatives.

Careful and sympathetic handling, combined with adequate explanation to the relatives, can make the distressing events surrounding a patient's admission to the ICU less unpleasant.

Medicolegal Problems in the Intensive Care Unit

By the very nature of intensive care, medicolegal problems will arise frequently. Patients will be admitted following violence, trauma, medical mishaps and poisoning. Criminal proceedings, inquests and litigation may all follow. Careful note-taking is essential for all patients in the ICU. It is important to remember that any note you make may be used in legal proceedings. When compiling notes:

1 Do not write unsubstantiated opinions such as 'this drunken man'; it is better to write 'this man smells of alcohol'.
2 Do not criticise previous treatments or colleagues.
3 Do not remove any items (e.g., drug charts) from the notes.
4 Remember to date and sign all entries in the patient's record.
5 If you do make a mistake in the notes, initial any corrections.

The Authorities

Police

Police enquiries will be made about patients who have sustained injuries in violent or suspicious circumstances. A statement may be requested about the nature of the injuries. The statement should contain only facts about the injuries; it should not contain any opinions. You may be asked whether or not the patient is likely to die, you should refer this matter to a more senior person; criminal charges, or the need for custody of an assailant, or other person, may be based on this opinion. In certain cases of a serious criminal nature, the police may ask for a forensic pathologist to examine the patient in the ICU.

Death certification

A death certificate can be issued by a medical practitioner only if:

1 The death is due to natural causes.
2 The doctor has been in professional attendance at some stage during the past 14 days.
3 He has examined the patient and is willing to certify both that the cause of death is known and that no suspicious circumstances surround the death.

In addition to completing a death certificate, it is useful to write a brief summary and the causes of death in the patient's record. A post mortem can only be carried out in the above circumstances with the consent of the relatives.

Coroner, Procurator Fiscal and Medical Examiner

In the following circumstances the death should be reported by telephone to the Coroner or his officer (in England, Wales and Northern Ireland) or the Medical Examiner elsewhere:

1 The body is unidentified.
2 No doctor attended the patient in the last 14 days of life.
3 During operation or recovery from anaesthesia.
4 Any sudden or unexplained death.
5 Medical mishaps.

6 Death related to an industrial accident or disease.
7 Death following violence, neglect, abortion, accident or misadventure.
8 Death occurring in suspicious or unnatural circumstances.
9 Alcoholism.
10 Poisoning.
11 Prisoners (including those in police custody).
12 Pensioners (service disability).

In addition, in Scotland the Procurator Fiscal, or his deputy, should be informed if death occurs in the following circumstances:

13 Smallpox or typhoid.
14 Foster children.
15 Accidents at home.
16 The residence of the deceased is unknown.

In the event of there being any doubt about whether a death should be reported to either the Coroner, Procurator Fiscal or Medical Examiner, it is better to discuss the case with them as soon as the doubts are raised. Early discussion not only prevents legal difficulties from arising later on, it also prevents unnecessary distress to bereaved relatives if, at a later stage, the authorities decide to investigate a suspicious death.

Giving evidence in court, inquests, etc.

If you are called to give evidence you should:

1 Consult your Defence Union well before the given date.
2 Read the notes before appearing in the witness stand. The notes will be made available to you in the witness stand, but it can be difficult to read the notes when under pressure.
3 Answer the questions (restricting yourself to the facts). Do not give interpretations, or expert opinions, unless you are qualified to do so.

Medical and nursing errors in the intensive care unit

Every time a procedure is undertaken or drug administered, a risk of error exists. In an ICU, many procedures are undertaken and many drugs administered to patients, and the likelihood of having to deal with an error is increased. In addition, the complexity and proliferation of equipment will periodically result in equipment malfunction, which may also harm a patient. If an accident of this sort occurs:

1 Inform a more senior member of staff who should guide and help you.
2 Document the error in the notes.
3 Inform your Defence Union (if you are directly involved).
4 Do not try to conceal from the relatives an error that has harmed the patient. Explain to them what has happened, in the presence of a witness, and then document this conversation in the notes.

If another medical or nursing colleague has been involved in a mishap, do not become drawn into any conversations with the relatives, or other staff, about suspension or other means of punishment; this is a matter for the hospital authorities.

Press reports

Many patients in the ICU will be of interest to the media. The hospital administration usually deals with press reports; if they do not, a limited number of people should issue reports, as the more people that are involved, the greater the confusion that can arise.

1 Do not divulge to the press confidential detailed information on the patient's injuries or illness.
2 Information should only relate to whether the patient is stable, improving, or increasingly unwell.
3 Indication of the severity of illness may be released.
   (a) 'Critically ill' is taken to mean there is a significant risk of the patient dying in the near future.
   (b) 'Seriously ill' is used to indicate a patient who is in no imminent danger of death, but who is requiring intensive support.
   (c) Other descriptions, such as 'recovering' and 'comfortable', may be used to describe the patient who requires close observation in an ICU, but who requires little in the way of support.

NOTES

Endotracheal Intubation

Indications

1 To allow prolonged artificial ventilation.
2 To relieve upper airway obstruction.
3 To allow control of the airway during resuscitation.

Endotracheal intubation requires skill and practice. Repeated attempts by the inexperienced at endotracheal intubation will result in hypoxia; if you cannot intubate a patient, ventilate them with a self-inflating bag and an oral airway.

Equipment

Mackintosh laryngoscope
Endotracheal tubes (adult male 9 mm, adult female 8 mm)
10 cc syringe for inflating the cuff
Stiff introducer
Tape
Lubricant (KY jelly)
Self-inflating bag
Suction apparatus

Method

The method described assumes the patient is already unconscious. If the patient is not unconscious and requires sedation and muscle relaxants, do not attempt to intubate, but obtain expert assistance from an anaesthetist.

1 Preoxygenate and artificially ventilate the patient, with a self-inflating bag into which high-flow oxygen is

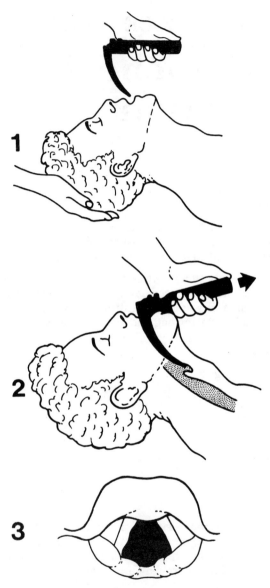

Figure PP1.1   Steps in endotracheal intubation

being administered, while the equipment is being checked and made ready.

2 Ensure suction apparatus is available.

3 Extend the head at the atlanto-occipital joint and push the head forward ('sniffing the morning air' position).

4 Holding the laryngoscope in your left hand, insert it into the right-hand side of the mouth, with the tongue underneath it.

5 Advance the laryngoscope blade over the tongue, until the epiglottis is seen.

6 At this point use the laryngoscope to pull the mandible upwards and forwards. (Do not lever the laryngoscope on the upper teeth at this or any other time.) This manoeuvre should pull the tongue and epiglottis anteriorly and allow the vocal cords to be seen.

7 Slide the ETT between the vocal cords, under direct vision, until the cuff is seen to disappear from sight just below the larynx.

8 Blow up the cuff until a gas-tight seal is obtained (checked by inflating the lungs using a self-inflating bag).

9 Tie the tube in place using cotton tape.

10 Artificially ventilate the patient and, while so doing, listen to both sides of the chest to ensure that the ETT is in the trachea and that it has not been advanced too far (leading to endobronchial intubation, which can be recognised by only one side of the chest inflating).

11 Connect the patient to the ventilator and visually check the chest moves.

12 Obtain a CXR to confirm correct positioning of the ETT; the tip should be halfway between the larynx and the carina.

13 If difficulty is experienced in pushing the ETT between the vocal cords (because of difficulty in visualisation) insert the introducer between the cords and slide the ETT over the top.

Complications

1 The most important complication is intubation of the oesophagus. If this is not recognised, hypoxia and death

will result. Immediately after endotracheal intubation, listen to the chest; if air entry cannot be heard, or you are unsure about correct placement of the ETT, take the tube out and ventilate the patient with oxygen-enriched air from a self-inflating bag.

2 Clumsy intubation may result in damage to the larynx and vocal cords.

NOTES

Arterial Cannulation

Indications

An in-dwelling arterial line may be inserted to allow frequent estimation of ABG without the need for multiple, painful arterial stabs, to allow continuous monitoring of systemic arterial blood pressure and for access to blood for routine laboratory tests, without the need for venepuncture.

Equipment

A 20-gauge, parallel-sided, catheter is the largest that is currently recommended. Some incorporate an integral guidewire, so that, once arterial puncture is identified by a flashback, the guidewire can be inserted up the artery and the catheter advanced over it. This has proved an invaluable technique, particularly in patients who have tortuous arteries due to atheroma.

A continuous flushing system, using heparinised saline (1 U/ml) is necessary to prevent clotting. Usually, a 500-ml bag of heparinised saline is pressurised, using a pressure infuser bag, to 300 mmHg. A giving set from this bag is connected to a proprietary flushing device, which allows a continuous flow of 3 ml/hr to flush the catheter. These devices also have a rapid flush position, which enables the lines to be cleared of blood after sampling.

If arterial pressure is to be displayed, the system will need to be connected to a transducer and monitor.

Sites of cannulation

The radial artery is the commonest site for arterial cannulation. When a catheter is *in situ*, or if thrombosis of the artery occurs after the cannula is removed, the blood supply to the hand is dependent solely upon the ulnar arterial flow. The presence of an adequate ulnar arterial flow should be demonstrated *before* cannulation of the radial artery.

1 The radial and ulnar arteries are compressed by the operator and the patient asked to open and close his fist 10 times (or has it done for him if he is unconscious).

2 With the hand open compression of the ulnar artery is released and the hand should become pink within 5 seconds. If it does not, the radial artery should also be released, to confirm the necessary colour change

3 If an inadequate ulnar arterial flow exists, contact a senior member of staff before cannulating the radial artery. Other sites of cannulation include the brachial, the femoral and the dorsalis pedis artery.

Method

1 Sterilise the skin surrounding the area of insertion.

2 Infiltrate the skin and deeper tissues with 1 per cent lignocaine *without* adrenaline.

3 An assistant should hold the limb still and extend the wrist over a folded towel. Do not overextend the wrist; this will make the radial artery difficult to cannulate.

4 With your left hand, stabilise the artery between your middle and forefinger.

5 Advance the cannula with your right hand, aiming for the artery.

6 When a flashback is seen, keep the needle still and advance the catheter over the needle and up the artery (or advance the wire up the artery and slide the catheter over it).

7 While removing the needle, press on the artery proximally to prevent blood loss.

8 If arterial puncture has been unsuccessful, remove the needle from the catheter and slowly pull the catheter back. You may have inadvertently transfixed the artery; slow removal of the cannula, without the needle, enables this to be recognised and the cannula to be advanced up the artery.

9 Attach the flush line to the arterial cannula. This and

all other connections in the system must have luer
locks.
10 Stitch the arterial line in place and cover with a trans-
parent dressing.

Removal of arterial lines

1 If the patient is thrombocytopenic, or has a coagulopathy, give platelets or clotting factors before attemp-
ting removal.
2 When the cannula has been removed, press on the
artery for five minutes, strictly by the clock.
3 Send the tip for culture.

NOTES

Central Venous Catheterisation

Indications

1 To measure central venous pressure.
2 To give drugs, or fluids, that are irritant to peripheral veins, or that may cause tissue necrosis should extravasation occur.
3 As a means of introducing a pulmonary artery flotation catheter (PAFC) or cardiac-pacing wire, or for some biopsy procedures.
4 As a means of obtaining rapid access to the circulation in patients whose peripheral veins may be difficult to find, due to shock.

Equipment

Central venous catheters are of two types:

1 Through cannula.
   The vein is cannulated using an IV cannula, and a catheter is then advanced through the cannula and sutured in place. Long IV cannulas may be of sufficient dimension not to require a catheter for subclavian or internal jugular vein catheterisation.
2 Catheter over guidewire.
   The Seldinger technique is increasingly popular. The vein is cannulated using a small IV cannula or needle, and a wire is passed down its lumen. The wire usually has a flexible end to prevent perforation of the vein. Once the wire is a suitable distance along the vein, the cannula or needle is removed, leaving the wire in place. One of a variety of catheters can be introduced over the

wire. The use of dilators enables large sheath intro-
ducers to be inserted into a vein with minimum risk;
these may be used subsequently for the introduction of
pulmonary artery flotation catheters, etc.

Catheters may be single-lumen devices or a single CVP
catheter with several lumina (multilumen) exiting at different
points near the catheter end. Multilumen catheters are useful
when inotropes or TPN need to be given as well as the CVP
measured. Catheter material is a non-irritant and non-
thrombogenic, plastic or silicone. Some catheters may be
heparin-bonded to prevent thrombosis.

Methods

There are many approaches to central venous cannulation.
The safest method is the method with which you are most
familiar. If you lack experience with central venous cannulation do not attempt a subclavian or internal jugular vein
approach until you have received tuition and supervision

The following points are applicable to all routes of cannulation:

1 Place the patient 20° head down to distend the central
   veins.
2 This is a sterile procedure; the skin should be sterilised
   accordingly over a large area surrounding the area of
   insertion. Wear gloves, mask and a gown.
3 All CVP cannulas are painful to insert and, unless the
   patient is receiving a general anaesthetic, infiltration
   of the skin and deeper structures with 1 per cent
   lignocaine is necessary.
4 If you are using the Seldinger technique and if, after the
   initial cannulation with a small cannula, you are
   unsure whether it is in the vein or the artery, connect
   the cannula to a pressure-monitoring device. Before
   passing the guidewire this will distinguish arterial
   from venous cannulation.
5 When passing the guidewire through a catheter, watch
   the ECG, to detect overadvancement of the wire and the
   development of arrhythmias, as the myocardium is
   irritated.

6 When using a guidewire technique *always* have some of the guidewire available to grasp. It must never be completely enclosed in the catheter otherwise it may be advanced with the catheter and lost in the circulation.

7 Once the catheter is *in situ*, stitch it firmly in place. Cover with a suitable dressing.

8 Obtain a chest X-ray to confirm correct positioning of the CVP line and the absence of a pneumothorax, before making recordings from it.

9 Before infusing drugs or fluids, or measuring CVP, ensure blood can be aspirated from the CVP line.

Median basilic vein approach

This large vein is situated on the medial side of the antecubital fossa. It can be cannulated easily with a large cannula and a long venous line advanced up the arm and into the large veins of the chest. Problems include difficulty in traversing the clavipectoral fascia, which can be overcome by abducting and rotating the arm. A high percentage of catheters will be malpositioned in the internal jugular vein. This can be prevented by turning the head to the ipsilateral side and placing a hand over the internal jugular vein during the catheter's passage.

External jugular vein approach

The external jugular vein is on the lateral side of the neck; it can be distended by placing a hand at the root of the neck, thus allowing easier cannulation. A guidewire can be passed down this cannula into the large thoracic veins. Guidewires are usually supplied with a J-tip to allow manipulation into the subclavian vein. Once the guidewire is in place, catheters can be advanced over it in the usual way.

Internal jugular vein approach

1 Place a pillow under the shoulders of the patient to extend the neck.

2 Turn the head to the contralateral side.

3 Find the midpoint of a line drawn between the mastoid process and the sternal head of the clavicle.

4 Feel the carotid artery and leave your fingers on the artery until the vein is cannulated to lessen the risk of accidental arterial puncture.

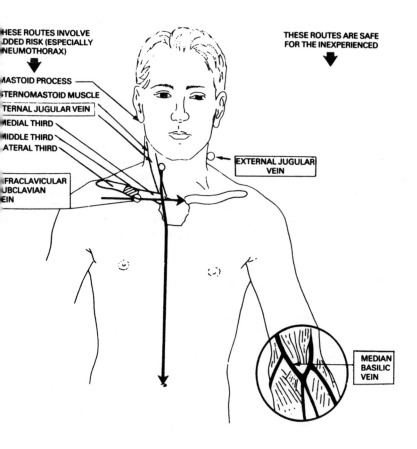

THESE ROUTES INVOLVE
ADDED RISK (ESPECIALLY
PNEUMOTHORAX)

THESE ROUTES ARE SAFE
FOR THE INEXPERIENCED

MASTOID PROCESS

STERNOMASTOID MUSCLE

INTERNAL JUGULAR VEIN

MEDIAL THIRD

MIDDLE THIRD

LATERAL THIRD

INFRACLAVICULAR
SUBCLAVIAN
VEIN

EXTERNAL JUGULAR
VEIN

MEDIAN
BASILIC
VEIN

*Figure PP3.1   Routes used for central venous cannulation (arrows
indicate the direction to insert the introducing needle)*

5 Palpate the area between the carotid artery and the
   sternomastoid muscle; it is often possible to feel the
   internal jugular vein.
6 With a syringe attached to the locating cannula, aim for
   the vein, if you can feel it; if not, enter lateral to the

fingers on the carotid artery, aiming 10–15° posteriorly, with the needle pointing towards the umbilicus.

7 Advance the cannula with an intermittent thrusting motion, maintaining suction on the syringe.

8 The vein lies 1–1.5 cm beneath the skin; once penetration has occurred, advance the cannula.

Infraclavicular approach to the subclavian vein

This is the most difficult approach to the central veins and has a higher complication rate. Except in special circumstances, it should not be attempted in restless children, patients with a bleeding diathesis, an apical bulla or abnormal anatomy in this region (following trauma). CVP lines inserted by this approach are easier to maintain, not being subject to the difficulties of beard growth in males and being more easily fixed. The method is as follows:

1 Place a small pillow under the upper thoracic spine, to bring the shoulders backwards.

2 Identify the sternoclavicular joint and the junction of the middle and medial thirds of the clavicle.

3 Introduce the cannula 1–2 cm below the clavicle, at the junction of its middle and medial thirds, in a horizontal plane (parallel to the coronal plane of the body); aim for the ipsilateral sternoclavicular joint.

4 Advance the cannula with an intermittent thrusting motion.

Many other approaches to central venous cannulation exist, including via the cephalic, femoral veins, supraclavicular approach to the subclavian vein and via the low approach to the internal jugular vein. It is important to identify one or two routes with which you feel familiar and to practise these routes. Experience in other routes can be obtained at a later date.

Complications

All routes of central venous catheterisation risk the following complications: right atrial/central vein perforation, systemic sepsis, misreading, malposition, air embolism and thrombosis.

All routes, except cephalic vein and external jugular vein, risk vessel and nerve damage.

Cannulation in the area surrounding the neck (except the external jugular vein approach) and clavicular regions, in addition, risk pneumothorax, haemothorax, thoracic duct damage (left side) and ETT damage.

NOTES

PRACTICAL PROCEDURE 4

Pulmonary Artery Catheterisation

Indications

Measurement of pulmonary artery pressure (PAP) and pulmonary capillary wedge pressure (PCWP) is useful in the management of patients with rapidly changing haemodynamics, or when the clinical picture is not clear. It is particularly indicated in patients with impaired myocardial function or respiratory disease, in whom the central venous pressure (CVP) provides little guide to left atrial pressure (LAP). It allows the measurement of cardiac output, pulmonary capillary wedge pressure (an indicator of LAP) and pulmonary artery pressures and the derivation of variables such as systemic and pulmonary vascular resistance. Knowledge of these variables allows fluid, inotropes and other vasodilator drugs to be administered in a logical fashion and their effects assessed.

Equipment

Pulmonary artery catheters are of various types. The manufacturer's instructions should always be followed closely. Double-lumen catheters have a balloon port plus a lumen for measuring PAP and PCWP and for sampling mixed venous blood. Triple-lumen catheters provide an additional lumen for monitoring CVP. Catheters designed for the measurement of cardiac output also incorporate a thermistor near the tip of the catheter and a hub for connection to a cardiac output computer.

Method

1 Monitor the ECG continuously, as there is a risk of arrhythmias.

2 Using an aseptic technique, insert a sheath introducer into a central vein (see Practical Procedure 3).

3 Attach three-way taps to the proximal and distal ports of the catheter and prime the catheter lumina with 0.9 per cent saline.

4 Check the integrity of the balloon by injecting air (1.5 ml or as stated in the manufacturer's instructions).

5 Insert the catheter through the sterile sheath adapter.

6 Connect the distal lumen of the catheter to a pressure transducer and display the catheter tip pressure waveform continuously.

7 Advance the catheter through the sheath introducer until a right atrial waveform is seen. The right atrium is approximately 10 cm from the subclavian, 10–15 cm from the internal jugular, and 35–40 cm from the antecubital and femoral veins. Respiratory fluctuations in pressure will confirm correct entry into the thorax.

8 Inflate the balloon with the recommended volume of air. Always inflate the balloon gently.

9 Advance the catheter further. Entry into the right ventricle causes a change in waveform to a right ventricular trace (Figure, PP4.1) and may be accompanied by ventricular arrhythmias (VE or VT). Note the length of catheter advanced to reach the right ventricle; this should be less than 35 cm.

10 Advance the catheter further. The pulmonary artery is entered when the trace has the same systolic pressure as the right ventricle, but a higher diastolic pressure (i.e. there is a step-up in diastolic pressure).

11 As the catheter is advanced further, a wedged pressure trace is obtained. This should be seen at a distance of less than 15 cm from the right ventricle. If not, *deflate the balloon*, withdraw the catheter into the right ventricle, reinflate the balloon and repeat the procedure.

12 Once a wedged trace is obtained, at a satisfactory distance from the right ventricle, deflate the balloon.

With satisfactory placement of the catheter, inflation and deflation of the balloon should result in PCWP and PAP waveforms, respectively.

13 Fluoroscopy is useful to aid correct placement if catheterisation proves difficult.

14 Do not leave the catheter in the wedged position for longer than is necessary to measure PCWP.

15 Secure the external catheter securely to skin.

16 The PAP trace must be displayed continuously to detect wedging if the catheter advances along the pulmonary artery.

17 Obtain a CXR to exclude pneumothorax and to confirm satisfactory placement of the catheter. The catheter should be seen to loop through the right ventricle into the pulmonary artery. Any 'slack' on the right ventricular loop should be rectified by slightly withdrawing the catheter to prevent the catheter advancing.

18 It is recommended that a pulmonary artery catheter should not be left in place for longer than 72 hours because of the formation of thrombus on it and damage to heart valves.

Cardiac output measurement

Cardiac output can be measured using the thermodilution technique if a catheter incorporating a thermistor close to its tip is used, and a cardiac output computer is available. With this technique, 10 ml of 5 per cent dextrose, at a known temperature (preferably 4°C), is injected into the CVP lumen and the change in temperature is measured in the pulmonary artery. Cardiac output is computed from the cooling curve obtained in the pulmonary artery.

1 Set the computer to measure cardiac output and ensure the correct catheter and injectate calibration has been selected.

2 Draw up 10 ml of 5 per cent dextrose.

3 Inject the dextrose as rapidly as possible into the proximal lumen of the catheter starting as soon as inspiration ends.

4 When the computer is reset, repeat the procedure, so that three readings are obtained. The cardiac output is the mean of the three values. The individual values should not vary by more than 5 per cent of one another.

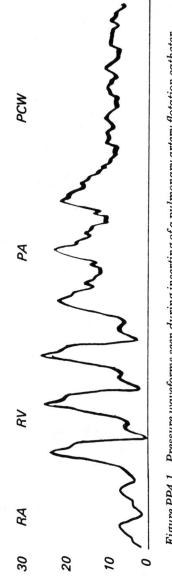

Figure PP4.1 Pressure waveforms seen during inserting of a pulmonary artery flotation catheter.

RA = Right atrium
RV = Right ventricle
PA = Pulmonary artery
PCW = Pulmonary capillary wedge

Interpretation

Hypovolaemia. The CVP, PCWP, systemic blood pressure and cardiac output are decreased. The PCWP can be used as a measure of the LAP to guide fluid replacement and optimise the cardiac output.

Left ventricular failure. The PCWP is increased and cardiac output is usually decreased. The CVP may be normal and does not reflect changes in LAP accurately in the presence of left ventricular dysfunction. Pulmonary oedema occurs at PCWP of 25–30 mmHg. Optimal vasodilator and diuretic therapy to lower PCWP, without lowering cardiac output, can be guided using a PAFC.

Right ventricular failure. The CVP is raised and the PCWP may be normal, in isolated right heart failure. The PCWP will also be raised if the right-sided failure is secondary to left ventricular failure.

Mitral regurgitation and VSD. See Chapter 4.

Cardiac tamponade. Cardiac output is reduced, CVP, PCWP, RVEDP and PA diastolic pressure all increase markedly to a similar level, with values above 20 mmHg.

Chronic pulmonary disease. The PAP is increased, as may be the CVP. The PCWP may be inaccurate if the PVR is increased.

Complications

1 The complications of central venous cannulation (see Practical Procedure 3).
2 Infection.
3 Cardiac arrhythmias are common during insertion, especially when the right ventricle (RV) is traversed. The catheter should only be inserted into the RV with the balloon inflated.
4 Pulmonary infarction may result from the injection of solutions under relatively high pressure into the distal lumen, or if the catheter is left in the wedged position for prolonged periods of time. The balloon should be deflated after every recording of PCWP, and PAP continuously displayed, so that continuous wedging can be rectified by slight withdrawal of the catheter. PCWP

should only be measured for one to two minutes at a time.

5 Balloon rupture may occur after prolonged use of a catheter. It may result in air being injected into the pulmonary artery. Since less than 1.5 ml is injected, this is usually harmless, but it is hazardous in the presence of right-to-left shunts. Carbon dioxide should be used for balloon inflation in these circumstances. Always stop inflating if no resistance is felt.

6 Catheter knotting is minimised by not advancing the catheter if the RA, RV or PA are not entered in the expected distances. If knotting does occur, the balloon should be deflated, the catheter withdrawn gently to the site of entry and, if necessary, the knot withdrawn through a venotomy. A guidewire inserted through the catheter is occasionally successful in unknotting the catheter.

NOTES

NOTES

Temporary Cardiac Pacing

Indications

Pacing is usually used in the treatment of the symptomatic bradyarrhythmias, but is occasionally indicated to terminate tachyarrhythmias, using overdrive or underdrive modes. It might also be used to allow the administration of drugs (used to treat tachycardias or hypertension) that would otherwise cause a dangerous bradycardia.

Equipment

1. A sheath introducer set with a Seldinger wire.
2. A pacing wire which passes through the sheath introducer and is compatible with the pacing box.
3. The pacing box usually incorporates knobs to control heart rate, voltage output and the mode of pacing (demand or fixed). A key switches from normal rate to overdrive ($\times$ 3 or $\times$ 10).

Method

1. The ECG must be monitored throughout the procedure and resuscitation equipment be immediately available.
2. Check all equipment, including the battery life of the external generator. Ensure that the pacing rate is not locked in the overdrive mode.
3. Arrange to have X-ray screening available during the procedure.
4. Insert a percutaneous introducing sheath into a central vein (see Practical Procedure 3).

5 Introduce the pacing wire through the sheath and advance it under X-ray control. Do *not* use force to advance it. Slight obstructions can be overcome by withdrawing the wire slightly and rotating it as it is readvanced. Excessive resistance indicates incorrect placement.

6 Allow the pacing wire to loop in the right atrium and rotate it, so the tip of the loop is in the region of the tricuspid valve. Slight withdrawal will then allow the tip to flick through the valve into the right ventricle.

7 Ventricular extrasystoles indicate that the right ventricle has been entered.

8 Position the tip of the pacing wire at the apex of the right ventricle, withdrawing and then rotating the wire as it is readvanced to aid positioning.

9 Connect the proximal and distal poles of the pacing wire to the anode (+) and cathode (−), respectively, of the pulse generator.

10 Check the threshold potential. This is the minimum voltage required for the pacing stimuli to capture the ventricles consistently (i.e. each pacing spike is followed by a QRS complex) and should be less than 1 V. If not, reposition the tip of the pacing wire (if the clinical condition allows).

11 Ensure that pacing is consistent during coughing and deep inspiration. Suture the pacing wire securely to the skin.

12 Set the output of the pulse generator to two to three times the threshold potential.

13 Check the patient's underlying rhythm, the battery life, all connections and the threshold potential, at least once daily. It is normal for the threshold to rise to 2–3 V over the first few days. Reset the generator's output to two to three times the day's threshold potential.

14 Monitor the ECG for the duration of temporary pacing.

Complications

1 The complications of central venous cannulation.

2 Breakage or disconnection of the pacing wire. The patient's underlying rhythm, without pacing spikes,

will be seen on the ECG. Reconnect, or replace, the pacing wire.

3 Displacement of the pacing wire results in intermittent or complete failure to pace. Reposition the pacing wire.

4 Exit block is the failure of pacing in the absence of displacement, or disconnection, of the pacing wire. It is probably due to excessive tissue reaction at the point of contact of the pacing wire with the endocardium. The pacing wire should be repositioned.

5 Infection at entry site.

6 Myocardial perforation by the pacing wire may lead to pericardial pain, a pericardial rub and diaphragmatic pacing. Rarely, cardiac tamponade may result.

Electrical safety

The pacing wire is in direct contact with the endocardium, and this exposes the patient to the risk of microshock, an intravascular current of 50 μA being enough to precipitate ventricular fibrillation. Handle the pacing wire as little as possible and only with gloved hands. *Never* handle the pacing wire with one hand and other electrical equipment with the other hand.

Failure to pace

In the case of such a failure:

1 Increase the pulse generator's output to its maximum setting (usually 20 V) and change to fixed pacing to avoid oversensing.

2 Check all the connections and the battery. Consider changing the pacemaker unit.

3 Start CPCR if cardiac arrest ensues.

Oesophageal pacemakers

In emergency situations an oesophageal electrode can be passed in a similar fashion to a NG tube. It is connected to an ordinary pacing-box via an amplifier which increases the maximum output to 30 V. Correct placement is confirmed by observing the presence of pacing on the ECG monitor. A transvenous pacing wire should be placed as soon as possible.

NOTES

Cardioversion

Indications

This is the use of an electric shock to terminate tachyarrhythmias. The shock depolarises the myocardium, interrupting the arrhythmia and allowing the resumption of sinus rhythm.

Equipment

Defibrillator with synchronisation facilities.

Method

1 The ECG must be monitored continuously and resuscitation equipment must be immediately available.
2 Check the rhythm *immediately before* cardioversion to ensure that spontaneous reversion has not occurred.
3 The shock is painful; anaesthesia must be provided in the conscious patient. If time permits, the patient should be fasted. Etomidate (0.3 mg/kg) or midazolam (0.1–0.2 mg/kg) are suitable anaesthetic agents.
4 Remove any glyceryl trinitrate ointment, as this may ignite on defibrillation.
5 Use a generous amount of electrode jelly, or jelly-impregnated pads, to avoid skin burns. Avoid jelly spreading between the paddles.
6 Charge the defibrillator. The charge chosen depends on the clinical situation. Very low levels (5–10 J) are used in the presence of digoxin; low levels (25 J) for atrial flutter; and higher levels (100–200 J) for ventricular fibrillation. Low energy levels (2 J/kg) should be used in children.

7 The defibrillator must be *synchronised* to discharge on the S or R wave, when defibrillating any rhythm other than ventricular fibrillation. If the shock coincides with the T wave, ventricular fibrillation may be precipitated.

8 Apply the paddles firmly at the apex and the right sternal edge, ensure that neither you nor anyone else is in contact with the patient or bed and deliver the shock.

9 If unsuccessful, repeat, using successively higher energy levels; do not exceed 400 J.

10 Continue ECG monitoring for several hours after defibrillation.

11 Observe for complications—burns, hypotension, transient arrhythmias and systemic emboli.

12 Note that repeated high-energy defibrillation may cause minor damage to the myocardium and chest wall muscles, leading to an increase in serum enzyme levels. The enzyme levels will be unreliable in diagnosis of myocardial infarction in this situation.

NOTES

NOTES

Chest Drain Insertion

Chest drains should be inserted in a calm, controlled manner. Although at times they may be life-saving, this must not remove from the operator's mind the dangers of hurried insertion; almost every structure in the chest and upper abdomen has been penetrated by a chest drain at some time.

Indications

A chest drain may be inserted to drain gas, usually air (pneumothorax), or fluid from the pleural space.

(a) *Air.* Pneumothorax may occur spontaneously, or following trauma to the lung from a sharp object, such as a broken rib or a sharp needle (used during central venous cannulation or intercostal nerve blockade).

A simple pneumothorax is one where the gas in the chest is not under pressure. This will require drainage, unless it is small and has occurred in a spontaneously breathing patient. If it is large, or has occurred in a patient receiving assisted ventilation, drainage will be required.

In a tension pneumothorax, the air is under pressure. The raised pressure in the chest pushes the mediastinum across to the opposite side of the chest, deviating the trachea and/or pushing the diaphragm downwards.

1 Difficulty in breathing occurs usually accompanied by bronchospasm, decreased air entry and a hyper-resonant percussion note.
2 If the patient is receiving artificial ventilation, an increase in airway pressure will be noted.

3 Mediastinal deviation leads to kinking of the vena cava and the increased intrathoracic pressure leads to a fall in cardiac output, a low blood pressure and a tachycardia.

4 The patient will be peripherally and centrally cyanosed, with a low PaO_2.

5 The patient may have a circulatory arrest.

(b) *Fluid.* The fluid can be blood (haemothorax), following trauma or surgery, or an effusion, resulting from trauma or tumour, lymphatic fluid (chylothorax) following damage to the internal thoracic duct on the left side or a collection of fluid from a misplaced central venous line.

The indications for drainage of fluid collections include: diagnosis, relief of respiratory, or haemodynamic embarrassment and if the collection is thought to be infected.

Radiology

Radiological assistance can be invaluable in deciding if a chest drain is necessary and where to place it. The clinical diagnosis of pneumothorax (either simple or tension) can be difficult in certain groups of patients, especially asthmatics. If there is doubt over the need for a chest drain, an erect, AP, portable CXR should be obtained. If the likelihood of a pneumothorax is great, but it is not proven and the patient's condition is stable, then while an X-ray is being taken and the film awaited, the operator should use this time to prepare. Unnecessary insertion of a chest drain into a patient who does not have a fluid collection or a pneumothorax is hazardous and risks damaging the lung. A collection of fluid may be difficult to differentiate from collapse and consolidation at either lung base; if there is no clinical urgency to drain these collections, an ultrasound should be obtained.

If an erect chest film is not possible and only a supine chest film is available, an anteriorly placed pneumothorax may leave lung markings going out to the periphery, causing confusion. A lucent area adjacent to the left or right heart border, giving a very sharp edge to the heart, may be the only radiological sign. A cross-bed lateral film should be taken and will demonstrate the presence of an anterior pneumothorax.

Insertion site

There are two common sites for the insertion of chest drains:

1 The upper insertion site is in the midclavicular line, in the second intercostal space. This insertion site is comfortable for the patient, and the skin is free from heavy contamination with commensal organisms. This site is used when a pneumothorax requires drainage.

2 The lower insertion site is found in the midaxillary line fourth or fifth intercostal space, posterior to the pectoralis muscle. There is only a thin covering of muscle (the intercostal muscles), making insertion easy. It is, however, an area that has a considerable number of skin commensal organisms; in addition, it may be uncomfortable for the patient. It is important to avoid the cannula tracking upwards subcutaneously and damaging the structures found within the axillary sheath. The lower site is used to drain fluid. Patients with both air and fluid may require the insertion of two chest drains, one at each site.

Equipment and insertion

There are three different types of chest drain available; each is inserted in a slightly different manner and is therefore described independently below. Each technique requires the chosen site of insertion to be shaved of hair, prepared with a sterilising solution and draped. Unless the patient is anaesthetised, adequate infiltration with a local anaesthetic (10 ml of 1 per cent lignocaine, without adrenaline) is necessary. Before inserting a chest drain, it is important to be able to aspirate air or fluid from the chosen insertion site, using a needle and syringe.

Plain plastic tubing

An incision large enough to accept a gloved finger is made in the skin and chest wall, using a scalpel. This incision is gradually deepened, using a scalpel and forceps, until the pleura is seen or felt. At this point it is incised, and the finger inserted through the hole. The finger is removed and, using the forceps, the drain is inserted through this hole.

Trocar and cannula

An incision is made in the skin approximately 1 cm in length. The trocar and cannula are introduced through this incision and pushed firmly, but under control, until the chest cavity is entered. At this point, the trocar is removed and a drain inserted. The drain may be plastic or rubber, soft rubber drains being particularly comfortable for the patient. Some types of rubber chest drain have wings on them that are folded down when an introducer is placed along the middle of the drain (Malecot). On removal of the introducer, the wings expand and allow the drain to rest against the chest wall, preventing dislodgement.

Integral disposable drain and trocar

This system consists of a trocar inserted through the middle of a plastic chest drain. Although its advantage is that the entire system is disposable and ready assembled for rapid use, it does require a considerable amount of force to introduce it. This system has been the cause of damage to many structures in the chest and upper abdomen; this may, in part, be attributable to the force necessary to insert it, in addition to its length, and care in its use should be exercised.

The skin should be incised with a scalpel for approximately 1 cm; further dissection down to the pleura is recommended. The trocar and catheter should be introduced through this incision and gradually pushed through the chest wall, in a controlled manner, so that rapid entry into the chest wall does not occur. When the trocar and catheter have entered the chest cavity, the trocar should be held stationary and the drain advanced, until 10–15 cm are in the chest cavity.

Drainage systems

Once the drain is inserted, it is connected to an underwater seal drainage system. This allows gas and fluid to escape, but does not permit air to re-enter the chest.

If there is a persistent gas leak, or pneumothorax, suction may need to be applied to a chest drain. A starting pressure of -5 kPa, increasing to -10 to -15 kPa, is usually adequate.

When there is a large air leak, it is important that the

FROM PATIENT

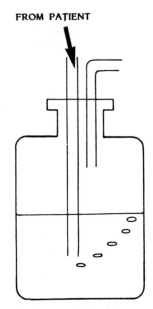

Figure PP7.1   Underwater seal drainage system, allowing gas and fluid to drain out of the chest without air entering the chest

suction apparatus flow rate is sufficient to match the air leak and does not obstruct the free drainage of air.

When transporting patients the underwater seal drainage system should be clamped (on the chest drain catheter itself), so that in the event of accidental disconnection of the under-water drainage system a pneumothorax does not result. Equally if the bottle, containing water, is lifted higher than the chest, water will not drain back into the chest. If temporary clamping of the chest drain is undesirable, a Heimlich flutter valve, connected to a urine drainage bag, is sufficient for transport.

Securing the chest drain

Once the chest drain has been inserted and connected to an underwater seal drainage system, it should be stitched in place. Although methods of securing vary between ICUs, most are agreed on the need for a suture, running around the insertion site which can be drawn up tight as the chest tube is removed, sealing off the site of entry (purse string suture) and preventing air entering and a pneumothorax developing.

A separate suture may be used to secure the chest drain in place, either by tying it tightly around the drainage tube, or by sticking a piece of 4-inch-wide adhesive tape to the chest drain and stitching to that.

A light dressing is all that is necessary over a chest drain that is adequately stitched in.

A CXR is taken after insertion of a chest drain to confirm resolution of the pneumothorax or decrease in pleural fluid and correct placement of the drain.

Removal of the chest drain

Chest drains should be left in for as short a time as possible. They are a potential source of infection and once they have ceased to function, they do not guard against the recurrence of pneumothorax. They should therefore be removed when one of the following has occurred:

1 The chest drain has stopped bubbling and swinging.
2 The amount of fluid drained per day has decreased, to less than 100 ml/day.
3 Intermittent obstruction in a patient with a pneumothorax receiving assisted ventilation (when it should be replaced with a properly functioning chest drain).

It is useful to clamp the chest drain for 12–24 hours prior to its removal to ensure that no fluid or air collects during this period. If the patient's condition deteriorates during this time, unclamping the chest drain may improve the situation. After removal, a further CXR should be taken to ensure that pneumothorax has not recurred.

NOTES

NOTES

Haemofiltration

Intermittent haemodialysis and ultrafiltration removes excess fluid accumulated over two to three days in a period of four to six hours. In patients requiring intensive care, rapid removal of fluid can cause significant hypotension and may limit the amount of fluid that can be removed. Continuous arteriovenous haemofiltration (CAVH) removes excess fluid slowly and continuously over the 24-hour period, avoiding the sudden volume depletion associated with intermittent techniques. The patient's own blood pressure drives blood through a modified dialysis coil, thus avoiding the complexities and hazards of a pump and removes a filtrate similar to glomerular filtrate. A mean systemic arterial blood pressure of 60 mmHg and access to the circulation are all that are required for this procedure to be undertaken.

Indications

1 Salt and water overload (pulmonary oedema, peripheral oedema, etc.), unresponsive to diuretic therapy.
2 In the management of patients with renal failure:
   (a) To make room for parenteral nutrition.
   (b) As an adjuvant or substitute for haemodialysis, in the less catabolic patient.

Contraindications

Bleeding from any site which would be exacerbated by the administration of heparin.

Equipment

Haemofilter

This is a modified dialysis filter which acts as a molecular sieve, with a pore size, for solutes, of 20 000 molecular weight

(MW). Small MW substances, such as creatinine, potassium, urea and many drugs, freely diffuse across this filter to give the same concentration in the filtrate as in the plasma. Large MW substances, such as albumin, cannot diffuse across the haemofilter. Arterial blood under pressure enters at one port of the haemofilter and emerges at a lower pressure at a port the other end, to be returned to the body. A third port enables the filtrate to be removed. The priming volume of the lines and haemofilter is small (100 ml).

Access to the circulation

Arteriovenous access

The most convenient access is created surgically using a Schribner shunt, either from the radial artery or the posterior tibial artery, to a nearby vein. Insertion of the Schribner shunt at the ankle is the most convenient site in critically ill patients; the space at the head end of the patient may already be cluttered by ventilators, infusion pumps, etc.

In an emergency situation, or when surgical access is not practicable, percutaneous cannulation of the femoral artery and femoral, or subclavian, vein can be accomplished, with large-bore cannulae inserted using the Seldinger technique.

Venovenous access

In some situations cannulation of an artery may not be possible; in such circumstances continuous venovenous haemofiltration can be performed, by removing blood from a large vein and using a roller pump to drive blood around the circuit. Particular care is necessary with this technique to prevent disconnection and air being entrained into the system, resulting in an air embolus. Double lumen venous catheters can be used for haemofiltration.

It is essential that all access points to the circulation are kept visible at all times.

Method

Connecting the circuit to the patient

A haemofiltration coil and extracorporeal circuit are flushed through to remove all preservative in accordance with the manufacturer's instructions. It is then primed with 0.9 per cent saline containing heparin (1000 u/l).

Taking care to avoid air entering the circulation, the circuit is connected to the arterial side of the shunt and blood slowly allowed to fill the filter lines. When blood reaches the outflow end of the venous connecting line the line is connected to the venous return cannula; blood is then allowed to flow freely round the circuit.

Filtrate removal

The volume of filtrate removed per hour depends upon:

1 The pressure gradient between mean arterial pressure and the pressure in the filtrate collecting system.
   (a) Mean arterial pressure will alter with manipulation of inotropes, blood volume, etc.
   (b) The pressure in the filtrate collecting system will increase as the roller clamp in the collecting system is tightened (lessening the difference between the two pressures), thus reducing filtrate removal. Releasing the roller clamp will increase filtrate removal. Adjustment of the clamp is the usual method of control of the amount of filtrate removed.
   (c) Hydrostatic pressure (i.e. the difference in height between the filter and the collecting system) will also have a part to play. The application of suction to the filtrate collecting system will further increase the pressure differential across the haemofilter, removing more filtrate.
2 The surface area of the filter; the larger the haemofilter surface area, the more filtrate that will be removed, for a given pressure gradient. The haemofilter area depends upon:
   (a) The size of filter, chosen from the manufacturer's range.
   (b) Blood clotting in the filter will reduce its surface area. The longer a haemofilter has been in use, the smaller the effective surface area it will have, due to progressive blood clotting.

When a haemofilter is first connected, it is usually possible to obtain 500 ml of filtrate per hour. As the haemofilter surface area gradually decreases due to clotting, or as the patient's condition deteriorates, this volume may become increasingly difficult to remove. The hourly target for removal of filtrate should be considerably less than this (usually less than 300 ml/hour), allowing a constant volume to be removed each hour, by gradually releasing the roller clamp.

Anticoagulation

Extracorporeal circuits require anticoagulation to prevent clotting; during CAVH, heparin is infused into the arterial, inflow, side of the haemofilter. The starting dose is usually 10–15 U/kg/hr of heparin, which is delivered by an accurate syringe pump. The heparin is diluted in 0.9 per cent saline so that at least 10 ml/hr of the heparin solution is infused, providing anticoagulation even if small amounts of heparin only are required.

1 If the haemofilter clots rapidly (recognised by increasing difficulty in filtrate removal and discoloration of the top of the filter), anticoagulation should be increased.

2 Only minor derangements of clotting times in the systemic circulation should occur. Activated clotting times, or the KPTT, are a useful indicator of heparin overspill and should not be allowed to exceed twice normal.

3 In patients with a pre-existing coagulopathy, a reduction in the dose of heparin may be necessary; in very ill patients, none at all may be needed.

4 Prolonged action of heparin has been seen in patients with hepatic insufficiency.

Volume replacement

1 Low-volume removal (2–10 l/day). If the patient is not salt and water overloaded and zero fluid balance is required, filtrate losses can be replaced using a haemofiltration solution and parenteral nutrition. Haemofiltration replacement solution has an electrolyte composition similar to plasma, but contains no potassium. Pharmaceutical problems make the packaging of bicarbonate into plastic bags difficult, and lactate, which is rapidly metabolised into bicarbonate

Table PP8.1

Component	Concentration (mmol/l)
Sodium	140
Chloride	100
Magnesium	0.75
Calcium	1.6
Lactate	45

by the liver, is used instead. Its composition is listed in Table PP8.1.

The composition of the parenteral nutrition solution can be varied to meet the needs of the patient.

    2 High-volume removal (more than 15 l/day). Higher volumes can be removed if a pump is introduced into the circuit; this produces significant clearance of low molecular weight substances and may be sufficient to diminish the need for haemodialysis. The majority of the replacement fluid will be as haemofiltration replacement fluid.

A variety of systems exists to simplify fluid balance; mechanical or electronic balances and computers.

The patient's temperature needs close control to avoid hypothermia, with the exchange of such large volumes. Warming the haemofiltration replacement fluid using a blood-warmer may be necessary.

Acid-based problems

The filtrate contains sodium bicarbonate in a concentration equal to that of the plasma. Failure to replace bicarbonate lost in the filtrate will result in a metabolic acidosis. Most of the bicarbonate can be replaced by the lactate in the haemofiltration solution. Additional bicarbonate replacement may be necessary as 8.4 per cent sodium bicarbonate, administered through a central venous line by syringe pump. If large amounts of bicarbonate-free replacement fluids (such as parenteral nutrition, or 1.8 per cent sodium chloride) are administered, more 8.4 per cent sodium bicarbonate may be required.

The amount of sodium bicarbonate required can be guided by measurement of the plasma bicarbonate.

Sodium chloride balance

Sodium chloride is lost in the filtrate in a concentration equal to that in the plasma. Failure to replace lost sodium chloride will result in hypotension. It can be replaced by the administration of sodium chloride-containing fluids, such as haemofiltration solution, or 1.8 per cent sodium chloride.

If the fluid replacement regimen contains electrolyte-free parenteral nutrition solutions, concentrated sodium chloride solutions (5 per cent) may need to be infused. Daily estimation of plasma chloride is a guide to the necessary rate of infusion of a concentrated sodium chloride solution.

Nutrition

The ability to remove large quantities of fluid can make nutrition considerably easier in these patients, without the constraints of a restricted fluid intake.

1 Amino acids are not filtered in significant quantities in the filtrate and only small increases (1–2 gm N/day) are necessary to compensate for the loss.
2 The administration of lipid emulsions (Intralipid) over four to six hours can cause the haemofilter to clog. Infuse fat emulsions over a longer period (20 hours) to avoid this.
3 Supplementation with trace elements and water-soluble vitamins should be increased to at least daily administration to overcome the increased losses during CAVH. During high-volume haemofiltration, administration two or three times a day may become necessary.

Drugs

Many of the commonly administered antibiotics, particularly aminoglycosides, diffuse freely across the haemofilter and may require increased doses during CAVH. Dosage should be guided by therapeutic drug monitoring.

Sedatives (e.g. midazolam) and analgesics (e.g. morphine) do not diffuse freely across the haemofilter and do not require an increased dose.

Venous access (during CAVH for infusion, drugs, etc.)

The complexity of this technique, with infusions of sodium bicarbonate, sodium chloride, parenteral nutrition, fluid replacement, analgesia and, often, inotropes, may necessitate several central venous lines; a triple lumen central venous line is of great value (see Practical Procedure 3).

CAVH is a technique that, once running well, should not be changed unnecessarily. All the different components interact with each other and unnecessary, frequent changes will cause considerable difficulties and administration errors. It is easier to remove a constant amount of filtrate and alter the input of the various fluids (especially the haemofiltration solution).

Haemofiltration is a versatile procedure, which correctly used is a convenient way of manipulating fluid balance in patients with impaired renal function.

NOTES

NOTES

Peritoneal Dialysis

Peritoneal dialysis (PD) has become popular in the long-term treatment of end-stage renal disease. There remain, however, acute situations where PD is a more appropriate choice than haemodialysis (see Chapter 8), in particular, in small children and when haemodialysis is unavailable.

Insertion of an acute catheter

1 The procedure is performed under strict aseptic conditions.
2 Empty the patient's bladder.
3 Sterilise the skin between the umbilicus and symphysis pubis.
4 Mark a point two-thirds of the way from the umbilicus to the symphysis pubis, in the midline. Infiltrate with 1 per cent lignocaine down to the peritoneum.
5 Make a small incision, with a scalpel, to allow the *tight* passage of the catheter. Too large an incision may result in leakage of fluid around the puncture site.
6 Keep the stylet perpendicular to the skin, rather than angled, and ask the patient to tense the abdominal muscles. Advance the stylet catheter through the incision using a twisting motion, until the peritoneum is punctured.
7 Once the peritoneum is punctured, withdraw the stylet slightly and advance the catheter until the side holes are within the peritoneal cavity.
8 Remove the stylet.
9 Allow two litres of dialysate fluid to enter the peritoneal cavity.

10 Replace the stylet so as to stiffen the catheter, but without allowing the point to protrude through the end of the catheter. Advance the catheter down towards the pelvis.

11 If the patient experiences pain, the catheter is impinging on the bowel. Withdraw it slightly and re-advance it, in a slightly different direction. Repeat, until no pain is experienced on advancing the catheter.

12 Use a purse string suture to secure the catheter to the skin. Fold two 4 cm × 4 cm gauze swabs in half and place caudal to the catheter, which is then bent over the swabs and dressed.

13 Connect the catheter to a closed, gravity-drainage system.

14 Allow the dialysis fluid to drain under gravity. If drainage is inadequate, the catheter should be repositioned.

15 If dialysis fluid leaks around the catheter, the purse-string suture should be tightened.

16 Commence PD.

Technique

1 In each cycle, dialysis fluid is allowed to enter the abdominal cavity under gravity (inflow) and then left to equilibrate (dwell time) before being drained out again under gravity (outflow).

2 Aim for a cycle of 2 l/hr:
   (a) 10 minutes inflow time.
   (b) 30 minutes dwell time.
   (c) 20 minutes outflow time.

3 Drainage of fluid may be aided by altering the patient's posture.

4 Add heparin to the first three exchanges (500 IU/l) to prevent clotting of the catheter.

5 Heparin (500 IU/l) should be used whenever the drained fluid is cloudy or bloody.

6 Accurate fluid balance records are essential: weighing the patient is desirable to prevent the dangers of over- or underhydration.

7 Monitor the plasma glucose and electrolytes regularly.

8 Protein is lost in the dialysate during PD, and thus it is necessary to increase protein intake (orally or IV).

9 Replace water-soluble vitamins.

10 The catheter should not be left in place for more than 72 hours, after which it should be replaced with a chronic catheter.

Choice of dialysis fluid

The principle of PD is similar to that of haemodialysis: fluid moving passively down an osmotic gradient and solute down a concentration gradient

Most acute PD needs can be met with commercially available preparations. When the intention is not to remove excess fluid from the body, use a slightly hypertonic solution, to avoid the risk of water being absorbed from the peritoneal cavity. If it is necessary to remove excess fluid from the body use a hypertonic solution. For maintenance dialysis, when it is necessary to remove sodium, use a solution with a low sodium content. The concentrations of the individual solutions can be obtained from local information sources and the one chosen should be that which best fits the patient's requirements.

Unnecessary use of hypertonic solutions results in hypernatraemia, dehydration and hyperglycaemia.

Complications

Pain

This may result from:

1 Malpositioning of the catheter usually causes pain in the rectum or around the bladder. The catheter should be repositioned.

2 Overdistension with fluid can cause both abdominal pain and pain referred to the shoulder. Reduce the exchange to 1 litre.

Bleeding

Blood in the effluent fluid is usually seen at the beginning of PD. It is usually self-limiting.

1 Apply pressure at the catheter entry site.

2 Add 500 IU/l of heparin to the dialysate until the effluent fluid is clear.

Rarely, the bleeding is from a damaged major vessel. In this case, resuscitation and surgical repair may be necessary.

Perforation of bowel

This is more common when acute catheters are inserted into patients who have undergone previous abdominal surgery. This presents by failure to return dialysate, faeculent drainage or watery diarrhoea containing dextrose.

1 Remove the catheter and insert another at a different site.
2 Continue PD using minimal dwell time.
3 Send drainage fluid daily for culture.
4 Give intraperitoneal and systemic antibiotics until cultures are negative for three days.
5 If the patient becomes shocked, or does not improve, with the above measures, surgical repair of the perforation is indicated.

Peritonitis

The incidence of peritonitis should be low, if sufficient attention is paid to aseptic technique.

1 Send some of the drainage fluid for microscopy, Gram stain and culture. The WCC of the fluid usually exceeds 300 per mm^3 in symptomatic peritonitis.
2 Instill and drain three exchanges, without antibiotics, as rapidly as possible.
3 Continue PD, adding appropriate antibiotics to the dialysate, in a concentration similar to the desired plasma concentration.
4 The choice of antibiotics is guided by the Gram stain and culture.
   (a) If the Gram-negative organisms are seen, give an aminoglycoside.
   (b) Both an aminoglycoside and a cephalosporin or penicillinase-resistant penicillin should be prescribed if mixed flora or no organisms are seen.
5 Antibiotics can be changed when sensitivity of the cul-

tured organisms is known and should be continued for seven days after the last negative culture.

6 Send drainage fluid daily for WCC and culture.

Spread of dialysate

1 Dialysate may spread subcutaneously and cause oedema of the abdominal wall. Stop PD if this occurs.
2 Spread across the diaphragm may result in a pleural effusion. PD can continue with the patient in a head-up position. The effusion should be drained, if causing dyspnoea.

Hyperglycaemia

This results from the peritoneal absorption of the dextrose in the dialysate. It is more common in diabetics and when hypertonic solutions are used.

1 Monitor blood glucose four hourly using a reflectance meter.
2 Give insulin as required, using a sliding scale (see Chapter 10).
3 Rebound hypoglycaemia may occur when insulin is used.

Pneumoperitoneum

Air frequently enters the peritoneal cavity with dialysate and may persist for a week after stopping PD. It is harmless, but may cause confusion in the interpretation of abdominal X-rays.

NOTES

NOTES

Epidural Analgesia

Indications

Relief of pain following trauma or surgery, when the pain is in an area supplied by a mid or lower thoracic, or lumbar spinal nerve root.

Contraindications

1 Hypovolaemia.
2 Coagulopathy.
3 Raised intracranial pressure.
4 Spinal tumour.
5 Diabetic neuropathy.
6 Infection around the site of insertion.
7 Patient refusal.

Equipment

Tuohy needle

This is a 16- or 18-gauge needle with a stylet. The lumen exits at 90° from the shaft, so as to direct the catheter in a cephalad direction in the epidural space, thus aiding correct placement and lessening the risk of dural puncture by the catheter. Disposable needles are available, and these may be sharper than reusable needles. Large wings are sometimes added to improve control of the needle. The usual length of the needle is 10 cm, although some 15 cm long are available for obese patients.

Epidural catheter

It is essential before starting this procedure to ensure that the catheter will fit down the Tuohy needle. Both end-hole and side-hole catheters are available.

Microbiological/particulate filter

This attaches to the end of the catheter and prevents the injection of bacteria and small particles of glass (from opening of ampoules) into the epidural space.

Method

1 Intravenous access is essential before starting.
2 The patient is turned onto his side, the skin prepared with sterilising solution in the area where the needle is to be inserted and the patient draped.
3 If the patient is conscious, the skin and deeper structures are infiltrated with 1–2 ml of 1 per cent lignocaine.
4 A large sharp needle is introduced through the skin and removed, to facilitate introduction of the Tuohy needle.
5 A Tuohy needle is pushed through the skin and interspinous ligament, with the lumen exit pointing cephalad. The stylet is removed and a 10 ml syringe of air, or a 20 ml syringe containing 0.9 per cent saline, is attached to the hub of the needle. The needle is advanced by applying pressure on the plunger of the syringe with one hand and steadying the needle with the other. Resistance to injection is felt as the needle traverses the ligamentum flavum. When the needle enters the epidural space, loss of resistance to injection is felt, and it is possible to inject air or saline.
6 The epidural catheter is threaded through the needle so that 2–3 cm are in the epidural space. At this point, the needle is withdrawn over the catheter. If the catheter fails to thread through the needle, excess pressure should not be used. *Under no circumstances should the catheter be withdrawn through the needle*, otherwise the catheter may be cut by the needle and left in the

epidural space. The needle and catheter should be removed together.

7 The catheter is aspirated to ensure that no clear fluid (CSF) or blood can be withdrawn through the catheter. Injection into the subarachnoid space, or intravascularly, can have adverse cardiovascular and neurological effects (see Chapter 17).

8 A 6 cm × 6 cm swab should be folded into four and its rounded edge placed adjacent and immediately superior to the exit point of the epidural catheter. The catheter should then be folded around the rounded edge of the folded swab and laid flat onto the skin. Two strips of wide adhesive waterproof tape should be laid from side to side and slightly overlapping, to cover the epidural catheter and swab. A further long length of adhesive tape should be laid along the body to secure the epidural catheter to the patient's back.

9 A microbiological and particulate filter is attached to the end of the catheter.

10 Three ml of 2 per cent lignocaine plain solution is injected into the epidural catheter as a further precaution against unnoticed, inadvertent, intravascular or subdural placement of the catheter.

11 In the event of intravascular injection of this local anaesthetic, transient hypotension and a bradycardia may be seen. If the patient is conscious, he may complain of a tingling sensation on the end of his tongue, or ringing in his ears, in which case further injection of local anaesthesia should not be carried out, until the catheter has been resited.

12 Subdural placement of the catheter is more difficult to recognise. Hypotension and analgesia may follow a test dose injection through an incorrectly sited catheter, particularly in the thoracic region. If this occurs, careful evaluation should be undertaken before a further dose of local anaesthetic solution is given. If there is any doubt, do not inject large volumes of local anaesthetic until help is obtained.

13 If, during insertion of the needle, the epidural space is accidentally traversed, the dura will be penetrated;

when the syringe is removed, clear fluid (CSF) will gush out. If saline has been used in the syringe to find the loss of resistance, CSF can be differentiated from saline by noting its temperature (by allowing a drip to fall onto the operator's skin). CSF is warmer than saline at room temperature. Alternatively use a Dextrostik; CSF contains glucose and 0.9 per cent saline contains none.

NOTES

Intercostal Nerve Blockade

The anterior aspect of the thorax and abdominal wall is innervated by the intercostal nerves. Dermatome levels can be identified by the following surface markings: nipple T4, xiphisternum T7, umbilicus T10 and suprapubic area T12. In addition to supplying sensation to the anterior thorax and abdominal wall, they also innervate the rib and adjacent tissues. If the appropriate intercostal nerves are blocked with local anaesthetic, cutaneous analgesia from the nipple to the suprapubic area can be provided.

Indications

To provide analgesia for incisions on the anterior abdominal wall and lower thorax and for the relief of pain following fractured ribs.

Equipment and Drugs

1 10 ml syringe.
2 23-gauge needle.
3 Bupivacaine hydrochloride (Marcain) is a suitable long-acting local anaesthetic. The maximum dose is 2 mg/kg every four hours. To reduce absorption of bupivacaine, a solution containing adrenaline may be used.

Method

1 Decide on which intercostal nerves need to be blocked to provide adequate analgesia. Remember that for mid-line or paramedian incisions, the cross-over of inter-

costal nerves means that both sides will have to be blocked.

2 Explain the procedure to the patient.

3 Identify the midaxillary line and the ribs that require to be blocked. You will need to block both the rib above and that below, the upper and lower extent of the wound, in addition to those supplying the wound.

4 Abduct the patient's arm and sterilise the skin over the area that you intend to inject.

5 Place the middle and forefingers of your left hand over the cephalic and caudal edges of the rib. Introduce the needle of the syringe containing the bupivacaine at 90° to the rib just cephalad to the caudal edge of the rib.

6 Advance the needle until the rib is met.

7 Gradually 'walk' the needle off the rib in a caudal direction, until it slips 1–2 mm under the rib, into the subcostal groove.

8 Aspirate the syringe to ensure no air (needle in the pleural cavity) or blood (needle in a vein or artery) is obtained.

9 Inject 2–3 ml of the local anaesthetic solution; take care not to exceed the maximum recommended dose. Slowly withdraw the needle.

10 Just before removal of the needle, inject subcutaneously 0.2–0.3 ml of local anaesthetic solution. This makes the next injection less painful.

11 Repeat at the required number of interspaces.

12 Even if a satisfactory block is produced, parenteral analgesia (in reduced doses) may be required for visceral pain.

13 Intercostal nerve blocks are effective for periods ranging from four to 24 hours.

Complications

1 Pneumothorax may occur particularly when patients receive this block from inexperienced operators. Document all blocks in the patient's records, so that others may be alerted to this possibility. Do not perform this block on patients requiring artificial ventilation.

2 Intravascular injection will produce systemic toxicity, including convulsions and cardiovascular and respira-

tory depression. Avoid this complication by aspirating, before injecting local anaesthetic solution.

3 Failure to produce analgesia will occur in some patients. Do not repeat the blocks, as this risks toxicity. Use alternative methods.

NOTES

Suggested Further Reading

General Textbooks

Chernow, B. and Lake, C.R. (eds.) (1983) *The Pharmacological Approach to the Critically Ill Patient.* Baltimore: Williams and Wilkins.

Goodman, L.R. and Putman, C.E. (eds.) (1979) *Intensive Care Radiology.* St Louis: The C.V. Mosby Co.

Macleod, J. (ed.) (1984) *Davidson's Principles and Practice of Medicine,* 13th edn. Edinburgh: Churchill Livingstone.

Oh, T.E. (ed.) (1985) *Intensive Care Manual,* 2nd edn. Stoneham: Butterworths.

Rippe, J.M., Irwin, R.S., Alpent, J.S. and Dalen, J.E. (eds.) (1985) *Intensive Care Medicine.* Boston: Little, Brown and Co.

Rubenstein, D. and Wayne, D. (1985) *Lecture Notes on Clinical Medicine,* 3rd edn. Oxford: Blackwell Scientific Publications.

Sibbald, J.W. (ed.) (1984) *Synopsis of Critical Care,* 2nd edn. Baltimore: Williams and Wilkins.

Tinker, J. and Rapin, M. (1983) *Care of the Critically Ill Patient.* Berlin: Springer-Verlag.

1 Cardiopulmonary Cerebral Resuscitation

American Medical Association (1986) Standards and guidelines for cardiopulmonary resuscitation (CPR) and emergency cardiac care (ECC). *JAMA,* **255,** 2905.

Baskett, P.J.F. (1985) Toward better resuscitation. *Br. J. Hosp. Med.*, **34**, 345.

Evans, T.R. (ed.) (1985) *ABC of Resuscitation.* London: British Medical Association.

Robinson, J. (1983) Hospital medical gas installations. *Br. Med. J.*, **55**, 807.

Safar, P. and Bircher, N.G. (1988) *Cardiopulmonary Cerebral Resuscitation* 3rd edn. London: W.B. Saunders Ltd.

2 Cardiac Arrhythmias

Bennett, D.H. (1985) *Cardiac Arrhythmias: Practical Notes on Interpretation and Treatment,* 2nd edn. Bristol: Wright.

Brownlee, W.T. (1985) Acute arrhythmias. *Br. J. Hosp. Med.*, **33**, 138.

Evans, D.W. (1984) Atrioventricular block. *Br. J. Hosp. Med.*, **31**, 328.

Goldman, M.J. (1986) *Principles of Clinical Electrocardiography*, 12th edn. Los Altos: Lange Medical Publications.

Hutchison, S. and Lorimer, A.R. (1984) Bundle branch block. *Br. J. Hosp. Med.*, **31**, 337.

Reid, D.S. (1984) Sick sinus syndrome. *Br. J. Hosp. Med.*, **31**, 341.

3 Shock

Chernow, B., Rainey, T.G. and Lake, R. (1982) Endogenous and exogenous catecholamines in critical care. *Crit. Care Med.*, **10**, 409.

George, R.J.D. and Winter, R.J.D. (1985) The clinical value of measuring cardiac output. *Br. J. Hosp. Med.*, **34**, 89.

Herbert, P. and Tinker, J. (1980) Inotropic drugs in acute circulatory failure. *Intens. Care Med.*, **6**, 101.

Norman, J. and Moles, M. (eds.) (1978) *Management of the Injured Patient.* London: Macmillan Journals.

Seely, H.F. (1987) Pathophysiology of haemorrhagic shock. *Br. J. Hosp. Med.*, **36**, 14.

Twigley, A.J. and Hillman, K.M. (1985) The end of the crystalloid era? *Anaesthesia*, **40**, 860.

Watkins, J. (1979) Anaphylactoid reactions to iv substances. *Br. J. Anaes.*, **51**, 51.

Wilson, R.F. (1980) The pathophysiology of shock. *Intens. Care Med.*, **6**, 89.

4 Myocardial Infarction and Cardiac Failure

Chamberlin, D. and Vincent, R. (1987) Acute coronary care. In: *Intensive Care*, 2nd edn. Gerson, G. (ed.). London: William Heinemann Medical Books.

Fleming, J.S. and Braimbridge, M.V. (1984) *Lecture Notes on Cardiology*, 2nd edn. Oxford: Blackwell Scientific Publications.

Henderson, A. and Lewis, M. (1982) Management of heart failure. *Med. Internl.*, **1**, 855.

Julian, D.G. (1983) *Cardiology*, 4th edn. London: Cassell.

5 Respiratory Failure

Berlauk, J.F. (1986) Prolonged endotracheal intubation vs tracheostomy. *Crit. Care Med.*, **14**, 742.

Browne, D.R.G. (1984) Weaning patients from mechanical ventilation. *Intens. Care Med.*, **10**, 55.

George, R.J.D. and Geddes, D.M. (1985) High frequency ventilation. *Br. J. Hosp. Med.*, **33**, 344.

Harrison, M.J. (1986) PEEP and CPAP. *Br. Med. J.*, **292**, 643.

Mushin, W.W., Rendell-Baker, L., Thompson, P.W. and Mapleson, W.W. (1980) Automatic ventilation of the lungs, 3rd edn. Oxford: Blackwell Scientific Publications.

Shapiro, B.A., Cane, R.D. and Harrison, R.A. (1984) Positive end-expiratory pressure therapy in adults with special reference to acute lung injury: a review of the literature and suggested clinical correlations. *Crit. Care Med.*, **12**, 127.

Shapiro, B.A., Harrison, R.A., Kacmarek, R.M. and Cane, R.D. (1985) *Clinical Applications of Respiratory Care*, 3rd edn. Chicago: Year Book Publishers.

Shelly, M.P., Lloyd, G. and Park, G.R. (1988) A review of the mechanisms and methods of humidification of inspired gases. *Intens. Care Med.*, **14**, 1–9.

Symposium on Anaesthesia and Respiratory Dysfunction (1982) *Brit. J. Anaes.*, **54**, 701.

Willats, S.M. (1985) Alternative modes of ventilation. Part I. Disadvantages of controlled mechanical ventilation: intermittent mandatory ventilation. *Intens. Care Med.*, **11**, 51.

Willats, S.M. (1985) Alternative modes of ventilation. Part II. High and low frequence positive pressure ventilation PEEP CPAP inversed ratio ventilation. *Intens. Care Med.*, **11**, 115.

6 Common Respiratory Problems

Boggis, C.R.M. and Greene, R. (1983) Adult respiratory distress syndrome. *Br. J. Hosp. Med.*, **29**, 167.

Branthwaite, M.A. (1985) The intensive care of asthma. *Br. J. Hosp. Med.*, **34**, 331.

Crofton, J. and Douglas, A. (1981) *Respiratory Disease*, 3rd edn. Oxford: Blackwell Scientific Publications.

Crompton, G. (1987) *Diagnosis and Management of Respiratory Diseases*, 2nd edn. Oxford: Blackwell Scientific Publications.

Moussalli, H. and Hooper, T. (1986) Management of chest injuries: 1. *Hosp. Update*, **12**, 751.

Moussalli, H. and Hooper, T. (1986) Management of chest injuries: 2. *Hosp. Update*, **12**, 889.

Pearn, J. (1985) The management of near-drowning. *Br. Med. J.*, **291**, 1447.

Stark, J.E., Schneerson, J.M., Higenbottam, T. and Flower, C.D.R. (1986) *Manual of Chest Medicine*. Edinburgh: Churchill Livingstone.

Tibbutt, D.A. (1977) Pulmonary thromboembolism. In: *Recent Advances in Intensive Therapy 1*. Ledingham, I.McA. (ed.). Edinburgh: Churchill Livingstone.

Westaby, S. (1985) Injury to the major airways. *Br. J. Hosp. Med.*, **34**, 210.

7 Fluid and Electrolyte Balance

Allison, S.P. (1984) Potassium. *Br. J. Hosp. Med.*, **32**, 19.

Askanazi, J., Starker, P.M. and Weissman, C. (eds.) (1986) *Fluid and Electrolyte Management in Critical Care*. Stoneham: Butterworth.

Baron, D.N. (1982) *A Short Textbook of Chemical Pathology*, 4th edn. London: Hodder and Stoughton.

Barton, I.K. and Mansell, M.A. (1984) Sodium. *Br. J. Hosp. Med.*, **32**, 15.

Bihari, D.J. (1986) Metabolic acidosis. *Br. J. Hosp. Med.*, **35**, 89.

Brenton, D.P. and Gordon, T.E. (1984) Magnesium. *Br. J. Hosp. Med.*, **32**, 60.

Clark, R.G. (1985) Fluid and electrolytes. In: *Care of the Postoperative Surgical Patient*. Smith, J.A.R. and Watkins, J. (eds.). London: Butterworth.

Linter, S.P.K. (1986) The anion gap. *Br. J. Hosp. Med.*, **35**, 79.

Stevenson, J.C. (1984) Calcium. *Br. J. Hosp. Med.*, **32**, 71.

Swales, J.D. (1987) Dangers in treating hyponatraemia. *Br. Med. J.*, **294**, 261.

Willats, S.M. (1982) *Lecture Notes on Fluid and Electrolyte Balance.* Oxford: Blackwell Scientific Publications.

Willats, S.M. (1984) Water. *Br. J. Hosp. Med.*, **32**, 8.

8 Oliguria and Anuria

Dettli, L. (1976) Drug dosage in renal failure. *Clin. Pharmacokinet.*, **1**, 126.

Lee, H.A. (1977) The management of acute renal failure following trauma. *Br. J. Anaes.*, **49**, 697.

Polson, R., Park, G.R., Lindop, M.J. et al (1987) The prevention of renal impairment in patients undergoing orthotopic liver grafting by infusion of low dose dopamine. *Anaesthesia*, **42**, 15.

Robson, J.S. (1977) The pathogenesis of acute renal failure. In: *Recent Advances in Intensive Therapy 1*, Ledingham, I.McA. (ed.). Edinburgh: Churchill Livingstone.

Schrier, R.W., Gardenswartz, M.H. and Burke, T.J. (1981) Acute renal failure: pathogenesis diagnosis and treatment. In: *Advances in Nephrology*, Vol. 10, Hamburger, J., Crosnier, J., Grunfeld, J.P. and Maxwell, M.H. (eds.). Chicago: Year Book Publishers.

Wardle, E.N. (1979) *Renal Medicine.* Lancaster: MTP Press.

Wilkins, R.G. and Faragher, E.B. (1983) Acute renal failure in an intensive care unit: incidence, prediction and outcome. *Anaesthesia*, **38**, 628.

9 Liver and Gastrointestinal Problems

Bonnett, F., Rotman, N. and Fagniez, P.L. (1985) Changing concepts in the evaluation and treatment of acute severe pancreatitis. *Intens. Care Med.*, **11**, 107.

Eiseman, B. and Norton, L. (1977) Massive acute gastrointestinal haemorrhage. In: *Recent Advances in Intensive Therapy 1*, Ledingham, I.McA. (ed.). Edinburgh: Churchill Livingstone.

Elias, E. and Hawkins, C. (1986) *Lecture Notes on Gastroenterology.* Oxford: Blackwell Scientific Publications.

Glazer, G. and Dudley, H. (1977) Acute pancreatitis. In: *Recent Advances in Intensive Therapy 1*, Ledingham, I.McA. (ed.). Edinburgh: Churchill Livingstone.

Hayes, P. and Bouchier, I.A.D. (1984) Drug therapy of portal hypertension and oesophageal varices. *Br. J. Hosp. Med.*, **32**, 39.

Knight, A., Bihari, D. and Tinker, J. (1985) Stress ulceration in critically ill patients. *Br. J. Hosp. Med.*, **33**, 216.

Murray, W.R. and MacSween, R.N. (1983) Hepatobiliary disturbances. In: *Recent Advances in Critical Care Medicine 2*, Ledingham, I.McA. and Hanning, C.D. (eds.). Edinburgh: Churchill Livingstone.

Murray-Lyon, I.M. and Trewby, P.M. (1977) Hepatic failure. In: *Recent Advances in Intensive Therapy 1*, Ledingham, I.McA. (ed.). Edinburgh: Churchill Livingstone.

Park, G.R., Shelly, M.P. and Mendel, L. (1987) The intensive care of patients following liver transplantation. In: *Liver Transplantation*, Calne, R.Y. (ed.). London: Grune and Stratton.

Triger, D.R. (1986) Management of bleeding oesophageal varices. *Br. J. Hosp. Med.*, **35**, 96.

10 Nutrition

Allison, S.P. (1977) Metabolic aspects of intensive care. *Br. J. Anaes.*, **49**, 689.

Echenique, M.M., Bistrian, B.R. and Blackburn, G.L. (1982) Theory and techniques of nutritional support in the ICU. *Crit. Care Med.*, **10**, 546.

Georgieff, M. and Geiger, K. (1983) Trauma-adapted intravenous nutritional support. In: *European Advances in Intensive Care*, Geiger, I. (ed.). Boston: Little, Brown and Co.

Grant, J.P. (1980) *Handbook of Total Parenteral Nutrition*. Philadelphia: W.B. Saunders.

Hulman, G., Fraser, I., Pearson, J.H. and Bell, P.R.F. (1982) Agglutination of Intralipid by sera of acutely ill patients. *Lancet*, 1426.

Silk, D.B.A. (1983) *Nutritional Support in Hospital Practice*. Oxford: Blackwell Scientific Publications.

Smith, H.S., Kennedy, D.J. and Park, G.R. (1984) A nomogram for the rapid calculation of metabolic requirements on intubated patients. *Intens. Care Med.*, **10**, 147.

Smith, J.A.R. (1985) Nutritional therapy. In: *Care of the Postoperative Patient*, Smith, J.A.R. and Watkins, J. (eds.). London: Butterworths.

Symposium Issue (1980) Enteral and parental nutrition. *Crit. Care Med.*, **8**, 1.

Symposium on metabolism and anaesthesia (1981) *Br. J. Anaes.*, **53**, 123.

11 Poisoning

Henry, J. and Volans, G. (1984) *The ABC of Poisoning. Part I: Drugs.* London: British Medical Association Publications.

Marsden, P. (1987) The intensive care of acute poisoning. In: *Intensive Care*, 2nd edn., Gregson, G. (ed.). London: William Heinemann Medical Books.

Proudfoot, A. (1982) *Diagnosis and Management of Acute Poisoning.* Oxford: Blackwell Scientific Publications.

Vale, J.A. and Meredith, T.J. (eds.) (1981) *Poisoning, Diagnosis and Treatment.* London: Update Books.

12 Head Injuries

Campkin, T.V. and Turner, J.M. (1987) *Neurosurgical Anaesthesia and Intensive Care*, 2nd edn. London: Butterworth.

McDougall, D.G. (1983) Management of severe head injury. In: *Recent Advances in Critical Care Medicine 2*, Ledingham, I.McA. and Hanning, C.D. (eds.). Edinburgh: Churchill Livingstone.

Potter, J.M. and Briggs, M. (1984) *The Practical Management of Head Injuries*, 4th edn. London: Lloyd-Luke (Medical Books).

Willats, S.M. and Walters, F.J.M. (1986) *Anaesthesia and Intensive Care for the Neurosurgical Patient.* Oxford: Blackwell Scientific Publications.

13 Neurological Diseases

Bates, D. (1985) Management of the comatose patient. *Hosp. Update*, **11**, 425.

Durocher, A., Servais, B., Caridroix, M., et al (1980) Autonomic dysfunction in the Guillain–Barre Syndrome. Haemodynamic and neurobiochemical studies. *Intens. Care Med.*, **6**, 1.

Kerr, J. (1979) Current trends in the intensive care of tetanus. *Intens. Care Med.*, **5**, 105.

Moore, P. and James, O. (1981) Guillain–Barré syndrome: incidence management and outcome of major complications. *Crit. Care Med.*, **9**, 549.

Trujillo, M.H., Castillo, A., España, J.V. et al (1980) Tetanus in the adult: intensive care and management experience with 233 cases. *Crit. Care Med.*, **4**, 19.

Ward, C. (1987) Status epilepticus. *Hosp. Update*, **13**, 190.

14 Endocrine Emergencies

Dagett, P. (1979) Endocrine emergencies. *Br. J. Hosp. Med.*, **21**, 38.
Griffith, D.N.W. and Ryan, D.W. (1986) Diabetic ketoacidosis. *Br. J. Hosp. Med.*, **35**, 82.
Hillman, K. (1987) Fluid resuscitation in diabetic emergencies – a reappraisal. *Intens. Care Med.*, **13**, 4.
McCulloch, W., Price, P., Hinds, C.J. and Wass, J.A.H. (1985) Effects of low dose oral triioclothyronine in myxoedema coma. *Intens. Care Med.*, **11**, 259.
Sonksen, P.H. and Lowy, C. (eds.) (1980) Endocrine and metabolic Emergencies. *Clinics in Endocrinology and Metabolism*. Vol. 9, No. 3. London: W.B. Saunders.
Wheatley, T. and Clark, J.D.A. (1987) Diabetic emergencies. *Hosp. Update*, **13**, 31.

15 Haematology

Hirsh, J. and Brain, E.A. (1983) *Hemostasis and Thrombosis: a Conceptual Approach*. New York: Churchill Livingstone.
Lasala, P.A., Chien, S. and Michelsen, C.B. (1986) Hemorrheology: what is the ideal hematocrit? In: *Fluid and Electrolyte Management in Critical Care*, Askanazi, J., Starker, P.M. and Weissman, C. (eds.). Stoneham: Butterworths.
Nunn, J.F. (1987) Clinical aspects of the interaction between nitrous oxide and vitamin B_{12}. *Br. J. Anaesth.*, **59**, 3.
Preston, F.E. (1982) Disseminated intravascular coagulation. *Br. J. Hosp. Med.*, **28**, 129.

16 Brain Death and Organ Transplantation

Cadaveric Organs for Transplantation (1983) London: HMSO.
Jennett, B. (1982) Brain death. *Intens. Care Med.*, **8**, 1.

17 Sedation and Analgesia

Cousins, M.J. and Bridenbaugh, P.O. (eds.). (1980) *Neural Blockade in Clinical Anesthesia and Management of Pain*. Philadelphia: J.B. Lippincott Co.

Cousins, M.J. and Phillips, G.D. (eds.). (1986) *Acute Pain Management*. Edinburgh: Churchill Livingstone.

Duthie, D.J.R. and Nimmo, W.S. (1987) Adverse effects of opioid analgesic drugs. *Br. J. Anaesth.*, **59**, 61.

Gareth-Jones, J. and Jordan, C. (1987) Postoperative analgesia and respiratory complications. *Hosp. Update.*, **13**, 115.

Merriman, H.M. (1981) The techniques used to sedate ventilated patients. A survey of methods used in 34 ICUs in Great Britain. *Intens. Care Med.*, **7**, 217.

Willatts, S.M. (1985) Paralysis for ventilated patients? Yes or no? *Intens. Care Med.*, **11**, 2.

18 Paediatric Intensive Care

ABPI (1988) *ABPI Data Sheet Compendium 1988–9*. London: Datapharm Publications.

Bray, R.J. (1985) The management of cardiac arrest in infants and children. *Br. J. Hosp. Med.*, **34**, 72.

Diaz, J.H. (1985) Croup and epiglottitis in children. The anesthesiologist as diagnostician. *Anesth. Analg.*, **64**, 621.

Insley, J. (ed.) (1986) *A Paediatric Vade-Mecum*, 11th edn. London: Lloyd–Luke (Medical Books).

Orlowski, J.P. (ed.) (1980) Pediatric intensive care. *The Pediatric Clinics of North America*. Philadelphia: W.B. Saunders.

Sarnaik, A.P. and Vidyasagar, D. (eds.) (1985) *Neonatal and Pediatric Intensive Care*. Littleton: PSG Publishing Co.

19 Microbiology

Banks, R.A., Lindley, K.J. and Posniak, A.L. (1985) AIDS: a problem for intensive care. *Intens. Care Med.*, **11**, 169.

Bartlett, J.G. (1983) New developments in infectious diseases for the critical care physician. *Crit. Care Med.*, **11**, 563.

DHSS (1986) *Acquired Immune Deficiency Syndrome. Booklet 3. Guidance for Surgeons, Anaesthetists, Dentists and Their Teams in Dealing with Patients Infected with HTLVIII*. London: DHSS.

Finn, A. (1985) Blood cultures. *Br. J. Hosp. Med.*, **33**, 272.

Hay, R.J. (1984) Managing fungal infections. *Br. J. Hosp. Med.*, **31**, 278.

Luce, J.M. and Hopewell, P.C. (1985) The acquired immunodeficiency syndrome: a San Francisco perspective. *Intens. Care Med.*, **11**, 172.

Sleigh, J.D. and Timbury, M.C. (1986) *Notes on Medical Bacteriology*, 2nd edn. Edinburgh: Churchill Livingstone.

Strachen, C.J.L. (1985) Prevention of postoperative sepsis. In: *Care of the Postoperative Surgical Patient*, Smith, J.A.R. and Watkins, J. (eds.). London: Butterworth.

Turner, A.C. (1981) Fever in the international traveller. *Med. Internl.*, **1**, 83.

20 Communication in the Intensive Care Unit

Hoy, A.A. (1985) Breaking bad news to patients. *Br. J. Hosp. Med.*, **34**, 96.

Knight, B. (1983) *The Coroner's Autopsy*. Edinburgh: Churchill Livingstone.

Practical Procedures

For this section few reading-sources are suggested. Practical instruction is of greater importance and cannot be replaced by reading.

Buchbinder, N. and Ganz, W. (1976) Hemodynamic monitoring. *Anesthesiology*, **45**, 147.

Dodd, N.J., O'Donovan, R.M., Bennett-Jones, D.N. et al (1983) Arteriovenous haemofiltration: a recent advance in the management of renal failure. *Br. Med. J.*, **287**, 1006.

Ellis, H. and McLarty, M. (1983) *Anatomy for Anaesthetists*, 4th edn. Oxford: Blackwell Scientific Publications.

Eriksson, E. (ed.) (1979) *Illustrated Handbook in Local Anaesthesia*, 2nd edn. London: Lloyd-Luke (Medical Books).

George, R.J.D. and Banks, R.A. (1983) Bedside measurement of pulmonary capillary wedge pressure. *Br. J. Hosp. Med.*, **29**, 286.

Gilbertson, A.A. (1984) *Intravenous Technique and Therapy*. London: William Heinemann Medical Books.

Latto, I.P. and Rosen, M. (eds.) (1985) *Difficulties in Tracheal Intubation*. London: Baillière Tindall.

Lauer, A., Saccaggi, A., Ronco, C. et al (1983) Continuous arteriovenous haemofiltration in the critically ill patient. *Annl. Int. Med.*, **99**, 455.

Peter, J.L. (ed.) (1983) *A Manual of Central Venous Catheterisation and Parenteral Nutrition.* Bristol: John Wright and Son.

Pilcher, J. (1982) Inserting a temporary pacemaker. *Med. Internl.,* **1,** 814.

Raj, P.R. (1985) *Handbook of Regional Anaesthesia.* Edinburgh: Churchill Livingstone.

Walesby, R.K. (1981) How to insert a chest drain and aspirate a pleural effusion. *Br. J. Hosp. Med.,* **25,** 198.

Index